THE GREATEST TREASON

The Bizarre Story of Hollis, Liddell and Mountbatten

Richard Deacon

CENTURY

London   Sydney · Auckland   Johannesberg

First published in Great Britain in 1989 by Century
An imprint of Random Century Ltd
20 Vauxhall Bridge Road, London SW1V 2SA

Century Hutchinson Australia (Pty) Ltd
89-91 Albion Street, Surry Hills, New South Wales 2010, Australia

Century Hutchinson New Zealand Ltd
PO Box 40-086, 32-34 View Road, Glenfield, Auckland 10, New Zealand

Century Hutchinson South Africa (Pty) Ltd
PO Box 337, Bergvlei 2012, South Africa

Set by SX Composing, Rayleigh, Essex

Printed and bound in Great Britain by Mackays of Chatham Ltd, Chatham, Kent

British Library Cataloguing in Publication Data
Deacon, Richard, *1911-*
    The Greatest Treason: the bizarre story of Hollis, Liddell and Mountbatten
    1. Anti-British espionage, history – Biographies – Collections
    I. Title
    327.120922

    ISBN 0-7126-4683-3

The publishers gratefully acknowledge the following sources for illustrations:

1, 4, 6, 7, 9, 11 Topham Picture Library
10 Associated Press Library
3 reproduced by kind permission of Mrs H. Sebastian

Contents

Introduction

When almost everyone in a position of influence except Churchill thought Britain, facing Germany entirely alone, would lose World War II a secret battle was waged in this country between Appeasers and pro-Soviet factions.

Not all the Appeasers were guilty of treachery: some honestly felt it was their patriotic duty to save Britain from defeat by making a deal with Germany and allowing that nation to fight it out with the Soviet Union. Similarly not all the pro-Soviet faction were subversive: some thought that only a deal between Britain and the USSR could defeat the Nazis and save democracy. Nevertheless there were potential traitors in the ranks of each faction.

The main personalities involved were members of the Royal family, politicians, ambassadors, intelligence and security officers and some senior members of the Armed Forces. Some of these attempted to set up undercover deals with the Germans, others became secret agents of the Soviet Union.

When at times like these it is difficult to determine where the national interest lies, it is more important than ever to be clear about what counts as treason. Such a situation could happen again, even if in a different form. T. S. Eliot said that 'The last temptation is the greatest treason: To do the right deed for the wrong reason.' It can, of course, sometimes be patriotic to do the wrong deed for the right reason, and maybe Eliot had this in mind. Treachery can only really be defined when it is discovered: only then can one assess the degree to which trust and allegiance have been betrayed.

Many traitors high up in the British Establishment remain to be uncovered both on the far right and the far left, both living and dead. The purpose of this book is to investigate at least some of them and to include royalty and the aristocracy just as much as commoners.

Sexual misbehaviour has always featured largely in the world of treachery. Homosexuals in particular perhaps tend to have a penchant for the double life and treachery, and they also lay themselves open to blackmail if they have not 'come out'. Traitors on both sides have abused their privilege. Sometimes this results in traitors appearing to switch sides and in the process even appearing as heroes to the very people they have betrayed. It is in this context that Admiral of the Fleet Lord Mountbatten of Burma is a key figure.

Treachery, linked to depravity in one form or another, continues, often in the most unexpected forms. The problem today is that treachery is much more skilfully disguised than in the past, and here Eliot's comment is particularly apt. It would not be exaggerating to say that treachery had become a science in some countries. Often it is developed in the very manner that Eliot suggested – 'the right deed for the wrong reason'.

1

Fantasies, Disinformation and Lies

> There are two schools of thought about our Intelligence Services. One school is convinced they are staffed by murderous, powerful, double-crossing cynics, the other that the taxpayer is supporting a collection of bumbling, broken-down layabouts. It is possible to think that both extremes of thought are the result of a mixture of unclear reasoning, ignorance and possibly political or temperamental wishful thinking.
>
> *(the late Lord Clanmorris)*

The above quotation aptly sums up the controversy with which this chapter and this book are essentially concerned. The late Lord Clanmorris, rather better known as John Bingham, the author of various spy novels, made this statement in the foreword to his book, *The Double Agent*, published in 1966. He should know exactly what he is talking about because for many years he served in various branches of the Security Services, mostly in MI5, but also with the British Control Mission after the war.

Little could he have known in 1966 how much truer his words would sound in the 1980s when both these extreme viewpoints were loudly voiced. On the one hand it was argued that the Security Service (MI5) was riddled with Soviet spies, while on the other it was suggested that the service was run by nincompoops who not only could not catch the villains in its ranks, but devoted their time to seeking out a Prime Minister as the chief target, and in the case of Sir Harold Wilson, allegedly going to the extent of trying deliberately to compromise him.'[1]

Problems confronting any counter-espionage service are accentuated when members of the royal family are involved. In such instances a service such as MI5 needs backing from the government of the day. For example, prior to World War I and in the early years of that war it was essential for the security services to pay attention to some of the activities of King Edward VIII both before and after he came to the throne and following his abdication, and it is obvious from the papers of Lord Davidson (then J.C.C. Davidson, Baldwin's liaison officer on intelligence affairs) that inquiries independent of MI5 were made on the Prime Minister's authority.

But when first in America and then in England in the 1940s the name of the late Lord Mountbatten of Burma was first raised as a possible security risk, backing for detailed investigation seems to have been sadly lacking. Yet American, French and other security services have on various occasions produced evidence which pointed to his having pro-German sympathies in the early days and pro-Soviet sympathies latterly. The response over here was that he was a World War II hero whose integrity should not be questioned.

The questions raised by all these matters are serious and, in the public interest, need to be answered. There are two tendencies in modern politics which sadly conflict and militate against such satisfactory answers. The first is the demand for a House of Commons Committee to monitor MI5 – a disastrous suggestion knowing how today political bias comes first and national interest second, so that any such operation would be wide open to exploitation one way or the other for political propaganda. The second is the somewhat sinister desire by some MPs for a new Act of Parliament which would defend the privacy of individuals. It sounds splendid until one examines how it might operate against the public being told how certain people behave.

A so-called 'yellow' press can sometimes do more good than a diffident serious press. This has been demonstrated in the USA in this century and it was also demonstrated in the United Kingdom in the early part of the last century when the press and media generally kept the public informed on skulduggery, fornication and improper behaviour in royal circles. Indeed, this very criticism in the press actually led to the improvement of behaviour generally in royal circles in the reign of Queen Victoria.

As an author who has written histories of the British, Russian, Chinese, Japanese, Israeli and French secret services it is clear to me that the great defect of the British character is a ridiculous obsession with the need for secrecy, sometimes long after the real villains are dead, or the issue is of no concern to present-day security. It is a factor which has done enormous harm to Britain's relations with the United States Intelligence and Security services. This obsession with secrecy is, of course, linked to Britain's equally absurd laws of libel which frequently benefit the rogues in our midst, and sometimes protect traitors, *even when what has been declared a libel has been the absolute truth*.

Equally damaging to the cause of establishing the truth is the manner in which the 'Thirty Years Rule' for placing official records in the Public Record Office for inspection is constantly broken. One of the most notorious examples of this is that of the holding back of the papers concerning Rudolf Hess even after his death. Another example is that of Section 3(4) of the 1958 Public Records Act which authorises MI5 to retain all their documents so that none are on public view. Rather more recently Sir Duncan Wilson's Committee recommended that MI5 at least agree not to destroy their old archives. This was a very small step in the right direction as many MI5 files had in the past been destroyed not only by directors of the service, but sometimes by their subordinates.

The policy of the Lord Chancellor's office is to refuse access to all records which identify individual Security Service officers – i.e. members of MI5. Sometimes (indeed quite often) the trial papers of cases in which MI5 operations have resulted in a prosecution are not released to the researcher. It might be argued that this is a matter of security. But security for whom? Security and obscurity for members of the Service, or for those who actually help the Service to bring such prosecutions?

I particularly pose this last question in the light of some quite extraordinary evidence produced in one of the reports of the Committee on the Judiciary of the United States Senate in 1975, concerning its investigation into Communist bloc intelligence activities. Having given testimony on this subject, Mr Josef Frolik, who had been a member of the Czechoslovakian Intelligence Service for 17 years, was asked whether since he defected to the West he had ever felt his life might be in danger. Frolik replied that he had received threats to his life both through the mail and by telephone calls until he changed his address and moved to another part of America. 'How did people know where you were living?' inquired Senator Thurmond. 'The most probable cause,' said Frolik, 'was that I was a witness in London during the trial of Mr Owen, a Member of Parliament. And during the trial, when I was called, my true name with my address were given to a number of people who participated in the trial. In a three or four month period when I returned to the United States I received a telephone call. And in this call I was told, "we will kill you anyway, you son-of-a-bitch." And they hung up. One day when I went to my office, we found inside nine rattlesnakes. I called the Hygiene Department and they said I am drunk and that there were no rattlesnakes in the town. We killed all of them, though one was five feet long.'[2]

Similar threats and actions against informants of the Security Service and opponents of Iron Curtain regimes living in Britain have been just as prevalent. There was the notorious case of Georgi Markov, the Bulgarian defector who found work with the BBC in London, and was struck dead by a mysterious assassin who not only got away completely, but was never identified. Markov was waiting for a bus on Waterloo Bridge when he felt a jab in the back of his right thigh. He looked around and saw a man with an umbrella hurrying to catch a taxi. It was ultimately established that via the jab in his leg he had been poisoned by the deadly ricin, derived from the seed of the castor oil plant.

Not only Markov, but other dissident Bulgarians also received anonymous threats that their lives were in danger if they continued to broadcast their anti-communist views to the world at large. Warnings of the Czech undercover network inside the United Kingdom, which actively sought to manipulate prominent Britons as informants, had been given on many occasions dating back to the late 1950s, but no action appears to have been taken to check its activities until some few years later. One of the most trustworthy and democratic of Czech emigrés to this country was the late Josef Josten, who enjoyed a worldwide reputation as a fighter for Czech freedom. Having lived in London for 30 years and founded the Free Czech Intelligence News Agency he was a consistent opponent of communism wherever it raised its head. A man of high courage, a former collaborator with Jan Masaryk, Josef Josten frequently warned about Czech infiltration in Britain and urged that diplomatic representation in many of the Warsaw Pact countries' embassies could usefully be cut down, thus forcibly decreasing the number of spies.

Attempts to silence Josten, even to the extent of trying to kill him, continued for some years. 'Josef Frolik gave me twenty names of those who had something to do with assassination attempts upon me, or checking my activities,' Josten told the author. On one occasion he suffered from a serious and unidentified illness which he was certain was caused by the administration of poison: 'They can now do this just by dropping a certain powder into one's shoes when left outside a hotel bedroom.'[3]

If this sounds too melodramatic to be plausible, one has only to turn to the testimony given by Frolik to the Sub-Committee of the US Senate investigating Communist bloc intelligence activities. Besides citing cases of liquidation carried out by Czech agents by means of gas poisoning and injections, Frolik stated categorically that 'between 1958 and 1973 there were three attempts made against the editor of the Free Czech Intelligence News Agency, Mr Josef Josten, who is living in London.' First his kidnapping, then his assassination were ordered. 'There were plans to put poison in his milk and later plastic explosive on the frame of Mr Josten's car. The British department of the Czech Intelligence Service convinced their superiors in Prague that such direct action would be politically stupid. In 1973 Mr Josten had dinner with a Czech agent, Marak, who was playing the role of a Czech exile in Switzerland. During the dinner a non-traceable drug was put into the meal of Mr Josten who is still seriously ill.'[4]

This testimony was confirmed to me by Mr Josten back in 1978. It brings one back to the vital problem of obsessive British secrecy which, far from protecting the Security Service (or the Secret Intelligence Service, for that matter), has often aided the moles inside it.

If it had not been for the fact that eventually a great deal, if not all, of such reports of the proceedings of the US Senate and other American governmental committees was published, those of us who wish to get at the truth would find it impossible. Even then, some of these very same reports cannot always be quoted in books or newspapers in the United Kingdom without the risk of libel actions. Frolik, for example, named the late John Stonehouse, MP, a former Postmaster-General and Minister of Aviation, as one who had been manipulated by Czech Intelligence. This statement was made during Stonehouse's lifetime and was not reported in the UK, even after his disappearance and attempt to create a new name and life for himself in Australia. Indeed, *The Times* obituary of Stonehouse stated that he was 'one of the youngest and most unpopular presidents of the London Co-operative Society where, as a founder of a group which set out to counteract alleged communist control, he was embroiled in bitter controversy.'[5]

This obituary writer not only ignores the evidence of Frolik, but dismisses quite lightly the 'alleged' communist influence in the Co-operative movement. On the one hand the media play down the Stonehouse Czech connection and portray him as a much maligned character, while, on the flimsiest of gossip and evidence, they devote a great deal of space to whipping up a campaign against the late Sir Roger Hollis as the most dangerous mole of all time.

It is this last theme with which I am concerned as a starting point for this book. The media, authors, politicians and various foreign Intelligence Services all played up this story of the former head of MI5 having been one of the major Soviet agents inside the British Establishment. It was all done largely on conjecture and the opinions of some counter-espionage agents whose mentality never really fitted the jobs they were given to do. In the end it resulted in a costly and disastrous attempt by the British Government to stop publication in Australia of a book, *Spycatcher*, by one Peter Wright who had served in MI5 for a relatively short period.

Malcolm Muggeridge once amusingly described Andrew Boyle as 'the keeper of the Queen's Moles'. The word 'mole' was factual before it became fictionally popular through the works of John Le Carré: Francis Bacon used it in its modern sense in his *History of Henry VII*. Yet only recently has it been accepted in its espionage context in established dictionaries.

As I once wrote in a review in the *Spectator*: 'Moles are difficult to catch, but sometimes easy to spot by investigative authors who can juggle with facts. One can make out a case for "molery" – to coin another word – against myself, for example. In New York in 1942 I was seen in the company of one William Otto Lucas who, even during the Second World War visited the Soviet Union and stayed with Zhdanov, then a fancied successor to Stalin. (He also managed to stay at Goering's hunting lodge in Germany, but a mole-hunter could overlook this fact.) In Bombay in 1943 I created somewhat of a scandal by taking a left-wing Hungarian girl to the Royal Bombay Yacht Club. In the 1950s, whilst in journalism, I tried to sign up Vladimir Petrov as a correspondent to advise on Australian football pools long before he defected. (I had been reliably informed that he knew more about Australian soccer than most Australian sporting journalists.) To cap it all, the remarkable Colonel Goleniewski, who claims to be the son of the late Tsar of All the Russias, has himself said I am a tool of the KGB.'[6]

As I added to these personal revelations, 'MI5, what have you been doing all these years? Where is Cmnd Paper XX 69 to unmask Richard Deacon?' In short, all of us who have played around in these deep waters, whether as actual agents, investigative writers or politicians, are liable to have our motives examined, and quite rightly so. I am happy to include myself in this corps and to be ready to answer any questions raised. At the same time I should like to add that though there has been in many cases questionable support for the Soviet Union and its allies sometimes this has come about through misdirected idealism and not treachery. If some evidence for this viewpoint of mine is needed, I can point to circumstances surrounding my one banned book, *The British Connection*,[7] which was serialised in the *Guardian* before publication. The book was withdrawn from publication after four days because of a libel action. But prior to this there had been all manner of attempts to strike out of the original script certain things I had written. Most of these, but not all, concerned my cautious attempt (it had to be cautious in the light of libel threats) to point in the direction of Anthony Blunt as one of the main Soviet agents. Attempts were made by the *Guardian*'s feature editor and one other member of the staff to confront Blunt with what I had said. Needless to say, at that stage, he remained silent. In the end it was Andrew Boyle's admirable book, *The Climate of Treason*, which finally convinced Blunt that with two investigative authors on his tail, his days as a respected figure were numbered, and that a single question in the House of Commons would at last produce the answer which previous prime ministers had carefully dodged.

However, despite the libel action against my book, which was settled out of court, let it be added, there had been every intention to republish it in slightly amended form. But suddenly pressure against this came from every quarter – from left-wingers (in one case from a person whose name was not actually mentioned in the book, though he claimed that statements pointed to him, and he was given an apology for this by the publishers), and, much more disturbingly from banking and big business interests. I felt at that somewhat perplexing time that the main threats came from such people in the City and business world who were anxious to cover up their own dealings with agencies behind the Iron Curtain. I had some anonymous threats by telephone and there was certainly hostility from some members of the Establishment, not least from some members of that élite secret society, the Cambridge Apostles. Not from all Apostles, I should like to add, but from those who had been active in the Soviet cause.

In the quest for the truth in all these matters there is a veritable jungle of fantasies, disinformation and downright lies through which one has to pass.

One of the most devious, yet sometimes highly skilful ploys of the Soviet Union and its allies in recent years has been the extension of *glasnost* to certain highly controversial areas of international politics. This quite often reveals itself by exploiting anti-Zionism in the interests of the USSR. Zionism has been extremely unpopular among some Conservatives everywhere for diverse and outdated reasons. This has sometimes been seen in the inept manner in which some British politicians and diplomats have handled matters related to both Palestine and Israel. It has occasionally shown itself in British Government pronouncements, despite the fact that Britain in particular and the Western World in general would be deficient in Intelligence without some collaboration with Israel's Mossad. In 1988, as a result of some incredible mishandling on an official level, relations between

British Intelligence Services and the Mossad were seriously damaged.

One Soviet ploy has been to confuse Western opinion by encouraging the propagation of the theme that behind the Palestinian problem and the controversy of the West Bank the USSR seeks a secret deal with certain Israelis. The truth is that as long as Israel exists as a resolute and democratic state so it is likely to remain an ally of the Western powers. It was only when the Jews were being persecuted all around the world, especially in many parts of Western Europe, and had no homeland of their own, that many of them did turn to Soviet Russia as a possible ally. But only if there is lack of support for Israel's security, or ambivalent politicising by Western powers over the Middle East, could such a situation develop again. One factor in this is the notorious pro-Arab section in the British Foreign Office which has persisted since the 1920s.

Yet out of such situations, especially when cleverly exploited by an enemy which has turned disinformation into a science and is increasingly scoring points by this means, suspicion and paranoia emerge. There is a strong element of disinformation being pumped out to support *glasnost* and *perestroika*. Behind *glasnost*, is the 'One World' sovietisation concept.

Fortunately Britain's Secret Intelligence Service has cleaned its stables over the past 20 years, and it is well aware of just how skilfully the USSR's new and carefully controlled disinformation techniques are deployed. If the era of Philby, Blunt and Blake was not long since dead, then one can be sure the British would never have won so valuable a double-agent as Oleg Gordievsky who worked for ten years both in Denmark and in London. Twenty years ago any such agent wanting to defect or to work for a Western power would have chosen the CIA not MI6. Gordievsky in effect gave the latter a clean bill of health.

But while MI6 has slowly re-established itself, MI5 will inevitably remain under a cloud until the allegations which have surrounded it for the best part of 40 years are fully examined. Britain's counter-espionage service is the one organisation which should never have been subjected to such hysteria on the one hand and downright skulduggery on the other. The late Sir Roger Hollis was Director-General of that service from 1956 until 1965, having joined it in 1938. Yet increasingly, especially in the last four years of his term of office, he was in charge of an organisation which was riddled with internal dissensions and trouble stirred up by small coteries of its officers. Not only did some of these people accuse Hollis of being a secret Soviet agent, but, when they failed to make out an adequate case against him, made the alternative suggestion that his Deputy-Director, Graham Mitchell, was a mole working for the USSR. When they made no progress in substantiating that allegation, a few of the more compulsive seekers after moles made further accusations against one or two other members of MI5. Suddenly it seemed as though everybody had become suspicious of everyone else, even closest colleagues. It demoralised the service.

To reject these accusations as being totally unfounded is part of the purpose of this book. However, let it be clearly stated that MI5 *was* infiltrated by the Soviet Union to a highly damaging extent and that there have been moles within it and one 'top mole' whose identity I shall reveal.

Certainly a vital purpose of this book is to explain exactly who these people were and how such infiltration came about, and how certain members of the British Establishment, not technically members of the security services, manipulated these people for their own questionable ends. As will be seen, it is a tangled story in which sometimes idealism and downright treachery were intertwined and where stupidity, suspicion and prejudice have been the main motivations.

2

'A Good Bottle Man'

The longest day must end in night,
Sing everything must change.
The blackest darkness turn to light,
Sing everything must change.
Rain follows sun, and sun the rain,
And then the clouds come back again'
Sing every change . . .
                        (poem by Roger Hollis in The Cliftonian, *July 1924)*

This is a book which, chronologically speaking, requires rather specialised treatment. It concerns matters which date back to the end of the last century and the beginning of this, and it especially covers the years between World Wars I and II. But, to put it into perspective, not least from the viewpoint of the reader who likes to know how these matters concern the present day as well as the past, it seems to make sense to start off with a close look at the life of Sir Roger Hollis, the man who has been so much maligned in recent years and who amidst continuing controversy has been mainly held to blame for alleged failures on the part of MI5. After examining his life and career, it will then be necessary to retrace our steps in time and go further back to examine the lives and careers of others.

Roger Henry Hollis was born at Wells in Somerset on 2 December 1905, the son of the late Right Reverend George Arthur Hollis, Bishop of Taunton. George Hollis was the eldest son of Henry William Hollis, JP, managing director of the Weardale Coal and Iron Company. Four years after having been ordained into the Church of England he married in 1898 Mary Margaret Church, the fourth daughter of Charles Marcus Church, a Canon of Wells Cathedral.

These details are not altogether irrelevant, because as a main plank of the case against Hollis, it has been argued that, in support of the Soviet defector Igor Gouzenko's account of a man from MI5 who interviewed him in Canada and then failed to pass on the information 'there was something Russian in his background'. The suggestion has been made that centuries ago the Hollis family were somehow linked to Peter the Great of Russia. Close investigation has shown no links whatsoever.

Roger was the third son among four brothers. The eldest, Michael, becoming a curate at Huddersfield, was known to Evelyn Waugh as 'Huddersfield Hollis'. He later became Assistant Bishop of the Diocese of Bury St Edmunds after considerable diocesan experience in India. The second son was Christopher, who became a Conservative Member of Parliament after serving in World War II in the RAF and was also an author of some distinction. The fourth son, Marcus, eventually joined MI6, Britain's Secret Intelligence Agency.

With four sons and no daughters, Margaret Hollis needed and indeed, judging from Roger, wonderfully achieved a remarkable relationship with her children both in their younger days and afterwards. Certainly there could have been nothing better in the home atmosphere, something which was admirably demonstrated in later years by letters from Roger to his mother. Elizabeth Goudge wrote:

When my father became Principal of the Theological College and moved across the road to the Principal's House his friend, Arthur Hollis, afterwards Bishop of Taunton, became Vice-Principal and I think three of his distinguished sons were born at Tower House. Mrs Hollis was not only lovely to look at, but she had a serenity surprising in a mother of a family of small boys, and a good reader aloud should always have serenity; it casts a spell. I have two memories of her that especially shine out, just as certain paradisial dreams do, clear and bright against the darkness of much forgetfulness. The first is of her reading aloud to a group of children in the panelled drawing-room at Tower House, a small, beautiful room half-way up the stairs. The sun was warm on the panelling, for it was summer, and there were flowers in the room and a sweet smell . . . Mrs. Hollis sat on a low chair, her wide skirts spread about her. She had a beautiful voice and I think the sweetest face of any woman I have ever seen. I had hard work to admit to myself that she was lovelier than my mother, but I had to in the end.[1]

Roger Hollis's early life was spent at Wells, where his father was at one time a priest. Later the family moved north and Roger was educated first at Leeds Grammar School and then at Clifton. It would seem that he always had a much closer relationship with his mother than his father, partly no doubt because she was in herself a remarkable personality who adapted easily to the needs of growing sons, but also due to the fact that in that particular era fathers who were also clergy of the Church of England did not always fill their paternal role in the best possible way. There have been many cases of tainted sons of C of E clergymen, Anthony Blunt being perhaps a supreme example. However, let it be stressed that in Hollis's case, whatever the shortcomings of the father, the mother maintained and even strengthened the family ties. It is interesting to note that it was generally to his mother he wrote letters. In many ways his mother gave him the balanced outlook on life which never seemed to leave him afterwards.

He went to Clifton with his brother, Marcus, unlike his other brothers, Christopher, who went to Eton, and Michael who was educated at Leeds Grammar School.

Roger Hollis was admitted to the Junior (Preparatory) School at Clifton in September, 1918.

Hollis seems to have done reasonably well at Clifton in the OTC, for in 1924 he was promoted from sergeant to company sergeant-major. At cricket he seems to have been rather less successful, being sent in first in house matches, but in 1923 at any rate registering 'ducks' in each innings. Nor did he seem to succeed as a bowler. But he was by all accounts a leading runner in the Long Penpole cross country race, and he composed verse for *The Cliftonian*. One of these was entitled *Carmen Amoebaeum*:

> Come gods above, and fairly aid my song;
> For me no lofty strain of hero's toil
> And old-time legend, mine the humbler broil
> Of human lives compound of right and wrong.
> My strain will rise to heaven's eternal light.
> What need for ever crawling, ever dumb?
> What reason? Strive to overtop the sum
> Of all, and learn to tell both wrong and right.[2]

There were several more verses, but the poem was rounded off by these lines:

> All hail! the joy of battle: hail to thee,
> Thou mighty Ares! Raise the warlike shout!
> Death may be hidden in that battle rout,

But such a death gives immortality.

Later on there were other poems in *The Cliftonian* by Roger Hollis, sometimes simple comments on the 'summer rain . . . I hear it from my bed falling warmly, softly' and one other 'To the Laburnum outside my Window.'[3]

Hollis kept in touch with his old school. As late as December, 1960, he was the guest speaker at a House supper (Watson's House) and referred to a recent visit he had made to Africa and the problems of African affairs.

In 1924 Hollis won a Classical Exhibition to Worcester College, Oxford. It seemed to herald the beginning of a career in which nothing could go wrong, yet in those days, rather more at Oxford than Cambridge, often the most promising came unstuck. University education was viewed somewhat critically by outside interests, not only in business, but in the professions as well: there was the feeling, quite often justified, that the university approach was out of touch with the realities of life itself. Though ostensibly reading English, he spent much of his time playing golf and thoroughly enjoying undergraduate parties. Hollis was essentially drawn towards interesting people – more in the sense of 'how can this person amuse me' than in 'how can he educate me'? For this very reason he drew his friends from a wide spectrum. Sir Dick White, a former head of MI5, in his contribution to the *Dictionary of National Biography*, said that in the view of his contemporaries at Oxford Hollis 'seemed to prefer a happy, social life to an academic one.'[4] Sir Harold Acton, the model for Anthony Blanche in *Brideshead Revisited*, also at Oxford at this time, describes Hollis as 'an agreeable friend'.[5]

It is true that Hollis made friends on the left as well as the right. Certainly he was for a time on friendly terms with Claud Cockburn, a sufficiently dedicated communist to become diplomatic and foreign correspondent for the *Daily Worker*. He was also a close friend of Maurice Richardson, another journalist and writer who for a time joined the Communist Party.

There was probably a strong feeling in young Roger Hollis that he needed to break away from his background and to take a good look around before he decided what to do.

Evelyn Waugh, who was a contemporary at Oxford, described Hollis as 'a good bottle man'. In his diaries he recorded that on 8 December 1924:

I moved to 40 Beaumont Street and began a vastly expensive career of alcohol. After a quiet day in cinemas, I had a dinner party of Claud, Elmley, Terence, Roger Hollis and a poor drunk called Macgregor. I arrived quite blind after a number of cocktails at the George with Claud. Eventually the dinner broke up and Claud, Roger Hollis and I went off for a pub-crawl which after sundry indecorous adventures ended up at the Hypocrites [Club] where another blind was going on . . . Next day I drank all the morning from pub to pub and invited to lunch with me at the New Reform John Sutro, Roger Hollis, Claud and Alfred Duggan.[6]

Two years later he recorded on 13 April 1926, a:

rather amusing afternoon at Wells. Roger Hollis and I lunched at the Swan and drank champagne and brandy mixed. After a time we were turned out. There was a market at Farrington Gurney. It was odd that we were not killed going there. After a time the man in the pub refused us drinks. I said I was Hobhouse of Castle Cary and that I would have him out of the pub in a month. He believed me and gave us heaps more to drink. We lay on a field for some time. Roger lit a pipe. I think the aunts thought I had been drinking.[7]

Another friend of Roger Hollis was Roger Fulford, who became President of the Oxford Union in 1927, and much later in life President of the Liberal Party in 1964-5. He was at Worcester College with Hollis, describing him as 'a good golfer who played regularly with Sam (as he was then known) Gaitskell. He read English under the Dean of the College and became, as he grew older, rather dissipated. He went down from the university prematurely in 1926 without taking a degree.'[8]

There seems to have been no clear explanation as to exactly why Hollis left Oxford so soon. Probably there were a number of reasons. At Worcester College today there is no special mention of him in any of its records. A member of the college writes: 'I have always understood that he left because he had run out of money. One can easily find parallel cases in that period.'

There was another even more vital reason why in those days many did not stay on at university: they had no confidence that a degree, even a good degree, would guarantee them a worthwhile job. Perhaps this was in Hollis's opinion a highly valid reason for leaving four terms before he took his finals. He had missed much time at school through illness and this may have contributed to a feeling that he was always somewhat behind in his work. Possibly he decided that a good social life was preferable to slogging away to get a good degree that might aid him very little. The only reason the 21-year-old Hollis seemed to give to his friends was that he had 'an itch to see the New World'.

Maurice Richardson, the literary critic, recorded that 'Roger Hollis and I had a romantic plan to abandon Oxford and seek our fortunes in Mexico. We got as far as applying for Mexican visas, but that was all. I never saw him after Oxford, but used to inquire about him during the early sixties from his brother, Chris, who either didn't know what he was doing, or else was diplomatically evasive.'[9]

Sir Roger Fulford said:

Like many people at that time whose families were not rich, he saw little hope of making a name for himself by toiling away for a degree in a subject where he was unlikely to get a first after a somewhat raffish time at the end of his Oxford career . . . I don't remember his saying anything about what he was going to do when he finally left Oxford. At that time the General Strike drove everything out of the minds of undergraduates.[10]

The General Strike of 1926 made an enormous impact on the minds of many undergraduates at Oxford, and undoubtedly some of them overreacted to it in an unintelligently romantic way. This particular tendency seems to have been a recurring error in Oxonian thinking over a lengthy period. Much has been written about the Cambridge Connection with relation to the number of prominent Cantabrigians who became Soviet agents, but far less has been told about the equally important Oxford Connection. It was from Oxford that the young Clemens Palme Dutt went to Cambridge to set up a Comintern network and a number of contemporaries of Hollis would be such communist figures as Tom Driberg (later Lord Bradwell), Ralph Fox, John Strachey and Tom Wintringham. Cecil Day Lewis, a former Poet Laureate, certainly ploughed the communist furrow for a number of years. Educated at Sherborne and Wadham College, Oxford, he was, like a number of leading young communists of this period, the son of a clergyman. He became a member of the CPGB for about three years, but was never one hundred per cent intellectually committed to communism. Yet his reputation as a scholar and a poet gave him a talent for winning recruits to the cause, some of whom lasted the course better than he did.

While Oxford University had quite a number of communists in the late 1920s, it never had as many as Cambridge and there was no under-cover secret society to support them, nothing remotely like the Cambridge Apostles. It was not until the middle 1930s that Oxford communists began to come into the news and by that time Hollis had long since left.

For about a year after he left Oxford Hollis worked in the DCO branch of Barclay's Bank, a job which was surely some indication of his desperate need to earn some money as it was hardly work to which he would be likely to be attracted. After this he made a brief visit to Canada and the United States without finding any worthwhile work. Letters home in that period suggested he had been to New York and some of the southern states. Then in 1927 he went out to the Far East to take up a journalistic post. According to Sir Dick White, this was with 'a Hongkong paper'. My own information was that he worked briefly as a reporter on the *Shanghai Post*, but it is possible that he wrote for both newspapers. At any rate when Hollis was in Shanghai he started to work for the British American Tobacco Company.

3

Laughing at Dreams

It is important that man dreams, but it is perhaps equally important that he can laugh at his own dreams. That is a great gift and
the Chinese have plenty of it.

(Lin Yutang in The Importance of Living*)*

Very occasionally Roger Hollis would in later life quote from the
modern Chinese philosopher, Lin Yutang, and this particular reference to dreams and laughing at them was one he particularly liked. Lin
and Hollis had a similar view of life in that one had to regard its ups and
downs with a judicious mixture of love and irony, cynicism and kindly
tolerance.

Hollis's duties with BAT took him far and wide across China. He
had to travel extensively at a time when the nation was involved in
fighting on more than one front. He seems not to have liked Chungking very much and expressed something akin to guilt about leaving a
colleague on his own in that city, referring to 'the little social life which
Chungking offers . . . thoroughly miserable.'[1]

He did a certain amount of writing while in China, and this included
one article in *The Times* some time between 1935 and 1937, entitled
'Japan on the Mainland'. It touched on the subject of Manchukuo and
the Sovietised Outer Mongolia. 'Japan has established her frontier
with Russia at what seemed at first a safer distance from her own highly
vulnerable cities. The idea that Manchukuo is in any sense a relief to
the over-population of Japan is false. The Chinese will work harder,
live cheaper and stand the climate better than their Japanese rivals,' he
wrote. Perhaps this opinion was prejudiced, but in his assessment of
the military situation Hollis was obviously much better informed.

The Kwantung Army is organising the Mongols and laying out
aerodromes for its own use. The Japanese have chosen their
ground well, for the passes of the high Mongol plateau are few
and far between, so they are able to carry out their plans in almost

complete secrecy. At present the door is shut tight and not even Japanese civil officials are allowed to visit this territory. The Manchukuo forces have quite openly seized the six northern counties or *hsien* of Chahar province, which gives them the opportunity of policing this part of the border of Sovietised Outer Mongolia.[2]

Hollis also wrote the occasional short story, again using the Far East as a background. One such story was entitled 'A Matter of Form' which is undoubtedly based to some extent on his own experiences. It started off by telling how:

Brian Leslie walked into the private office with a thrill of importance. He was young, and it was his first job "on his own", so it was excusable. For a month he had been working with Frobisher, taking over the area, but today Frobisher was due to leave on his long train-journey to Peking and civilisation, and Brian would be in full charge.

The office was sited 'on the borders of Mongolia' and Brian was full of excitement as he was given the keys and the code to solve the telegraph messages. There was one disappointment – Frobisher had not told him what was in the safe, or what the combination was. He had said he didn't think there was anything important inside, if indeed there was anything at all. He personally did not use the safe.

Brian deduced that in some way the safe was faulty, so he consulted Head Office and they told him to send it to them and they would replace it. The old safe was duly loaded on to an ox-cart and taken to the railway station. Next came a request from the railway police that the safe should be opened as they wished to examine it, because no package could be shipped until they had done this. Brian declined to give permission and sent his personal clerk to sort matters out. The clerk was promptly arrested and put in jail. Brian protested and went down to demand his clerk's release, but was told this would only be done just as soon as the safe was open. In the end the safe was blown up and nothing was found inside it. The Chief of Police explained that often such safes were full of heroin, but he bowed and told Brian: 'Now it will be quite in order for you to ship your safe. Of course, in the case of your honoured company such inspection is a mere formality!'[3]

One wonders on what incident this short story was based. Those who knew Hollis well are convinced it would have some basis in fact, and that almost certainly it would have been based on some story concerning BAT. Certainly Hollis visited a variety of offices and branches either belonging to BAT or linked to that company ranging from Shanghai, Peking, Chungking, Hankow and the borders of Mongolia to the Yee Tsoong Tobacco Distributors at Tsinanfu in Shantung Province. Most of the evidence of what he did and the people he saw at this time came through letters sent home to his mother. These were mainly hand-written, but occasionally typewritten. They were all addressed to 'Meg'. In those days there came a point when boys shied off 'Mummy' or 'Mums', while not being altogether happy with the alternative of 'Mother'. Incidentally, in his correspondence with his mother his father seems to have been left out almost totally. One has the feeling that Roger Hollis was glad to escape paternal influence. Chapman Pincher claims that when Hollis was interrogated in 1970 in the belief that he might confess to having been a Soviet agent, he gave as his reason for leaving Oxford without a degree to go to China 'to get away from the family and the Church'.[4] For 'family and the Church' perhaps one could read 'father'.

Many of Hollis's letters contained references to the tuberculosis which he suddenly contracted and which eventually caused him to leave BAT. Once he was obviously writing a letter to his mother in bed for he said 'this typewriter seems to make a most awful racket, even though it is all tangled up with the bed clothes: I'm sure I shall soon have one of the Sisters reminding me that some of the patients are really ill, even if I'm not.'[5]

Whatever his other problems in coping with a new job, Hollis certainly must have had a devastating test of his own character in facing up to his tuberculosis problem at so early an age:

Hall, the doctor who examined me, thought I had made an amazingly good recovery, so good, in fact, that he wants to see me again in three months time to make sure I'm not going along too fast. I shall, of course, have to be very careful for another year or two, because apparently one can never absolutely get rid of the bug once it is there, but I'm living a perfectly normal life except that I avoid late nights and violent exercise.[6]

In a letter to his mother he referred to sharing an apartment with 'two pleasant but not over-intelligent Americans, who spend their time at the club playing bridge when they are neither working nor sleeping.'[7]

It has been said by many people, including some in the counter-Intelligence Services, that Hollis was anti-American. No doubt he felt, as many of us did at that time, that America was being very unrealistic in setting itself apart from the rest of the world.

But what of Hollis's alleged Soviet contacts in China? They range from unsubstantiated allegations that he was a close friend of Richard Sorge, later the Soviet Union's ace spy in Tokyo, to Ursula Maria Hamburger (better known later on as 'Sonia' in the Soviet Swiss network) and to Agnes Smedley, the American woman who lent aid both to the Chinese and the Russians. However, the truth remains that there has been no positive evidence of Hollis even having met these people. The latter was a gregarious character and she had a habit of turning up in the most unexpected company, so it is no surprise that Hollis, when invited to give an account of his early life, recalled having met Smedley, but denied having had any later connection with her.[8] This admission has been expanded by some writers into the charge that during a nine-year stay in China Hollis became 'friendly' with Agnes Smedley.

As to Sonia, though she has given considerable details of her life in China in this period in a book published in East Germany, there is no mention in this of Hollis. As various people have alleged that Hollis met her in China and maintained a close relationship with her afterwards both in Switzerland and in Oxford where she lived for a while, it is important to seek evidence supporting this, and also to take a look at 'Sonia's' career. Ursula Ruth Kuczynski was the daughter of a German Jewish professor who taught economics at Oxford University prior to World War II. She went out to the USA in the mid-1920s, worked in a bookshop in New York and met Rolf Hamburger, who was finishing his studies as an architect. She went back to Germany and married him in 1929. Already a communist, when her husband obtained a post as an architect in Shanghai, she went out with him in 1930.

'I was thrilled by the prospects of being able as a German Communist to cooperate with the persecuted comrades in China,'[9] wrote Ursula. In her account of her life in that country she mentions many names of people she met, including 'a well known lawyer named Dr Wilhelm'; an eccentric bachelor, Bernstein, who had been interned by the British in India in World War I; Professor Stumpf of the German-Chinese University; Matsumuto, 'a good-looking Japanese who represented UFA motion pictures'; Agnes Smedley, then correspondent of the *Frankfurter Zeitung*; and 'Miss Ting Ling, who had been for quite a long time with the Chinese Red Army'.

At the time 'Sonia' was living in Mukden, Hollis was mainly based in Hankow. The set in which Hollis moved while in China was very different from that of 'Sonia'. In any case it is almost certain that 'Sonia' and her fellow-conspirators would keep well away from those of the BAT fraternity in China, or of similar Anglo-American companies. They were all suspected of being at best supporters of imperialism, or at worst undercover Intelligence agents for the West.

In October, 1934, he wrote to his mother about 'streaking up the Yangtse River on my way back to Hankow' while at the same time telling her of his trip back to China after leave in the UK via Berlin and Moscow:

> Berlin . . . struck me as a wonderful city, but I did not at all like the militaristic Hitlerism which one found everywhere. Uniforms, strutting self-importance and fantastic salutation on all sides . . . The Russian customs at Nuigoreloji was very thorough, but harmless apart from that, after which we boarded the trans-Siberian train and woke up next morning at Moscow. We were met by a representative of Intourist, who drove us to their head-quarters at the National Hotel . . . Intourist then put us into another Lincoln car with a very charming young lady as a guide, and sent us off to see the sights.[10]

The guide was apparently 'most enthusiastic, as was to be expected', but Hollis commented that he had:

> never seen anything which depressed me so unutterably as Moscow. It was like driving through a huge drab slum of three and a half million people, everyone ill-drest [sic] in the most deplorable ready-mades, though not in rags, I admit . . . Lenin's tomb . . . looked rather like a high class public lavatory, but we couldn't go in as it didn't open until five o'clock . . . It was a positive relief to get back to our compartment on the train. I suppose you are as anxious as ever for the human side, so let me assure you that my companion in the compartment was not the charming young guide, whom we left at Moscow, but a schoolmaster from Shang-hai of the plebian name of Tebbs, whom I met on the train at Berlin.[11]

Nothing much here to suggest that Hollis was in any way enamoured by the Soviet Union, and later in this same letter he wrote 'Manchuria we reached about three hours late with a feeling that here at last was China and civilisation again ... I am not at all sorry that I did the journey, but if I do it again it will be from China home, when one can more easily travel light and make arrangements for one's own feeding.'

Outside his work Hollis showed his principal interest to be golf and he was most irritated when the attack of tuberculosis interfered with this. In February 1935, he wrote that 'weather like this makes me long to hit a golf-ball again. It seems like years since I last did so.' Once he wrote to his mother that he had had 'rather an unpleasant experience ... I woke up on Monday with an attack of bleeding like the one I had after the West of England golf championship ... I'm going to be X-rayed as soon as we can arrange it, and I'll let you know the worst.'

To Roger Fulford he once said that he now knew what Thomas de Quincey must have suffered when he contracted tuberculosis. De Quincey, like Hollis, had gone to Worcester College to study in 1803, reading German philosophy and learning the language. 'De Quincey found solace in opium, but I need something more than dreams to live on. It is curious that both de Quincey and I should have left Worcester without a degree.'

Fulford was also convinced, judging from what Hollis told him when they served together in MI5 much later, that Hollis had picked up some worthwhile information which he passed on to British Intelligence contacts while he was in China: 'I believe he passed on some news of Soviet espionage activities in China and actually named one of their agents.' But Fulford could not recall the name and was not sure that he had ever been told it.

Both Chapman Pincher and Peter Wright have alleged that Hollis returned to the United Kingdom in 1936 via Russia, stopping off at Moscow where he was recruited as a Soviet agent. The truth is that he returned to Britain by ship from China across the Pacific Ocean to Canada and then over the Atlantic to Britain. Letters to his mother at home, showing date stamps and ship stamps, prove this quite clearly. Much of this correspondence was discovered after the death of the first Lady Hollis, and is now supplemented by a document freely available at the Public Record Office. Of course this does not prove Hollis's *innocence*, admittedly, but it does show that Peter Wright had not done his research very effectively. Indeed, Wright's allegation regarding this return journey shows just how much it is based on guesswork and unsubstantiated statements.

It was tuberculosis which forced Hollis to give up his post in China.

Such a disease might well have defeated a lesser man, but he was determined to fight it. As soon as he got home he sought further treatment, rehabilitated himself and eventually sought a new career.

4

Hollis in Quest of Soviet Plots

I said to Roger Hollis, 'You know I think we spend too much time worrying over the Russians. What do you think?' He answered: 'I do not think I should think that, if I were you'.
(Sir Roger Fulford, a wartime member of MI5, in a letter to the author)

Roger Hollis was confronted with two simultaneous problems when he returned to Britain – to seek a cure for his tubercular ailments and to find a worthwhile job. In the late 1930s nobody got a really first-class job without making great efforts. The former hearty and mildly dissolute undergraduate had at last realised that what was most important in life was a worthwhile job. Possibly the shock of a sudden and devastating illness had brought about a change of outlook.

It is true that about this time there was a certain cover-up on Hollis's health problems in his own family circle, but in the light of needing to look for work this is understandable. There is evidence that he spent a very short period in Switzerland and saw a Swiss doctor. Naturally, those who argue the case that Hollis was a Soviet spy use the theme of a visit to Switzerland as a possible opportunity for making contact with 'Sonia' who by that time was in charge of the Soviet network and living not far from Montreux. Another factor in the wishful thinking of Hollis's denouncers was that Hugh Sykes Davies, then a member of the Communist Party and also of the Cambridge Apostles, also had treatment for tuberculosis in Switzerland about this time.

While in China Hollis had established a relationship with Peter Fleming, already somewhat of a specialist on Chinese affairs, and through him Hollis tried to obtain a job on *The Times*. This attempt failed, as did other approaches to W. D. & H. O. Wills in Bristol and to Cadbury. Meanwhile he worked for a few months in the accounts department at Ardath, an associate of BAT.

Surprisingly, perhaps, for a man in his position both health-wise and job-wise it was in this uncertain period of his life that Hollis married. Possibly there was some family pressure for him to 'settle down',

and equally he may have been led to believe that family contacts as a result of marriage might lead the way to a job. He was then 32 and at a
difficult age to find the right job. At that age it would have been far too
risky to start again at the bottom of the ladder, as it were. He needed to
get a relatively senior post. On 10 July 1937, he married in Wells
Cathedral Evelyn Esme, daughter of George Champeny Swayne, a
solicitor of Burnham-on-Sea and Glastonbury. The best man at the
wedding was one Jack Swayne, a cousin of the bride and not a close
friend of Hollis. The honeymoon was spent very briefly in the New
Forest.

Almost immediately after this Hollis was making desperate searches
for a serious and important post and going out of his way to build up a
reputation for himself. In October 1937, he gave a lecture to the Royal
Central Asian Society on 'The Conflict in China', which received
favourable attention both inside and outside the society.[1] It is said that
he owed the good luck to be introduced to the ranks of MI5 through
his wife's family's connection with Colonel W. A. Alexander, a
Regular Army officer who had good reason for hating the Comintern
as he had lost a great deal of his personal fortune in supporting the
anti-Soviet North Expeditionary Force in the Russian Civil War. As a
result of this Alexander was chosen by Major-General Sir Vernon
Kell, head of MI5, as the man to combat the problem of subversion in
Britain. Certainly Alexander was one of those who recommended
Hollis to Kell.

Another who recommended Hollis for the MI5 job which he
eventually got was Ray Meldrum, a relation of Hollis's wife. It is clear
that his wife's family were concerned that, without a degree and in ill-
health, he would have difficulty in finding employment. On the other
hand it would be foolish to think that he owed his job in MI5 solely to
influence. Obviously in such a service influence and strong recom-
mendations from experts in the field were essential, especially in the
period just before World War II. But Hollis himself seems to have felt
that what he witnessed in China might be put to some use. Certainly he
must have been well aware of Soviet subversion and espionage in
China. BAT was a company which was always well informed politically
and which expected its staff to be equally well informed on what was
going on in both official and underground sources. To succeed in
business in China at that time such information was all-important. It
was most probably this experience which clinched his appointment by
Vernon Kell as a member of MI5. Kell had been somewhat of a
Chinese expert himself in his early career. He had actually passed an

examination as an interpreter in Chinese and had not only seen service in the Boxer Rebellion in China, but had been made Intelligence Officer on General Lorne Campbell's staff in Tientsin.

But this was not the only thing which Kell and Hollis had in common. Ill-health had also interrupted Kell's military career and in 1904 his job prospects must have seemed as grim because of recurrent outbreaks of asthma, the effects of dysentry and pains in his back which were so acute that for the rest of his life he could barely sit upright in a chair, though few would have guessed this from his upright carriage while walking. Thus it is not unlikely that Kell saw in Hollis a case which resembled his own.

I continue to assess Hollis alongside Kell, because Kell inspired in him a sense of duty and commitment. Kell more than anyone else realised the threat of Soviet subversion inside Britain in the early 1920s. In 1923 a notice appeared in the *London Gazette* to the effect that he had officially retired from service. The *News of the World* then announced in banner headlines 'The Spy Destroyer: Famous Secret Service Officer Retires', but in fact his retirement was just a bluff. The powers-that-be were anxious to conceal the fact that he was still head of MI5, because they realised that since the war the counter-espionage service was faced with a new permanent problem – that of communist subversion and saboteurs in factories. As Lady Kell declared years afterwards: 'He simply wanted to put people off. That was about the year he really did get down to work. He didn't actually retire until 1940.'

It has been said that MI5 in this period immediately before World War II was still relatively amateur and not nearly as sophisticated as it became during the war and after Kell's retirement. Relatively amateur it may well have been, but it was the patriotic and enthusiastic amateurs who did more than anything to combat the Soviet subversion. The sophisticated members who were recruited later were often not even remotely patriotic and sometimes pursued political ends of their own. Hollis was plunged almost immediately into compiling evidence on the Comintern and maintaining surveillance of the British Communist Party, which was to be his special subject. He worked in B Division under Jane Sissmore, a former barrister. B Division later came under the overall control of its section head, a certain Guy Liddell.

Within three years Hollis had become the acknowledged expert in MI5 on communist subversion, as Sir Dick Goldsmith White, a former head of MI5, has testified in his entry for Hollis in the *Diction-*

ary of National Biography. Mentioning that Hollis 'began his new career in MI5 in 1938', Sir Dick went on to say: 'By qualities of mind he was in several ways well adapted to it. He was a hard and conscientious worker, level-headed, fair-minded and always calm. He began as a student of international communism in which he became an authority. With small resources he managed to ensure that the danger of Russian-directed communism was not neglected.'[2]

Sometime later Hollis was firmly attached to 'F' Division. Along with Kemball Johnston and Roger Fulford, he was charged with keeping watch on the communists, while Graham Mitchell (later to become Hollis's deputy) maintained a similar role regarding the fascists and members of such organisations as Mosley's Blackshirts and the right-wing society known as The Link.

Over several years since its founding Kell had forged a remarkably efficient, if small and certainly not highly funded organisation. He had established a close relationship with Scotland Yard and the Special Branch of the Metropolitan Police. This arrangement dated back to the earliest days of MI5 in 1909. For years leading statesmen and politicians had dismissed the possibility of espionage in this country as a figment of the imagination. So when at last Kell was given the task, albeit reluctantly by the powers-that-be, of creating a counter-espionage service, all he was allowed was a small room in the War Office which became known as MO5, but no staff at all. For several months MO5, or MI5 as it soon became, comprised one man who was told to keep his expenses to a minimum.

Kell's first step to overcome this ridiculous parsimony by the War Office was to arrange that MI5 must cooperate with Scotland Yard. Thus through Kell the military were put in touch with a problem which had been worrying the police for years – how to cope with potential spies. It was this move by Kell that paved the way to the complete round-up of German agents in the United Kingdom when war broke out in 1914. Kell had insisted from the very beginning that once a person was suspected of being a spy, however much evidence against him or her might be lacking, constant watch was to be kept on that individual. It was a policy which paid handsome dividends.

A less determined man than Kell might have given up hope of making MI5 work in almost any one of those pre-1914 years. He soon found that the outdated Official Secrets Act was one of the biggest obstacles to catching spies. He pointed out to the War Office that in case after case Germans had been found gathering information about ships, factories, arms supplies and harbours, but that nothing could be done to check them because in law the spies were committing no offence. Typical of the mentality of the judiciary in coping with such cases was that of Lord Chief Justice Alverstone, who, when sentencing one German spy to a mere 18 months' imprisonment, declared that relations between Britain and Germany were 'most amicable' and added that he was sure nobody would condemn the 'practice of which the prisoner had been found guilty more strenuously than the leaders of Germany'. Kell pressed for changes in the law.

Gradually he managed to obtain permission for extra staff for MI5. He was given the services of Captain Frederick Clark, Captain R. J. Drake and Inspector Melville from Scotland Yard, as well as a barrister, Walter Moresby, who handled the legal side of the department's work. Later on Kell was fortunate in that the man chosen to head the newly created Special Branch at Scotland Yard was Basil Thomson, the son of an Archbishop of York, a man of great force and drive who had had experience in the Colonial Service in various parts of the world. Thomson was a formidable ally who had made a study of the Anarchist movement in London's East End and the problem of handling immigrants pursuing political ends. But soon he found that the problem of German spies in Britain was of much greater urgency.

By the time war was declared in August 1914, Kell's service had been expanded to include four officers, one barrister, two investigators and seven clerks. Requiring larger premises, MI5 was moved from the War Office to the basement of the Little Theatre in John Street, off the Strand.

Kell held office as head of MI5 from 1909 until 1939, a record equalled by no other Director-General of that organisation. Possibly, his persistence in pressing for changes in the Official Secrets Act was vital to the safety of the nation from World War I onwards. Without such changes the German spy network inside Britain, which was quite considerable in the early years of the century, would probably never have been broken. By the time World War II came Kell had something like 100 persons working for him in some capacity or another, even if most of them were only called upon occasionally. He had not only infiltrated the communist and fascist ranks in Britain, but had most efficiently penetrated the organisation which was handling recruitment for the Spanish Republican Army, the International Brigade. Thus, in 1939, after the declaration of war, some 6000 people were rounded up and interned as suspects, though only 35 of these were Britons.

By this time Kell realised that age and ill-health would prevent him from achieving in World War II what he had done in World War I. It has been suggested that his retirement was forced on him because some had tried to make him a scapegoat for the fact that the Germans had been able to penetrate the hitherto impregnable anchorage of Scapa Flow to sink the battleship, *Royal Oak*. There was a story that the Germans had had a long-term spy living in the Orkneys: this later proved to be nothing more than a propaganda story from Berlin.

Kell was a deeply religious man who was always impressed if a prospective candidate for MI5 had a religious background. Curiously enough, though, this tendency also had an unusual qualification: Kell was said to be opposed to employing Roman Catholics on the grounds that sometimes their religious beliefs might come before their patriotism. Probably this had some relation to IRA-watching. One of his colleagues said of him:

> If he learned that Hollis's father was a bishop, that would almost make Hollis home and dry for a job. Not that I am suggesting that Hollis wasn't a sound choice, but simply that Kell tended to think on those lines.

On the outbreak of World War II certain sections or divisions of the service were moved to Wormwood Scrubs Prison. Soon bus conductors on routes which ran close to the Scrubs realised that a number of highly delectable young females were dismounting by the Scrubs, and it was not long before one wag among them used to shout out 'This way off for MI5!' Whether anyone protested about this is not recorded. Hollis worked in 'A' Block at the Scrubs and Roger Fulford was asked by his fellow Oxonian to join him in the spring of 1940, taking a post in F-4 section which mainly handled the pacifist and anarchist groups.

'I was working in "B" Block and he was in "A" Block,' Fulford told the author. 'I was doing postal and telegraph censorship – very roughly similar work to his, and we worked in adjoining cells at the Scrubs and talked of our cases each day, going through them without any sort of reticence and doing it completely openly.'[3]

In 1929 Fulford had stood unsuccessfully as the Liberal condidate for the Woodbridge Division of Suffolk. Later he became a distinguished author on a variety of topics with a penchant for writing about queens (Victoria and Caroline in particular), while at the end of his career in 1965 became President of the Liberal Party. Fulford had, of course, been at Oxford with Hollis and later remembered him at this time as being 'a conservatively-minded Liberal, but certainly one who was receptive to both sides of a question.'

In July 1940, after Kell had departed, his protegé Hollis was promoted to take over the post of head of the section dealing with what was sometimes called 'Military Subversion'.

Fulford wrote:

In August or September [1940] Hollis's wife had a child. That September the bombing began – that is to say, September 1940, and our office was hit by enemy bombs in that month. My memory may be wrong, but our records were kept under the careful eye of Miss Beeching. It is obvious that for the records of an office of this kind, their safety was of the first importance . . . Although my memory may desert me here, I know that the MI5 records – though never severely bombed – were in some disorder as a result of the bombing. It was not, I think, realised by the Government civil servants concerned that if once the Security Service records were destroyed or interfered with, the mischief would be considerable.[4]

As to whether there was any such 'mischief' as a result of the bombing only MI5 could tell. And, even at this distance in time, not only would they probably not tell, but the powers-that-be would continue to forbid them to tell.

Roger Fulford went on to say that 'we had always thought that a move from London might be necessary to safeguard ourselves, and we accordingly went in the October. There was a good deal of chaos naturally while we were moving down from London, and there was a good deal of confusion between London and Oxford [their destination]. During that period the various spies were, of course, active and no doubt did much harm'.

Fulford made no further comment on this somewhat puzzling statement. Did he mean that because of missing documents and the bombing MI5 had temporarily lost touch with the realities of their own work? Some others, mainly two female secretaries to whom I have spoken, allege that from the time Kell left office there was increasing confusion in the service and that some executives seemed to be permanently unable to cope with events. 'All of a dither, all the time,' said one, 'and we were just told to take a sandwich in the office at lunchtime and keep watch on the phone.'

Roger Hollis had a recurrent bout of tuberculosis almost immediately he moved to Oxford. Prior to this he had lived at 18 Elsham

Road, on the borders of Holland Park and Hammersmith. In Oxford from 1940 to 1942 his address was at 29a Charlbury Road, described by Fulford as being 'rather dingy lodgings'. For a time Hollis was treated at a sanitorium near Cirencester, but he still continued to work even from his bed. 'I went over to see him several times to discuss cases in which we were interested,' said Fulford:

> and I generally went accompanied by the head of a branch. I remember saying to Roger on one of these occasions, after the Russians had come into the war, 'You know I think we spend too much time worrying over the Russians. What do you think?' He answered: 'I do not think I should think that if I were you.' He was freed from the sanitorium about the next Christmas, and I had taken his place when he had to leave the office. I went, so far as this is of any importance, largely on different work – that is to say, the religious fanatics like Jehovah's Witnesses, and going round various regional offices which we had, lecturing the Police on such things as the Jehovah's Witnesses and those who were preaching disloyal opinions.[5]

Fulford insisted that Hollis had been 'thoroughly grounded in the position of the office under dear Sir Vernon Kell . . . a very fine man and one who carefully guarded the traditions and secrets of the service. Roger Hollis – and I remember this very well – acknowledged these traditions as the main basis of the service.' Respect for such traditions was undoubtedly weakened to some extent by the fact that in the summer of 1940 many people were allowed to join MI5. A small, tight little service such as this had been up to that date could not effectively cope with a sudden large-scale invasion by outsiders. True, there may well have been delays in increasing its strength so that the service could operate efficiently in a war situation, but in some ways the swift increase in numbers was disruptive.

Some members of B Section were, if anything, rather too anxious to see the results of their work manifested in swift imprisonment for all suspects. Hollis, quite rightly, believed that the correct procedure was to know everything about one's quarry, but not to lock him up unless absolutely necessary. This was not the policy of a weak man, but rather that of one who wanted the maximum information first. By this time he was fully aware of the bonuses that could be achieved by 'turning' enemy agents and using them to pass false information to the enemy.

On the other hand there was on occasion a tendency to be lenient with communists who were under supervision. This was not so much a fault of MI5 as of the Home Office. Roger Fulford recalls 'one occasion when we had a microphone fitted up inside a public meeting [a Communist meeting] and unfortunately a policeman in undress uniform tripped over the wire and alerted the whole hall as to what we were doing. Morrison was Home Secretary at the time and he summoned me to him to explain the danger of what had been done, and we certainly did not carry out such things unless there was good reason for it.'[6]

It is interesting to note what Kim Philby had to say on this subject in his own personal account of what went on in this period. Referring to the 'unsatisfactory relations between SIS and MI5' contributing to his appointment to Section IX of SIS, Philby said it was then necessary for him to:

> place our relations on a new and friendly basis. My opposite number in MI5 was Roger Hollis, the head of its section investigating Soviet and communist affairs. He was a likeable person, of cautious bent . . . Although he lacked the strain of irresponsibility which I think essential (in moderation) to the rounded human being, we got on very well together, and were soon exchanging information without reserve on either side. We both served on the Joint Intelligence Sub-Committee which dealt with communist affairs and never failed to work out an agreed approach to present to the less well-informed representatives of the Service departments and the Foreign Office.
>
> Although Hollis had achieved little in respect of Soviet activity, he had been successful in obtaining an intimate picture of the British Communist Party by the simple expedient of having microphones installed in its King Street headquarters. The result was a delicious paradox. The evidence of the microphone showed consistently that the Party was throwing its weight behind the war effort, so that even Herbert Morrison, who was thirsting for communist blood, could find no legal means of suppressing it.[7]

There are still some people who, recalling the service when Kell was in charge, argue that it was a major error to sack him so suddenly, mainly on the grounds that he would have been invaluable in staying on until his successor was fully briefed. 'Sir Vernon was a sick man, but then he had been sick for many years and had still run an efficient service,' said one. 'He could probably have given vital advice to a newcomer. To get rid of a key man like Kell at a moment's notice was a Churchillian blunder.'

The new chief of MI5 was Sir David Petrie, whose background was the Indian Police. He had been Director of the Indian Government's Intelligence Bureau. One of his first actions was to try to forge closer links between MI5 and MI6, but this eventually became counter-productive in various ways. Sometimes it created hostility between the two services and, as the war progressed, resulted in a more serious problem in the establishment of close links between pro-Soviet members of these organisations. This, however, is a theme which will emerge later on in this narrative.

It was under Petrie's administration that MI5 was brought into contact with the newly created 'Double-Cross' (XX) committee who were concerned with taking over captured (or sometimes merely recruited) enemy agents and then using them to disinform the enemy. There were six separate divisions of MI5 at this time. Lieutenant-Colonel T. A. ('TAR') Robertson was in charge of the double-agents of XX: Victor Rothschild (now Lord Rothschild) was head of the Counter-Sabotage Division (largely scientific); Colonel Charles Butler headed administration; Major Herbert Bacon was the head of 'C' Division which in many ways was all-important in that it had the task of vetting newcomers to the service; Major Bertram Ede headed 'F' Division which was in charge of overseas control; and Captain Guy Liddell was in charge of 'B' Division, with Dick Goldsmith White (later Sir Dick White) as his assistant director. It should be noted that Hollis, Kemball Johnston and Fulford in 'F' Division kept watch originally on the communists, but later all such work was closely controlled by Liddell as head of the counter-espionage section, 'B' Division.

With all these changes and switches in overall responsibility going on Hollis' task was far from easy. He coped, and probably as a result paved his way to promotion, by being quietly reasonable and concentrating on the immediate task. Some of his rivals for promotion did exactly the opposite: they set out to lay down new ideas and to undermine the theories of their superiors. Nobody at the top seemed to clamp down on such disruption.

As one MI5 secretary of this era told me: 'The bitchiness of the men in charge was sometimes unbelievable. They not only mistrusted one another, they tried to manipulate each other's secretaries and set them against the bosses. This may have applied only to a few of the bosses, but this alone made its effects felt throughout the offices.'

Nevertheless Roger Hollis emerged more or less unscathed, and within three years he was the acknowledged expert in MI5 on communist subversion. Sir Dick White has stated that 'in the subsequent extensive wartime expansion of that service he was one of the few professionals to hold his own against the competition of outside talent and to rise to a senior position. The personal qualities responsible for his rise were those of integrity, objectivity and imperturbability in times of crises.'[8]

These qualities became doubly important because all the time that Roger Hollis was trying to tackle these problems he was already being undermined by colleagues in one or other of the Secret and Security Services for reasons more sinister than mere professional rivalry. Kim Philby expressed the opinion that 'no single person could cover the whole field' of communism, adding that he threw his weight behind the solution of keeping the whole field of anti-communist and anti-Soviet work under 'my direct supervision'.[9]

Throughout 1940-1, however, a number of pro-Soviet recruits were drafted into the Intelligence and Security Services. In theory communists were barred from MI5, as they were from the SIS and SOE, but in practice all three organisations took on covert CPGB members both past and present. Usually such recruits were kept in the background and were only known to their case officers. Some of the allegations made against Hollis have concentrated on the fact that he is said to have rejected a report by Maxwell Knight, another MI5 operative, that 'the Comintern is not dead', the theme being that the United Kingdom was still being infiltrated by Soviet agents. It has been said that this report was later read by Churchill after it was passed to him secretly by his personal assistant, Major Desmond Morton. The truth is that the Comintern, largely on Stalin's own instructions, was already dead and other forms of infiltration had been set up long since, which made the main thrust of this report redundant. And in any case, it was Guy Liddell, Hollis' superior officer, who actually turned down Knight's thesis on the grounds that 'Max was allowing his personal distaste for communism to swamp his judgement'. Further, Churchill had laid down on 22 June 1941, a personal order that MI6 should cease to decode Soviet wireless traffic since it would be wrong to spy on our friends. Hollis was always doubtful about the wisdom of this decision: he regarded it as merely a political move on Churchill's part to win friends on the left. In 1941 in response to Churchill's order there was a directive (allegedly by Guy Liddell) that MI5 should scale down its surveillance of the Russians in London.

What is much more important is the report which Hollis made in September 1945, to T. E. Bromley (Sir Thomas Eardley Bromley, who in 1943-5 was Assistant Private Secretary to the Permanent Under-Secretary of State at the Foreign Office). Hollis's report asked the Foreign Office to take note of a document which 'is from a source in this country which had proved reliable in the past'. Among various points which the document made were the following: 'Communists will set up an independent administration in the Russian zone of occupation if the Western Allies agree on a central body for their territory. The part of Germany assigned to Russia will be subject to immediate sovietisation in order to form the nucleus of a future Soviet Germany.'[10]

There is a note at the end of this document made as a commentary on it by the late Sir Con O'Neill, who resigned from the Diplomatic Service in 1939 and served in the Army Intelligence Corps in World War II while also attached to the Foreign Office for part of that time. Sir Con discounted the significance of the Hollis report, noting that 'the people of all European countries comprising not only the lower orders have expressed great enthusiasm for their Russian ally and cannot or will not realise that the victors of Nazism do not stand for democracy, but for a totalitarian system.'[11] In other words there was nothing to be done about it.

In 1982 I asked Sir Con O'Neill whether he would care to amplify or explain further his written comment on this report. After that long passage of time, he admitted that he had

no recollection of it whatsoever. This should not surprise anyone. To read such a report and comment on it would take perhaps three minutes; not much out of a working day of ten hours, itself not much out of a working stint of some three years. I am not trying to throw doubt on the existence of the report, or the likelihood of my having commented on it . . . I spent about 20 minutes a day on such Intelligence reports, or two hours in a six-day week, or perhaps 300 hours in a three-year stint of work. Now, as to the report itself. Maybe I am only exercising hindsight, but it does seem to me that the report is obvious, banal and commonplace with the exception of item 6 [i.e. the part in which it is indicated that Russia intended to withdraw her own troops as soon as the national government in its zone was fully established]. I think that everyone working in the Foreign Office on Germany assumed from hundreds of different reports, events and trends that points

1-5 [in the Hollis report] were indeed valid elements among many others in the situation of Germany.

It surprises me that I should have 'discounted the significance of this report'. I think I should have accepted it (apart from item 6), but regarded it as being unimportant because obvious.[12]

I had suggested in my correspondence with Sir Con that in the possibly sub-edited PRO version of comments on this report something had been arrived at which was not strictly in context, as indeed has been the case with many other such reports. Sir Con's comment on this was:

I do incline to believe with you that something has gone wrong, because the rest of my comment bears no relation whatever to the report it is supposed to be dealing with. The point I am making – about the enthusiasm people in Western Europe felt at that time for their Russian allies – is an important one which I felt strongly at that time. It was this strong residual pro-Russian feeling, as strong in this country as anywhere and deriving from the indebtedness we felt to the Russians for having done so much to win the war ... which more than anything else inhibited our Government from applying correct and necessary policies to Germany until by about 1948 Russian conduct had made it totally manifest that we could not work with them. But this point bears no relation to the report which is supposed to have evoked it.[13]

Perhaps this essentially frank explanation reveals more about the muddled minds of the British Foreign Office at this time than anything else. It is no surprise that some of their members, many years later, could not recall what they thought at the time. The most extraordinary thing about all this is how they, who had adequate access to all the facts, should so blithely jog along, as it were, with a less well-informed public in making their official comments. 'Whose finger on the trigger?', to quote a famous newspaper query of much later years. This was neither Churchill's nor Attlee's, but the British Foreign Office, longing to avoid having any kind of finger on any kind of trigger.

In this period of uncertainty and desire not to offend uninformed public opinion (the curse of all democracies) Hollis had a dual task to perform in his work: he had to try to assure the liberals that communism was still a threat, while equally having to calm down the fanatics who saw the hand of communism everywhere.

In Hollis's work in MI5 in the forties we can see the boy who strove to 'learn to tell both wrong and right', the man who laughed at dreams, and the conscientious, cautious, level-headed and even slightly dull colleague that his contemporaries have recalled.

5

Guy and Alice

Liddell can be regarded ... as a link with past usage, and as
something of a pioneer (albeit perhaps an unconscious one) of
those who today aspire to authentic Baroque string playing.

(Edward Croft-Murray)[1]

To trace the background of Guy Liddell, (a background which was as
exotic as Hollis's was ordinary) we must go briefly back in history.

Just after the end of World War I Britain was threatened by subversion on a scale to the extent of which most historians have paid little
attention. 'February, 1919,' wrote Sir Basil Thomson, chief of the
Special Branch of Scotland Yard, 'was the high-water mark of revolutionary danger in Great Britain. Everything was in favour of the
revolutionaries. Many of the soldiers were impatient at the delay in
demobilisation. Russia had shown how apparently easy it was for a
determined minority, with a body of discontented soldiers behind
them, to seize the reins of power.'[2]

While it is quite true that such a situation as Sir Basil indicated never
developed to the point of widespread rebellion, Britain was menaced
by subversive activities for the next two years. Workers' councils talked
of 'direct action' and opposed the sending of troops to Russia to fight
the Bolsheviks. Electrical engineers talked of plunging London into
darkness unless their demands were met. The Police Union balloted
in favour of a strike.

There were attempts to form Soldiers' and Workers' Councils on
the same basis as in the Soviet Union. Revolutionary leaflets were
distributed in the Army and the Sailors', Soldiers' and Airmen's
Union was set up as a revolutionary body in close touch with workers'
committees. In many industrial centres riots broke out: an attempt was
made to seize Glasgow City Hall. During this same period a Russian
violinist, Edward Soermus toured the country, and his concerts were
attended by large numbers of working men and women who came
more to hear his revolutionary speeches than his music.

All this may seem almost hard to believe some 70 years later, but at that time a feverish political *malaise* had infected a vast section of the people. While the real meaning of Marxist-Leninist philosophy was lost on the masses, they were excited by the idea that the underdog could seize power. This was the problem which Sir Basil Thomson, in his capacity as anti-saboteur chief at Scotland Yard, had to tackle, and advise the Cabinet on it. What made matters difficult for Thomson was that he and Lloyd George, then Prime Minister of a Coalition Government, did not see eye to eye on the best way of tackling it. Thomson wanted tough measures and wider powers: Lloyd George was anxious not to seem to be antagonistic to the workers.

It was early in 1919 that parallel to Vernon Kell's newly formed MI5, the Special Police Branch was set up as a separate organisation under Thomson's control to deal with Bolshevik attempts to spread their doctrines in Britain and to keep watch on subversive agents. As I have indicated it is probably true to say that neither before nor since – not even during the height of Soviet popularity in Britain during World War II – was the United Kingdom nearer to becoming indoctrinated with communism than in 1919. The Council of the Third International was so confident of the success of its organisation in Britain that it forecast 'a revolution in the United Kingdom within six months'. Basil Thomson felt that Lloyd George took an appalling risk in hiding from the Cabinet the true facts about communist infiltration in Britain.

It was in this period that a man who very much later became a key figure in MI5 and the Intelligence world generally was recruited into the Special Branch. This was Captain Guy Maynard Liddell, who was looking for worthwhile work after leaving the Army. He was originally given the task of surveillance of communists under the direction of O. A. Harker (later Brigadier Harker) who was a liaison officer between the Special Branch and MI5 and the Foreign Office. Later on this was the very post to which Liddell was promoted.

The Liddells were an aristocratic Northumberland family whose links had long since been established inside royal circles. Henry Thomas Liddell (1797-1878), the eldest son of Sir Thomas Henry Liddell, the sixth baronet in the family, had been created the first Earl of Ravensworth in July, 1821. His father had rebuilt Ravensworth Castle in 1808. The son became groom-in-waiting to Queen Victoria and Deputy Ranger of Windsor Great Park, while another son was Permanent Under-Secretary of State for the Home Department under Lord Derby. The Liddell baronetcy dated back to 1642, but from the late 1800s onwards the principal friend and influential benefactor and mentor to the family over some generations had been Sir Almeric Fitzroy, Clerk of the Privy Council from 1898 to 1923.

Guy Maynard Liddell was born on 8 November 1892, the son of Captain Augustus Frederick Liddell, CVO, who had been comptroller and treasurer to the household of members of Queen Victoria's family, notably Prince and Princess Christian. Prince Christian came from the house of Schleswig-Holstein-Sonderburg, and was a favourite of Queen Victoria, whose third daughter, Princess Helena Victoria, he married in 1866. At one time he was the senior general in the British Army, as well as being the Ranger of Windsor Great Park. Guy was the third son and he became somewhat of a favourite in Court circles, not only with the Clerk of the Privy Council, but with Prince Christian's unhappily married daughter, Princess Marie-Louise. She and Guy shared an interest in music and the Princess encouraged him to take part in drawing-room quartets at an early age. It was as a result of this that the young Liddell started to play the cello.

Another interesting relative of Guy Liddell was the original model for *Alice in Wonderland*, Lewis Carroll's masterpiece, Alice Liddell being the daughter of the Very Reverend George Liddell, Dean of Christchurch, Oxford, Vice-Chancellor of Oxford University, one-time headmaster of Westminster School as well as being Chaplain to Queen Victoria and 'domestic Chaplain' to the Prince Consort.

To probe the life and times of Guy Liddell is indeed not unlike ex-ploring the kind of existence which Alice herself found in Wonder-land. When Lewis Carroll wrote that 'Here, you see, it takes all the running *you* can do, to keep in the same place. If you want to get some-where else, you must run at least twice as fast as that,' he might well have had a character such as Liddell in mind.

These parallels with the world of Alice were to be imaginatively and brilliantly brought out in a novel by the late David Mure, who served in the 'Double-Cross' organisation in the Middle East in World War II. When he found that nobody would listen to his own theories on the devious roles Liddell eventually played both in the Special Branch and MI5, he decided to write a novel which would throw some essentially coded light on the man. *The Last Temptation* was the result, a novel in code, leaving judgement to his readers. The book had all the charac-ters in *Alice in Wonderland* from Alice (a devoted friend of Liddell whose identity will become clearer later in this book) to Humpty Dumpty (Winston Churchill), the Red Queen (Anthony Blunt), the Red Knight (Kim Philby) to Jabberwock (Adolf Hitler) and the Red King (Josef Stalin).[3]

While David Mure did not reveal the identity of 'Alice', or indicate that he was referring to Liddell, to those of us who knew something of the inner story of those days it was not difficult to guess. After the book was published David Mure wrote to me, saying that in *The Last Temptation* 'I then put myself in Guy Liddell's place and dealt with these problems as I would have done. Curiously enough, members of the wartime MI5 including Lord Rothschild became convinced that by some means I had obtained access to the diaries which Liddell is supposed to have left with that organisation and that I was in close touch with his former secretary, Miss Margo Huggins. In fact I had no access to secret papers, nor did I know the secretary'.[4]

The only interpretation one can put on this is that David Mure had produced out of his own remarkably astute fictional reconstruction of the Liddell story a singularly accurate picture of certain events.

Music was undoubtedly a major influence in Liddell's life from a very early age. It could almost be said that he lived in a world of music, not only through those around him, but in his thoughts. All his life he had something of that facility for which Sherlock Holmes was famed, turning to music for inspiration whenever he wanted to think out the whys and wherefores of a problem. Those who knew him well paid tribute to the fact that he was as much interested in past techniques in music as those of the modern world and that he often re-introduced such practices. In this instance Edward Croft-Murray's comment which appears at the head of this chapter is of special interest. In a letter to *The Times*, referring to a photograph that journal had printed of Liddell playing the 'cello, he wrote:

> I think he is shown playing in the modern manner with the supporting spike. But, on the one occasion on which I had the pleasure of making music with him, he used the old 'gamba stance' as Christopher Simpson recommends in his *Division-Violist, 1659*, with the instrument placed 'decently betwixt your knees'. He was, indeed, the first living performer I had met to use this traditional method, and, on my commenting on it, he told me that he had learnt it from his first teacher and that he always employed it when playing informally. Liddell can be regarded, then, both as a link with past usage, and as something of a pioneer (albeit perhaps an unconscious one) of those who today aspire to authentic Baroque string playing.[5]

He was encouraged early on to develop his interest in music not only by Princess Marie-Louise, but by his younger male friends such as Peter Montgomery, another talented musician and the second son of Major-General Hugh Maude de Fellenberg Montgomery, who later became a homosexual friend of Anthony Blunt and in World War II a member of the Intelligence Corps.

Dean Liddell's mother, Charlotte, the daughter of the Honourable Thomas Lyon, was also the grand-daughter of the eighth Earl of Strathmore. Thus both Anthony Blunt and Guy Liddell were related to the present Queen Mother.

Another influence in young Liddell's life was the fact that Dean Liddell's son, Edward Henry, married Minnie Cory. Much has been written about Lady Cory's famous musical evenings at 28 Belgrave Square. She was a pupil of Paderewski and the violinist, Kreisler, who always played at the Belgrave Square parties when he was in London. Rom Landau has described these musical evenings in the following terms: 'The evening would begin at eight-thirty with a dinner to which as many as thirty would sit down, among them, possibly the Prime Minister and his wife. Soon after ten the other guests would arrive, and some of the great names in politics, society, finance, diplomacy and the arts would be there . . . Round midnight there would be supper for a hundred to two hundred guests.'[6]

Among those guests would be Guy Liddell, not simply because of the Cory connection, but because he accompanied his family's princesses, Helena Victoria and her sister, Marie-Louise. Much later in life, when the ageing Princess Helena-Victoria was in a wheel-chair, it was often Liddell who took her in and out of concert halls as well as No. 28.

Another artistic friend of Liddell's younger days was the second Viscount Churchill, Viscount Victor Alexander Spencer Churchill, who was a godson of Queen Victoria. With professional courtiers such as the Churchills and the Liddells it was normal to have royal god-parents. Victor Churchill, for example, had Queen Victoria as a god-parent, as did his sister. But none were given to the Liddells. Had Guy had rich royal sponsors, he would undoubtedly have gone to Eton like his brother and Victor Churchill. The latter, always called 'Peter', was a Page of Honour to King Edward VII, and was mentioned in des-patches in World War I, in which he became a GSO major. In the early 1920s he became a radical rebel, as well as an art critic on the *New Statesman*. A lifelong homosexual, despite the fact that he had had two wives, he told in his autobiography, *All My Sins Remembered*, how he started such affairs with a Maltese sailor.[7]

Between the wars Peter Churchill was a close friend of the late Lord Bradwell (Tom Driberg), with whom he closely cooperated in writing for the 'William Hickey' column of the London *Daily Express*. The Churchill-Liddell-Driberg connection was to become quite important by the time of the mid-thirties. Both Driberg and Churchill were informants to Liddell after he joined the Special Branch.

The Liddell family had close links with Ireland and often spent time in that country. While a number of Guy Liddell's earliest acquaintances were of a homosexual persuasion, those of them who had family links to Northern Ireland were terrified of such inclinations leaking out to their families or family friends. In Protestant Northern Ireland of those days homosexuality was almost equated with Roman Catholicism, however irrational that might seem. For some Protestants buggery was seen as a Catholic permissive form of birth control!

Not only was Liddell fascinated by the fact that *Alice in Wonderland* was written about a relative of his, but he once told Cyril Connolly that:

> as a child I always regretted the fact that I never met the model for Alice, and I kept telling myself that one day I should meet someone like her with whom I could happily explore some of the more improbable avenues of life today. I was always on the look-out for someone named Alice. It just had to be someone with that name. *In the end it wasn't.* To me *Alice in Wonderland* put life in its true proportions. After all much of life is just a fog.[8]

That phrase 'life is just a fog' is interesting in the light of something Kim Philby wrote about Liddell:

> 'I was born in an Irish fog,' he [Liddell] once told me, 'and sometimes I think I have never emerged from it.' No self-depreciation could have been more ludicrous. It is true that he did have a deceptively ruminative manner. He would murmur his thoughts aloud, as if groping his way towards the facts of a case, his face creased in a comfortable, innocent smile. But behind the façade of laziness, his subtle and reflective mind played over a storehouse of photographic memories. He was an ideal senior officer for a young man to learn from, always ready to put aside his work and to listen and worry at a new problem.[9]

I have italicised those words *'In the end it wasn't'*, as told to me by Cyril Connolly. It is true this comment comes as a secondary source, but it raises again the question as to who was the substitute for Alice.

Life became increasingly difficult from a financial standpoint for the Liddell family as the years passed. There were retreats to Scotland and Ireland only to find that farming in the west of Scotland was in a bad state, with tenant farmers often behind with their rents. While Guy Liddell's elder brothers had been to Eton and Charterhouse respectively, he himself went to a relatively minor school in Scotland. Nor was there any prospect of a university education for him, and perhaps for this reason his mother encouraged his talents for music. She had been taught by a German violinist and perhaps because of this she helped to arrange for Guy to go to Germany to study in the period shortly before World War I. By this time his two brothers were captain and subaltern respectively in the local Scottish regiment, a militia battalion which his father had commanded in the South African war. His father seems to have looked with some disapproval on the musical career which his son had chosen and the fact that in no way had he distinguished himself in games or athletic pursuits. There was a lack of understanding between father and son and the mother's influence was much greater in consequence.

It was to Dresden that young Liddell went to seek instruction in music. From what he told people in later life he did not particularly like his instructors and felt that his fellow students held them in far too much awe, and at the same time he developed a foreboding about Germany generally: 'a menace that will remain with us for an indefinite period, not just in this generation, but in others to follow', was how he put it to one close friend.

During this period he returned home for brief holidays from time to time where he was received with some contempt by his military brothers. David Mure describes their reaction in his novel as follows:

> his beastly brothers, who couldn't make it plainer that they regarded him as notably lesser breed without the law. Every now and then one of them had a brother officer to stay to whom I was duly explained and apologised for. I once heard such an apology in progress: 'There he is, little squirt. All brown! Brown suit, brown tie, brown shoes, brown face. All brown like his fiddle. Damn disgrace to the family.'[10]

The fictional picture once again tallies with what Liddell himself related to friends in self-deprecatory tones about his early life.

Towards the end of his period of study in Germany his mother informed him by telegram that his father was seriously ill. He returned home speedily only to learn that his father was dead and that his financial affairs were such that he died virtually bankrupt. There was much work to be done in sorting out family affairs with Guy devoting himself to this and to securing some worthwhile life for his mother.

Liddell cancelled his return to Germany and shortly afterwards World War I began. He realised full well that he could not afford to seek a commission like his brothers, but that, with family fortunes being at a low ebb, he must join the ranks. He entered a newly formed London unit of a Royal Artillery battalion and spent some months training in home territory. During this time he managed to store away his 'cello at a country public house where he would occasionally call in at nights and, with a pianist accompanist, play for the customers, thus earning the price of a few drinks for himself and his pals.

A problem occurred when the Army chaplain, a man with a singular absence of any sense of humour, sent for him one day and asked him whether he proposed to change his religion. Totally baffled by this astonishing query, Liddell replied that he was a Christian and a member of the Church of England. 'But you are listed as a Hindu,' insisted the chaplain with disapproval on his face.

'Ah, sir, I think that was a little joke on the part of the sergeant-major.'

'How could that be?'

'Well, you see, sir, some time ago I was given the chore of cleaning out all the rubbish, pig swill and other odds and ends each Sunday morning, and the way I was dressed the sergeant-major who had been out in India called me "his Hindu".'

'And I suppose you took this job to get out of going on church parade?' inquired a still somewhat unsympathetic chaplain.

'Well, yes, sir, it did excuse me, but it was a job that had to be done.'

'Then we shall have to rectify this matter in your records, and I trust this unfortunate experience will make you more aware of church duties in future.'

The Army List shows that Liddell served from late 1914 until 1920, though it is certain that he was not actively employed in the Army during 1919. He was promoted first to sergeant and sent over to France where he spent twelve months in the front line. Deaths of comrades helped to pave the way to further promotion and he was appointed Temporary Second Lieutenant on 30 March 1915, and then, after being wounded, made Acting Captain on 3 August 1917. He was mentioned in despatches on 1 January 1916, and 4 January 1917. Like his two brothers he won the Military Cross, which was awarded on 1 January 1918. For what it was awarded remains a mystery, as, according to the Ministry of Defence, the Honours Gazette of that date 'consists purely of a list of the names of recipients and regrettably in such instances no citations exist.'[11]

This seems remarkably odd unless, of course, by that date Liddell was engaged in Intelligence matters and for that reason no details for the award could be given. That is a possibility, but on the other hand one cannot help recall Raymond Asquith's comment that, when it came to giving awards in World War I, the Dukes seemed to be the bravest of men and after them the earls and baronets! A cynical view, but it is one which has frequently been substantiated. For three brothers all with connections to royalty and high society to get the MC is surely a pointer in the direction of Raymond Asquith's barbed comment. The award of the MC to Liddell may have been partly a device for ensuring he got a worthwhile job at the end of the war.

After being wounded, Liddell had a brief spell as a divisional intelligence officer and, as a result, came to know Stewart Menzies, the man who years later became head of MI6. Menzies had been adjutant of the Second Life Guards and joined Field Marshal Haig's counter-espionage division at Montreuil in 1915. Undoubtedly such experience and contacts enabled Liddell to clinch the new job at Scotland Yard which, at first, he somewhat reluctantly accepted, still being inclined to take the risk of life as a musician, either as performer or teacher.

It was in the period immediately before he was recruited into the Special Branch that Liddell met someone who became an important influence in his life, possibly the one person who more than anyone else encouraged him to keep up his playing of the 'cello. She was, if one likes to put it that way, his 'Alice in Wonderland'. Her name was Joyce Wallace Whyte. Her broadmindedness and commonsense were to help to preserve in him a sense of balance in what often seemed to be the mysteries of life behind the looking glass.

Born at Bromley in Kent in July, 1897, she was the daughter of Robert Whyte, an Australian merchant. After being educated at a school known as Coed-bel at Chislehurst and later at Bromley High School, she went to Girton College, Cambridge, in 1916, remaining there until the end of the summer term, 1919. That she was highly popular almost from her first day at Girton is recalled by a contemporary, Mrs Hilda Sebastian, of Coggeshall, Essex, who writes that when she arrived at Girton, 'Joyce Whyte had a lovely fair plait of hair down her back and was a delightful companion. She was my daughter's godmother later on, and I remember my grandchildren going to the Mansion House children's party to meet her.'[12]

While at Girton Joyce Whyte distinguished herself both in musical and sporting activities. She was secretary to the college orchestra and the tennis club and her other activities included war-work for the YMCA canteen and the Red Cross Fund as well as organising concerts for war charities. As Girton College lay outside the Cambridge town boundary it was responsible for its own fire safety precautions, and Joyce along with other students helped run an amateur fire brigade. It was quite hard work from all accounts, involving practice between the hours of 7.30 and 8a.m. The *Girton Review* for the years 1916-19 records that as a member of the Girton Tennis Club 'J. W. Whyte played a very good and steady game throughout,' and she eventually became captain of the University women's tennis team.

It was perhaps as a violinist that she particularly shone, often taking part in a trio which included a pianist and 'cellist. It was this particular activity which drew her close to Guy Liddell, whom she met through mutual friends. They often used to play together on various outings and she even nicknamed him 'Cello'. The *Girton Review* particularly praised her for her 'courage in attacking such a work as the Pugnani-Kreisler and her skill in giving us such a creditable performance'.

Her special subject was ancient history and she maintained her academic interests for some years, acquiring an MA in 1925. Her meetings with Liddell were sometimes at her home at Bromley, occasionally at Cambridge and in London. To Liddell, who was still in his later twenties and had not had much experience of girls of his own age, she was a delightful platonic companion who was cherished above all others. Liddell always regarded her as the personification of Alice in so many ways, her down-to-earth commonsense, her liveliness and inquisitiveness about all and sundry and what he once called 'the eternal relevance of her questions'.

Joyce Whyte is said to have been not only the first female undergraduate to be seen riding a motor-bicycle, but the first female 'President' of a university Communist Society. This report surprises most of her contemporaries at Girton as well as those who met her in later life when her views generally seemed to be, outwardly at least, quite orthodox. She was, however, tutored by Dr. Eileen Power, the first woman to preach to the fertile mind that there was such a word as socialism. In June 1927, she married Sir Cuthbert Lowell Ackroyd, an Alderman and Magistrate of the City of London, who took office as Lord Mayor of London in October 1955. Whatever may have been her youthful interest in communism, she certainly showed no such tendencies whatsoever afterwards. All who knew her testified to her integrity and essential open-mindedness as well as her orthodox opinions.

Nevertheless Sir John Ackroyd says that his mother told her children and her sisters that 'she was a member of the Cambridge Ladies Communist Party while at Girton, round about 1918. Her grandfather was a Liberal and she was always somewhat of a rebel. In later life at Lord Mayoral functions she used to suit her conversation to that of her neighbours by very often taking the opposite viewpoint, whether that of Eden or Macmillan, etc. They seemed to love it!'[13]

In the years after the Great War communist activities at the university were kept extremely quiet and secretive and frequently the names of the real leaders were concealed by various devices. It is interesting to note that the British Labour Party in 1933 brought out a pamphlet which stated: 'The influences of the Communist International are not radiated by the light of day or through the illuminated obscurity of the night. With the exception of a few leaders, it is not known who are members of the CPGB. It is a secret society. It publishes no financial statement . . . Even the composition of the Executive Committee of the Party is not known.'[14]

The nucleus of the group of communists at Girton, in which Joyce Whyte must have been one of the earliest, was strengthened some few years later when Katherine Raine arrived at the college as a science exhibitioner from Ilford Grammar School. Arthur Koestler has written of this period that 'the Comintern carried on a white-slave traffic whose victims were young idealists flirting with violence.'

Here then is irrefutable proof of a close communist connection in the early life of Guy Liddell, of the sort that people have tried in vain for years to discover in the case of Roger Hollis.

Guy Liddell, as we have seen had a passionate hatred of German militarism and the possibility of this being revived worried him: to that extent he was vulnerable to left-wing propaganda.

We must assume that the fact that his friend, Joyce Whyte, was a communist intrigued him. During 1919 Liddell often visited her at Cambridge and, on occasions, she travelled on her motor bicycle to meet him at his mother's home. His brothers regarded Joyce Whyte as somewhat of a freak, but then they were almost ridiculously conventional in their views of what was orthodox behaviour and dress, and for a girl to ride a motor-bicycle was almost beyond the bounds of decency!

Guy and Joyce played tennis together as well as thoroughly enjoying their musical sessions. Guy was frequently persuaded to join in impromptu concerts arranged by Joyce. They even went together to a lecture-cum-solo performance by the Bolshevik violinist, Edward Soermus, who was later deported from Britain. It may be that Liddell fell in love with his new friend. He always claimed that he was too poor to marry. Had he made a proposal to her at that time, it is possible that he would have been accepted and that she would gladly have helped support him while he tried to make a living as a professional musician.

Joyce's interest in communism surely gave him reason to question some of his own theories about the world in general. Perhaps she was responsible for creating deep down inside his mind a certain sympathy for the far left. If he told her that his job entailed tracking down and investigating communists, she did not allow it to interfere with their friendship, and even introduced him to some of her fellow communists, male as well as female.

One of these was a young communist named Wilfred Francis Remington Macartney, who had already had a somewhat remarkable career. In 1915, at the age of 15, he had failed an army medical examination because of poor eyesight, but had managed to join the RAMC 3rd Field Ambulance as a driver and was sent to France. There he somehow managed to secure a commission in the Royal Scots, but after some months his eyesight deteriorated and he was forced to resign his commission. After treatment he was recommissioned in the Essex Regiment, then stationed in Malta, and from there he was posted first to Egypt and then to Greece. Here he came to work for Compton Mackenzie, who was then head of British Intelligence in Greece and the Eastern Mediterranean. Mackenzie described Macartney as 'a pink-faced, cherubic, grinning youth with glasses . . . he was energetic and efficient and I do not recall one occasion on which he involved us in any trouble. He had no scheme for his own aggrandisement, unlike so many . . . He led at the age of a schoolboy the kind of life that a schoolboy may dream of leading after a course of spy novels and spy films.'[15]

Eventually he left the army with the rank of lieutenant in 1919, having been attached to the Berlin-Baghdad railway mission in Constantinople after the Armistice. It was about this time that he became a communist, apparently influenced by visits to Germany and having been appalled at a system which meant starvation in that country for millions. It may well be that he came into Joyce Whyte's circle not so much because he was a fellow-communist, but on account of his social background and the fact that he was working as an underwriter in the City. Mackenzie made the comment that 'Communism became Macartney's religion', but that despite this 'he was still monkeying around with the demi-monde of finance.'[16]

Liddell established quite early on that Macartney was a communist and that he was on record as saying that he would not hesitate to use violence if it would further the cause. As a result he warned Alice Whyte to beware of Macartney. He was astonished at her reaction. She felt that Liddell was betraying his own department by revealing what he knew to her. Somewhat bewildered, he replied that he only wanted to save her from getting mixed up with a person who might one day be arrested for his activities. Her response was that she could very well look after herself, but that Guy should bear in mind that, if she was so minded, she could warn Wilfred that he was being watched. This would put Guy totally in the wrong with his department. She then explained that she did not believe in violence and subversion as a means of upholding communism, but preferred to change 'the system' by reasoned argument and influencing people – 'infiltrating their minds, if you like'.

One of Liddell's tasks at this time was to liaise with the Foreign Office in respect of his probes into communist subversion. While he seems to have established a fairly easy and close relationship in that Ministry quite early on, his boss, Sir Basil Thomson, was not at all happy about what the Foreign Office and MI6 were planning in regard to Russia. Positive records are not available on this subject, but such slender items as have been allowed through into the Public Record Office leave no doubts about all this. Thomson was anxious to know exactly what undercover moves were being conducted by MI6 inside Russia. He was especially concerned about the secret operations and manoeuvres of Sidney Reilly. Up to about 1921 Reilly had been hailed by some as one of the finest and bravest British agents of all time, despite his somewhat obscure origins in Odessa. Captain Sir Mansfield Cumming, head of the SIS, described him as 'a man of indomitable courage, a genius as an agent, but a sinister man whom I could never bring myself wholly to trust.'[17]

There is an interesting memorandum written in 1921 in the archives of the White Russian Military Agent in Constantinople: 'George Sidney Reilly is being sent by the British Government to Poland, the Ukraine and the Crimea to study conditions there and to open . . . British information sections . . . Officially he is visiting there to purchase sugar surplus. His person and activity are exceedingly mysterious ... He is very close to the government – on the highest level – and performs missions ... No doubts exist that at the same time he maintains contact with the Bolshevik delegation in London ... Among the people to whom he was close in Russia was Manusevich-Manuilov, notorious for his activity as a criminal and provocateur ... He lived for a long time in St Petersburg at Novo-Isaakiyevskaya 22, circulating in the business and banking world ... Rumour credits Reilly with an unsavoury, if not even a criminal past ...'

6

'The First Man'

Savinkov is the only man who counts . . . with all the stains and
tarnishes there be, few men tried more, gave more and suffered
more for the Russian people.
(Sir Winston Churchill on Savinkov and 'The Trust')[1]

It was quite astonishing how British people both on the right and the
left were persuaded into accepting the alleged anti-Bolshevik organisation known as 'The Trust' as a means of creating a more civilised
society and government in Russia in the 1920s. The relevant point
today should be that 'The Trust' in its original form as a masterly exercise in infiltration of Western civilisation continues. 'Trust Number
One' has long since been rather more successfully and subtly succeeded by 'Trust Number Two' and 'Trust Number Three'.

The object of the first 'Trust' was to set up a bogus anti-Bolshevik
organisation which would lure counter-revolutionaries and other
enemies of the new regime back to Russia where they were promised
underground support. On arrival they would be arrested and summa-
rily dealt with by the authorities. Two skilled operators were chosen by
Felix Dzerzhinsky, head of the Cheka (the Russian secret police), to
carry out the planning. They were A. A. Yakushev and a Cheka official
named Artuzov, both of whom operated under the cover of an organisation calling itself MOTSR (the Monarchist Association of Central
Russia) and the Moscow Municipal Credit Association. The first important refugee to be impressed by 'The Trust' was Savinkov, the War
Minister in the former Kerensky Government.

Savinkov had a lengthy history of terrorist and revolutionary activities before he threw in his lot with the White Russians. He was a cour-
ageous man but he had come to rely on morphine and it was well
known in the ranks of the Cheka, doubtless from intelligence gleaned
from his old comrades in the revolutionary ranks, that under the influence of the drug he could be induced to undertake the most reckless
missions. 'The Trust' proposed that he should return to Russia, give

himself up and 'confess' his 'crimes', afterwards announcing that he would support the Soviet Government. The argument used to support this madcap scheme was that, because he would then denounce the White Russian cause, his life would be spared and he would be inside Russia ready to seize power the moment The Trust launched their counter-revolution.

It is said that Sidney Reilly advised Savinkov to have nothing to do with this plan. If that was so, he was, I believe, merely trying to mask his own role in the affair. The truth is, as recent archival discoveries have shown, that British Intelligence agents as well as Soviet counter-intelligence chiefs were involved in this somewhat complicated plot. They included not only Reilly, but Commander Ernest Boyce, one of the two area chiefs of British Intelligence in Russia, and Captain George Hill, another British agent. Hill's father had been active in the Jewish merchant-Masonic networks of Czarist Russia, working on a pre-Trust Bolshevik project, an assignment very relevant to his son's posting to Salonika about 1915-16. Hill had been active in supporting this project for some years prior to this and had been the personal courier to and from England of private documents of the Bolshevik playwright, Maxim Gorky.

On 10 August 1924, Savinkov set off for Russia and nineteen days later *Izvestia* announced that he had been arrested. Then came the news of his renunciation of the White Russian cause and a statement that he 'Honoured the power and wisdom of the GPU'. But the suspicions of the White Russians were aroused when Sidney Reilly reported that he had had a letter from Savinkov which stated that he had met men in the GPU 'whom I have known and trusted from my youth up and who are nearer to me than the chatter-boxes of the foreign delegation of the Social-Revolutionaries.'

Why should Savinkov write to Reilly, and not to one of the leading White Russians in exile? It seems not to make sense. But if, as I now believe, Reilly was all the time a secret agent of the Cheka, then the pieces in the jig-saw puzzle of his relationships with the Americans as well as the British, fit much better. If the Savinkov letter was forged, Reilly could be relied upon to swear that it was genuine, thus giving the death blow to Savinkov's supporters.

By this time American Intelligence operatives were beginning to have the gravest doubts about Reilly. This arose partly out of the so-called 'Sisson' documents, sold to America's Intelligence for what was reported to be a large sum of money. The full story of this mysterious transaction has not yet been told and varying versions of it have been bandied around for years. But one thing is certain, it went a long way towards creating suspicions in the United States of motives behind British foreign policy.

Ostensibly, the Sisson papers were concocted to demonstrate to the USA that the Bolsheviks, after gaining power, remained the agents of the German General Staff. According to reliable American sources and to Sir Robert Bruce Lockhart (then Britain's principal adviser on Russian affairs), these forgeries were sold to the Americans by Commander Ernest Boyce. But other evidence suggests that the man behind the forgeries was Sidney Reilly, who was no stranger to this kind of trading. He certainly knew all about the American covert involvement in financial aid to the anti-Bolsheviks; therefore he must have known that it was a waste of time to sell anti-Bolshevik propaganda to them. Could it be that the object of this operation was to upset Anglo-American relations?

Censorship of Cabinet papers and public records has hushed up a great deal of the intrigue behind the scenes in connection not only with the Sisson papers, but the notorious Zinoviev Letter as well. In 1924, allegedly from Grigori Zinoviev, President of the Third Communist International, to A. McManus, the British representative on the executive of the International, this letter openly incited revolution in Britain. Until recent years it has generally been accepted that the document was a forgery, but there is no absolutely conclusive proof of this, in fact rather the reverse. The index to the 1921 Minutes of Cabinet papers shows substantial blank areas where the weeder of the papers has tried to cover all traces by removing not merely certain entries, but the headings as well. But the game has been given away by a cross-reference to 'Secret Service' under the 'Scotland Yard' index. In September of 1921 an incident occurred which probably explains a great deal of the censorship. Having had constant reports of Soviet subversive activities through the Government Code and Cipher School, Lord Curzon, then Foreign Secretary, made a protest to the Soviet Government. However, in order not to compromise the GCCS and give away their interception of secret messages, he based his protest on Soviet documents obtained by the Secret Service. Almost immediately he discovered that the documents were forgeries.

The Foreign Secretary was livid. In private he castigated his staff and the SIS; publicly, however, he still maintained the documents were genuine. Two years later, in April 1923, Curzon's temper got the better of discretion. He made one of the most monumental blunders of his term of office. He not only confronted the Russians with evidence

of the intercepted messages, but actually revealed to them the success
of this highly secret enterprise in code-breaking.

A covert intervention by the USA on the side of the anti-Bolsheviks
started as early as the end of 1917. Officially the decision to intervene
was not made until July 1918, and then grudgingly. Outwardly the
State Department put forward the view that 'in principle' the government was still opposed to intervention and that American troops were
only being sent to Russia to aid the Czechoslovak Legion.

But behind the scenes it was a very different story. There the State
Department was secretly showing more resolution in intervening than
any of the Allies. Within a month of November 1917, the Americans
had started surreptitiously to finance the anti-Bolshevik forces. At the
same time a secret intelligence network was set up with centres in
Kiev, Salsk, Tsaritsyn, Astrakhan, Vladikavkaz, Nizhni Novgorod,
Kirov, Saratov and even Ekaterinburg, all of which were controlled by
the Information Service of the Consulate-General in Moscow.

De Witte Poole, an American Consular officer who had been in
Russia for some few years, and who was in close touch with the anti-
Bolshevik forces, was convinced that Reilly was a double-agent. If
Bruce Lockhart did not know the extent of American machinations in
Russia, Sidney Reilly most certainly did. He had actually been involved both with William G. MacAdoo, President Wilson's son-in-
law, and Oliver T. Crosby, MacAdoo's agent in London, in connection with certain financial deals. Exactly how Reilly had insinuated
himself into these financial negotiations is not clear from State
Department records, though it is highly probable that Poole had some
idea, but dared not, of course, mention anything of this to Lockhart, so
strict were the embargoes on United States covert intervention at that
time. The clue to Reilly's involvement comes from a Czech Intelligence message of 27 April 1918, inquiring when 'can we expect the
promised funds which Kalamatiano tells us Reilli [sic] had arranged to
transmit for our troops?'[2] There is no trace of the reply to this query,
but it would seem that one was received, as on 6 May a further telegram to Crosby indicated that 'despite careful inquiries no signs of any
funds being received in this whole area.'

From this one must assume that Sidney Reilly had not carried out
his instructions. Somewhat coincidentally another interesting message
was sent by De Witte Poole from Stockholm to Secretary of State
Lansing shortly afterwards, requesting that 'all American Consular
agents in Western Siberia be informed that Kalamatiano must not
attempt to return to Central Russia until further notice to do so and in

no case under his present Russian name Hay --- [name indistinct].'
This message was sent in code, and it was considered sufficiently
serious for Lansing personally to relay warnings to all other key
American agents and Consular officials in Russia.[3]

The agent they wanted to save was an American subject, X. B. Kalamatiano, one of Poole's spy controllers, who in turn supervised as
many as twenty observers. Thus he was in charge of something like
three-quarters of the American intelligence network in Russia. It is
clear from Poole's warning that Kalamatiano's cover had been blown,
and from later messages sent by the Czech Intelligence there seems
little doubt that they suspected Reilly had informed on him. Not long
afterwards Kalamatiano was captured by the Bolsheviks and, according to Soviet sources, they discovered a list of agents on him. It is true
that the number given by the Soviets – thirty – does not exactly tally
with the known figures of Kalamatiano's agents – twenty – but the fact
remains that from that date the American intelligence operation was
drastically curtailed and never regained the supremacy it originally
had.

Why have the facts about the substantial financial aid given to the
anti-Bolsheviks by the United States been kept hidden all this time?
The answer may well be that the State Department, who paid the
funds through intermediaries other than the Ambassador in Moscow,
wished to conceal the fact that at least half never reached their intended destination and may well have been redeployed by Reilly, or
others, possibly even to the Bolsheviks themselves.

Yakushev, one of the earliest Trust operators, had been interrogated by the Cheka about his previous work during the Tsarist
regime and his chief questioner was Artuzov who dwelt at some length
on Yakushev's extra-marital affairs. During this interrogation Artuzov
stated that the Cheka knew that Yakushev had met a 'Mr Massino' in
the dressing-room of a female dancer in 1917 and that together they
had discussed the future of Russia and that 'Massino had mentioned
the concessions the British Government would request for its continued support.' 'Massino' was none other than Sidney Reilly.[4] During
1917 Reilly had been sent to Petrograd as a specialist in Levantine
affairs under the alias of Massino.

In May 1925, it was reported that Savinkov had 'committed suicide' by
throwing himself out of a window while under house arrest. Prior to
this, according to reports of his trial appearing in various Western
newspapers, Savinkov was alleged during interrogation to have dis-

closed all the secrets of his organisation and betrayed all its members. This allegation has neither been confirmed, nor denied. It is possible that the so-called frank confessions of Savinkov outside the court might be nothing more than disinformation put out by the GPU to camouflage the extent of its infiltration of the Savinkov organisation. Once Savinkov had been shown to be a complete turncoat the GPU could act boldly on information which presumably came from his babbling. It was on 29 August 1924, that Savinkov was sentenced to death, this sentence later being commuted to ten years imprisonment. He was given a comfortable two-room apartment in the Butyrki Prison and treated well. His death by a jump or fall from his apartment window in May of the following year remains a mystery. Maybe it was murder made to look like suicide in the hope that others would believe that Savinkov had not confessed after all. Thus the Cheka would have the best of both worlds. Stories of his confessions would spread panic and confusion in the White Russian ranks, while the suggestion that he had committed suicide rather than talk would help to lure others to their destruction.

Some people inside the British Secret Service saw Sidney Reilly as the greatest agent on their books. (Many years later Ian Fleming was to declare that James Bond 'was not to be compared to the superb Sidney Reilly'.) To his supporters in London Reilly was a man who had developed a fanatical patriotism for his adopted country and who, in some ways, was more British than the British.

American Intelligence had a dossier on him which claimed that he began his business career at the turn of the century in the Far East with the lumber firm of 'Gunberg and Reilly' and that a little later he was also a director of the Danish firm, 'Danish Western Asian Co'. In 1906, according to this account, after the Russian-Japanese War he participated in an enterprise called 'Mandrekovich and Shuberskiy', which helped to rearm the defeated Russian fleet.[5]

On one occasion while in London Reilly had established contact with Leonid Krassin, the Soviet Representative to the British Government. It was suggested that Reilly and Krassin were engaged in currency smuggling. In the United States Reilly had sought to establish himself with the President's son-in-law, while in Britain he set out to charm and capture the support of Winston Churchill himself. In securing Churchill's ear and confidence his intermediary was Churchill's private secretary, Eddie Marsh (late Sir Edward Marsh), a Bohemian patron of the arts and homosexual who had almost strayed into the Civil Service. Marsh had been a member of the Apostles secret society when at Cambridge and he maintained his links with later members of that society, including Anthony Blunt and others. Some people have claimed that despite his record as an ardent pursuer of females, Reilly was bisexual.

There were conflicting viewpoints about both Reilly and The Trust in London. Some both in Whitehall and the Secret Service were doubtful about both; some mistrusted Reilly, who was then strongly supported by Sir Robert Bruce Lockhart, but felt that The Trust was one last chance to overthrow the Bolshevik regime.

Meanwhile Reilly continued to play many roles both inside Britain and later inside Russia. It is still far from clear as to how many countries he was working for as an agent in 1925. He had dabbled in espionage for the Americans on a freelance basis, he retained certain contacts with the Japanese, though these had diminished, and, though the British Secret Service appeared to be his prime employer, he also helped French Intelligence. In December 1924, Reilly brought from Russia documents concerning the imminence of a communist revolution in Paris and northern France. As a result Herriot, the French Premier, ordered the arrest of certain alleged communist ringleaders. It was always said afterwards that they were the wrong people!

When Reilly returned to Russia in 1925, he went with the reluctant approval of the British Secret Service and on the understanding that, if things went wrong, he would get no help. He was given a forged passport in the name of Nicolas Steinberg and on 25 September 1925, he crossed the frontier into Russia from Finland.

The first news received came to Commander Boyce: he had a postcard from Reilly, dated 27 September, franked in Moscow, indicating that he had arrived safely. Then, a few days later, a news item in *Izvestia* stated that on the night of 28-29 September, 'four smugglers attempted to cross the Finnish border. Two were killed; one, a Finnish soldier, taken prisoner, and the fourth, mortally wounded, died on the way to Leningrad.'

Piecing together these two items of evidence it might be construed that Reilly arrived in Moscow, and that somehow the GPU discovered him and followed him back to the Finnish border. For it had been Reilly's intention to return to Finland on the very night that the four men were reported to have been caught. From that moment the British Secret Service and the Foreign Office disclaimed all interest or responsibility; even Reilly's wife was given to understand that her inquiries were an embarrassment. In desperation, hoping that the move would attract some attention to the mystery of her husband's disappearance, she had the following notice published in the deaths column of *The Times* on 15 December 1925: 'Reilly – on the 28th Sept., killed near the village of Allekul, Russia, by GPU troops, Captain Sidney George Reilly, MC, late RAF, beloved husband of Pepita N. Reilly.'

The announcement certainly induced a flood of newspaper stories and articles about Reilly and his exploits in Britain, but it drew no statement either from the Foreign Office or from the Russians. Then, in the following year, the awful truth, which many had long suspected, emerged – that The Trust had been used as a 'front' by the Soviets.

Mrs Reilly remained unconvinced that her husband was dead, despite the notice she had put in *The Times*, and even as late as 1930 declared that this question was 'as open today as it was six years ago'. There was some reason for this element of doubt, for M. Brunovski, a Latvian who had been released by the Russians after four years in a Moscow prison, said that he had learned that 'an important British spy lay in the hospital at Butyrski Prison'.[6]

The Soviet version of what happened when Reilly crossed the border was not given until the journal *Nedelya* published an account in June 1966, which, it must be assumed, is also the official Soviet report, stating that 'in January 1925, the GPU gave Yakushev the assignment of investigating the possibilities of luring Sidney George Reilly to Helsinki and thence to Moscow.' It had all been most carefully planned: Reilly was to be allowed to cross the border, to be smuggled to Moscow and there to take part in discussions with The Trust Council. He crossed the border safely and was met by a Soviet agent who posed as an emissary of The Trust. After thorough interrogation and being subjected to solitary confinement Reilly wrote to Dzerzhinsky on 13 October 1925, saying he was ready to cooperate with the Soviet: 'After prolonged deliberation I express willingness to give you complete and open acknowledgement and information on matters of interest to the GPU concerning the organisation and personnel of the British Intelligence Service and, so far as I know it, similar information on American Intelligence and likewise about Russian emigrants with whom I have had business.'

On 8 June 1972, *Russkaya Misl*, a Russian emigré paper published in Paris, contained a lengthy article about Sidney Reilly, written by Revolt I. Pimenov, a Soviet dissident. This stated categorically that Reilly was a Soviet spy all the time he was apparently working for the British during the civil war. According to Pimenov, Reilly did not die in 'that carefully staged frontier incident', but in imminent danger of being uncovered by his Intelligence Service colleagues in Britain, he was simply 'coming in from the cold'. In effect, the *Russkaya Misl* article refuted the *Nedelya* version of events saying that once Reilly crossed the border he reverted to his former 'work-place' with the Leningrad Cheka. There he worked as a top investigator in the criminal branch for two years and also became a candidate member of the Soviet Communist Party under his old name, Sigismund Georgivich Relinski.

It could, of course, be argued that the Pimenov article falls into the category of Soviet disinformation, but this hardly seems likely – why should the USSR, within a period of a few years, wish to disseminate two different stories about Reilly?

Soon after his disappearance some people in MI6 and MI5 suspected that Reilly was still alive and that he had made a deal with the Bolsheviks.

Damning evidence against Reilly, as indeed it was against Philby, is the secrets which he is known to have passed to the USSR – secrets that could only have come from him. The Russian dossier of his interrogation suggests he gave them a great deal of accurate information; even the inaccuracies in his statement to the GPU ring true, for they were essentially the kind of inaccuracies he would have introduced deliberately to boost his own image. Mr Robin Bruce Lockhart, Sir Robert's son, points out that the Russian dossier mentions that Reilly used the name of Sidney Berns in the USA, and denies that this was so. Presumably Mr Lockhart was relying on British Intelligence knowledge of Reilly's activities during this period, but Reilly was not then working for the British, so they would not necessarily know what cover name he was using. But Walter Krivitsky, the Soviet Intelligence chief who defected from Russia in the late thirties, supplied some confirmation of the Berns pseudonym when he informed the Americans that the Russians first penetrated the American Secret Service through a man known as Sidney Berns and that this code-name was carried on by a substitute until 1936.[7]

As Krivitsky was the man who revealed the presence of other traitors in the British Foreign Office and elsewhere, this seems to be conclusive proof that Reilly was a Soviet agent all along. Since he wrote his original biography of Reilly, *Ace of Spies*, Robin Bruce Lockhart has considerably revised his views of Reilly and has in effect demolished his own myth about the agent in that first work by a new book, *Reilly: The First Man*. Now he claims that both his own father and Captain George Hill had proof that Reilly not only survived, but went on to work for the GPU. Moura Benckendorff, who features later in this

story as Moura Budberg and who had been Sir Robert Bruce Lockhart's mistress in 1918, wrote to him in 1932 that she had recently met
Reilly in Russia.[8]

The testimony of Captain Hill is also interesting. When the USSR
entered the war against Germany in 1941 Hill was posted to Moscow as
British SOE liaison officer to the NKVD. Robin Bruce Lockhart said
that 'to the astonishment of everyone, including Hill himself', this
former SIS agent, said to have been a chief organiser of the Lockhart
Plot to overthrow the Bolsheviks in 1918, was chosen by the Russians
'from the short list of names put forward by the British'.[9]

It was undoubtedly memories of the work Hill had done as a guerrilla behind the German lines in World War I which encouraged the
ultra-suspicious Stalinists to choose him as the link man in 1941. Hill
was promoted first to colonel, then to the rank of brigadier and he
spent four years in his liaison post with the NKVD, about which he
eventually produced an unpublished account.[10] Hill eventually made
inquiries as to what had happened to Reilly through his principal
NKVD contact, but the latter professed total ignorance on the subject,
later changing to the excuse that 'this is something I cannot discuss'.
Robin Bruce Lockhart writes that shortly before his death Hill told
him how he:

> ran into, seemingly accidentally, one Sergei Nekrassov, a former
> Tsarist cavalry officer who had been Hill's star agent in 1918.
> Nekrassov told Hill he had 'reluctantly' come to terms with com-
> munism. Over a bottle of French brandy – rare in wartime Mos-
> cow – which Nekrassov produced, Hill's former agent told him
> that Reilly was indeed still alive and had been doing extremely
> valuable work for the GPU and then the NKVD ever since he
> arrived in Moscow in 1925.

In addition to this Robin Bruce Lockhart also revealed that Colonel
Ossipov (Hill's opposite number in the NKVD) at a farewell party for
Hill in 1945 'vouchsafed that Reilly had been working for the NKVD,
and that he knew him to have been very much alive up to early 1944.'[11]

Most important of the new revelations on Reilly is contained in a letter which Reilly wrote to Sir Robert Bruce Lockhart (undated except
for the words 'November 24th'). This states that:

> the term 'Bolshevism' has been applied so promiscuously that for
> the purpose of this letter, I find it expedient to define more clearly

the sense in which I am using it: I am not concerned at the moment with Bolshevism as a Super-Marxism, as a system for the social reconstruction of the world. I believe that in-so-far as this system contains practical and constructive ideas for the establishment of a higher social justice, it is bound by a process of evolution to conquer the world, as Christianity and the ideas of the French revolution have done before it, and that nothing – least of all violent reactionary forces – can stem its ever-rising tide. Incidentally, I should also like to state here that the much decried and so little understood 'Soviets' which are the outward expression of Bolshevism as applied to practical government, are the nearest approach, I know of, to a *real* democracy based upon true social justice and that they may be destined to lead the world to the highest ideal of statesmanship – internationalism.[12]

During World War I the British lost a submarine, L55, in about 100 feet of water in the Gulf of Finland. Sidney Reilly was asked to ascertain details of the exact location of the craft and whether anyone had suggested salvage operations. As he was often in and out of Finland during the immediate postwar years, Reilly was easily able to accomplish this mission. Shortly after his disappearance in 1925 it became known in London that the USSR had discovered where the craft was and that Soviet technicians had taken soundings in the area. Two years later the Russians actually raised the L55 and so discovered all her secrets. Three years were spent studying and repairing the submarine which was finally put into service with the Soviet Navy.

I have copies of many Special Branch memos from Liddell enquiring as to Reilly's progress. If Reilly was employed by MI6 (the overseas intelligence service), how is it that he seemed to be of special interest to Liddell at Special Branch (concerned only with internal affairs)?

The evidence that Reilly was in many respects 'The First Man' seriously to infiltrate British Intelligence at a high level on behalf of the USSR is increasingly impressive.

With Reilly's disappearance the British Secret Service lost the nucleus of a small but apparently useful network inside Russia, not to mention the more serious risk that his knowledge of both MI5 and MI6 could be used to its detriment. He would be well able to advise the USSR on how to circumvent the then highly efficient traps which the British set for their agents. His suggestion was to mount spying operations against Britain from a base in Holland, according to what Krivitsky told Isaac Don Levine.

But perhaps the most recent and authoritative statement on Reilly comes from Ilya Dzhirkvelov, who served in the Soviet Intelligence Service from 1943 until 1980 when he decided to quit Russia for the West. 'I came across documents which made it clear that Reilly was not killed in the frontier incident,' states Dzhirkvelov, 'but was taken alive by the Soviet Security Police. The Soviet authorities announced that he had perished, in the hope that the news would cause confusion and defeatism among his supporters. According to Reilly's file, Reilly ultimately provided detailed information about the work of the British and other Western Intelligence Services and of the Russian emigré organisations hostile to the Soviet regime.'[13]

The Failure of the ARCOS Raid

In 1926 Liddell married the Honourable Calypso Baring. Perhaps it is significant that Joyce Whyte had just broken the news to him that she was getting engaged to Cuthbert Lowell Ackroyd, a prominent businessman in the City of London. Ackroyd eventually became Lord Mayor of London and was made a baronet.

Never from then onwards was there ever a hint of even the remotest interest in communism on the part of Lady Ackroyd. She and her husband led the most highly respectable and conventional lives, he being a Church Warden and Church Commissioner for England and involved in countless charities, while she was concerned in the WVS, local education in the Bromley area and the Church of England Children's Society.

Meanwhile Liddell, as some of his contemporaries testify, was still very much resentful of how he personally and his family, too, had suffered from the failure of their royal patrons to protect them, and may have felt that his marriage to a daughter of the illustrious banking house of Baring was some kind of compensation.

But apart from this the connection with the Baring family was quite important from the viewpoint of his own work. It will be noted that he was already using this link as a means of establishing contacts with the State Department in Washington. In the sphere of intelligence-gathering Liddell was much more active than a counter-intelligence officer is supposed to be: all evidence suggests that he built up his own position more by this means than by actual results in his true work. 'Ask Guy, he will know', became a frequent saying among the Intelligence fraternity.

Without doubt Liddell was especially interested in the Baring Bank's links with Russia. Prior to World War I it was said in London that the Barings knew more about Russia than anyone else in the City, and Sir Mackenzie Wallace, *Times* correspondent in St Petersburg, was very close to the Barings. The second Lord Revelstoke (the baronial title taken by the family) was one of Britain's four delegates to the

Allied conference at Petrograd in 1917. Possibly equally important from Liddell's assessment of international affairs was the link with Russia of Maurice Baring, the fourth son of Lord Revelstoke, who was an authority on Russia. He had not only served in the Foreign Office, but had been a war correspondent in Manchuria in 1904 and for the *Morning Post* from 1905 to 1908. In World War I Maurice Baring had been a lieutenant in the Intelligence Corps.

In May, 1927, Scotland Yard's Special Branch was informed of the theft of a confidential military document which, it was believed, was somewhere in the offices of the All-Russian Co-operative Society (known as ARCOS) in Moorgate Street, London. The Home Secretary gave him orders to raid the ARCOS premises. The pretext for this was Clause Nine of the Official Secrets Act, but, as the Russians claimed some form of diplomatic status and immunity under the Trading Agreement, great care and precision was needed in carrying out the raid. Moreover this was not just a case of raiding premises housing some half dozen people, but several hundred.

After the British General Strike of 1926, N. K. Jilinsky had been posted to London to keep a tighter control of the ARCOS offices. His task was to avoid any actions which might lead to a breaking-off of ties between the British Government and the USSR and to keep an eye on Communist Party hotheads who had bungled matters during the General Strike. Jilinsky put an end to open subversion, but concentrated instead on obtaining jobs for communist seamen in British merchant ships and using them as spies and couriers. It was under his guidance that a staff of more than three hundred was established in the ARCOS offices.

Thus the Soviet quest for British agents was intensified, but for long-term purposes and not to foment trouble in the unions, or to pursue the courtship of the TUC which the USSR had now decided was hopelessly linked to the capitalist cause from their point of view. By 1927, following the lessons of the General Strike, the TUC had in fact become much more realistic and less politically biased. Jilinsky worked with remarkable speed and efficiency. He succeeded in suborning key technicians in the Air Ministry. He was, in fact, surprised at the ease with which he was able to find willing agents among British subjects, and this may have made him careless or too ambitious. At any rate MI5, with help from the Special Branch, discovered that the Russians had obtained the services of a former British Army officer named Stranders, and soon afterwards a British technician serving with the Royal Air Force was arrested and charged with the theft of top-secret documents. During his trial the authorities had become alarmed by the revelation that these documents had been transmitted to the ARCOS offices.

A key figure in all that led up to the ARCOS raid was none other than the Wilfred Macartney known to both Guy Liddell and Joyce Whyte. In 1924 Macartney had been introduced to George Edward Monkland from ARCOS. At this time Macartney, who had been contacted by Soviet agents, was asked to ascertain the quantity and quality of war material shipped by Britain to the Baltic states, Poland, Latvia, etc.

He should not have foolishly believed he could trust Monkland to find out the information. Compton Mackenzie gave his opinion that Macartney, 'with a stupidity which verged on imbecility, left the questionnaire with Mr Monkland in his flat, and promised to return later for the answers.'[1]

Monkland, while apparently accepting the sum of £25 from Macartney for services to be rendered, promised to provide the information wanted. The fact that he accepted so large a sum – £25 then was worth almost £500 in today's money – and the considerable doubts as to whether he was in any position to obtain the whole intelligence that Macartney wanted – makes Monkland somewhat of a puzzling figure. Monkland, it should be mentioned, was also well known both to Joyce Whyte and Guy Liddell. The question now arises as to whether Monkland was an intermediary set up by Liddell, or if he played along with both sides.

What little information there is concerning Monkland's reaction to Macartney's request for intelligence amounts only to the fact that he is supposed to have obtained an introduction to Admiral Sir Reginald Hall and told him about the approach from Macartney. But why should he have done this when he knew Guy Liddell and had a more relevant and direct approach to the Security Services than Hall could possibly have had?

Despite the intervention of Admiral Hall, nothing much happened on the counter-intelligence side for a long time. Compton Mackenzie makes the point that:

> it would be tedious to relate in detail the steps by which the Intelligence authorities proceeded to deal with the information handed to them by Sir Reginald Hall, but it may be observed that the apparent ineptitude they displayed over several months was equalled only by the obvious ineptitude of Macartney himself.

That the Intelligence Department was at this time engaged in preparing the ARCOS raid adds force to any criticism of its competency.[2]

Both Kell and Liddell were kept informed about developments in alleged espionage between Macartney and Monkland, and these particularly centred upon another long questionnaire, on matters concerning the RAF, for which Macartney had asked Monkland to provide the answers. Monkland was then given a somewhat outdated RAF handbook marked 'Secret' to pass on to Macartney. Macartney was seen to have passed on this handbook to a Soviet contact.

Somehow, despite the fact that both MI5 and the Special Branch were working on this case, almost everything went wrong. According to Krivitsky after he defected a few years later, 'the GRU had a tip-off from someone inside Scotland Yard that an attempt was being made to pass bogus information on to us with a view to recovering this material in a raid. We had advance information about the ARCOS raid.'[3]

Krivitsky gave no names of any such informants, but the fact that it was certainly someone inside Scotland Yard points in the direction of Guy Liddell, because only he was in a position to know the full details of the Macartney-Monkland link. That the Soviets had been given warning of the raid seems to be confirmed by the fact that Macartney told Monkland 'to get rid of the documents'. It also looks as though there was some attempt to enable Macartney to escape from possible arrest. London's Passport Office had already issued a passport to Macartney, but a search of its official files after the ARCOS raid showed that his letters of application and photographs had disappeared from the files.

Certainly there were inexplicable delays before the raid on the Moorgate premises of ARCOS was made. By the time the Special Branch men arrived at the offices the Soviets had already either removed or burnt their secret papers, so nothing of any value was discovered. Sir Wyndham Childs was convinced that they had been effectively warned what was about to take place. He described how:

there were several hundred employees in the building, so it can be imagined how difficult it was to carry out the search effectively, and it was not until the following Sunday that we were in a position to ascertain the results of our search. The particular document we were looking for was never found, but we discovered conclusive evidence that ARCOS was being utilised as a focus for the dissemination of revolutionary propaganda.[4]

What little information was obtained as a result of the ARCOS raid was mainly what the Special Branch and MI5 already knew – addresses of Communist Party headquarters in such areas as Canada, the Argentine, Columbia, Guatemala, Uruguay, Mexico, Brazil, Chile, South Africa, Australia and the USA. But what the British fatally failed to find was the names of the chief Soviet agents and re-cruiters in Britain, or, more importantly, the links with the USA via couriers or any evidence of the infiltration of the British Foreign Office and the Security Services.

The raid did not come to an end until midnight on 16 May 1927. By this time Macartney was already making plans to leave the country and members of the American Embassy in London seemed to be con-vinced that he had been secretly advised to escape before any action against him was taken. There was a note in their records, dated 5 December 1927, that 'the forewarning of ARCOS and the withdrawal of Macartney's passport file fuelled speculation that the Soviets had achieved effective penetration of the Metropolitan Police, the Special Branch and possibly MI5.'[5]

The handling of this whole affair by both Special Branch and MI5 was not merely incompetent, but in many ways inexplicable unless somebody inside one or other of these services was deliberately delay-ing operations. Why was Macartney not arrested immediately after the raid following information from Monkland? The fact is that through-out the summer of 1927 Macartney was freely travelling about between London, Paris and Berlin, and, according to Compton Mackenzie, 'writing idiotic letters to Mr Monkland, all of which the Intelligence Department had photographed by the Post Office in transit.'[6]

Possibly by this time Macartney felt he was safe and that no action would be taken against him. At any rate he returned to London in November 1927, and had a rendezvous with a young German named Georg Hansen, said to have been the chief contact with the Soviets. Even then there was a delay of three days before arrests were made. Charges were brought under the Official Secrets Act and eventually resulted in a trial in January 1928, before Lord Chief Justice Hewart. Much of the evidence was heard *in camera*. Both men were sentenced to ten years' penal servitude, with a concurrent sentence of two years' hard labour.

It is said that Liddell personally accompanied the Special Branch men who broke into the ARCOS offices, and no reason for this was given. Considering how the raid failed almost totally to provide the authorities with the information they wanted, it is incredible that no serious steps seemed to have been taken to conceal that the British government had broken the Soviet codes. The result was that those codes were almost instantaneously changed.

Superintendent Arthur Askew, of Scotland Yard, told the author that some time in the early 1920s there was a disagreement between Sir Basil Thomson, head of Special Branch, and Liddell:

> I never knew exactly what it was about, but from then on Thomson was distinctly cold towards Liddell and it became obvious that he did not altogether trust him. This seemed all the more strange because Liddell was the type of man who got on well with everybody. Thomson must have had sound reasons for taking this line, however, because he always made carefully considered verdicts on all those who worked for him.[7]

Ill luck dogged Sir Basil in retirement. In December 1925, he and a young woman named Thelma de Lava were arrested in Hyde Park and summoned for committing an act in violation of public decency. Sir Basil pleaded 'Not Guilty' and said that he was carrying out investigations in Hyde Park into reports of soliciting by women with a view to writing both a book and articles for the newspapers on this subject. It was perfectly true that since retirement he had written both books and articles on various criminal cases and subjects connected with crime. Some of these had made him highly unpopular with the authorities. Nevertheless he was found guilty and fined five pounds. He appealed against the sentence, but lost. Both Admiral Hall and Reginald McKenna, a former Home Secretary, gave evidence on Sir Basil's behalf, testifying to the high regard each had for him and paying tribute to his character. Two friends, Major Douglas Straight and Mr H. V. Higgins, testified that Sir Basil had discussed with them the writing of an article on prostitution in Hyde Park before the incident occurred. Even the chairman of the Court of Appeal expressed surprise that in such a case, where a joint offence was alleged, the couple should not have been tried together. Thomson had many enemies in the police hierarchy, especially in the Metropolitan area where he knew a great deal about the corruption and chicanery then prevalent in that force. The question arose as to whether Thomson had been framed by people either within or with access to the Special Branch.

Superintendent Askew recorded that, when the verdict was

announced, Liddell said to him with a smile of satisfaction: 'Sir Basil has had it coming to him for a very long time. This should teach him to lay off telling stories out of school in books and articles.' Askew added that when he tried to find out exactly what Liddell had against Thomson, 'the man just smiled and commented: "Let's just say he spent too much time chasing shadows."'[8]

The Strange Death of Ernest Oldham

> Kensington police are trying to trace the identity of a man, aged about 35, who was found dead in a gas-filled kitchen at 31 Pembroke Gardens, Kensington ... His shirt bore the initials 'EHO'.[1]

This police report strikes a particularly odd note because 31 Pembroke Gardens was, in fact, the home of the man with a shirt bearing the initials 'EHO'. Why should the police have any problem in establishing his identity? Unless, of course, someone higher up, probably at Scotland Yard, had wanted the minimum of publicity for this discovery.

The man in question was Ernest Holloway Oldham, the very first Soviet spy to be discovered inside the British Foreign Office and the man who recruited Captain Herbert King, who was eventually caught as a result of information from Krivitsky. The full details released by the police about this character were that 'he was five feet six inches in height, well built, clean shaven and had dark brown hair and eyes ... wearing a brown suit with collar and tie to match.'[2]

Oldham was born in September 1894 and in 1913 he passed a competitive examination for a second division clerkship in the Board of Education. He left this department to go to the Board of Trade in January 1914, and then in April of that year was transferred to the Foreign Office. It was not until 9 February 1917, that he was called up for active service in the Army, from which he was quickly demobilised after the Armistice on 11 December 1918. He was, according to some, rather more fluent in a number of languages than he officially claimed to be. Certainly he had an excellent record as a hard and efficient worker so that it was no surprise when he was promoted to junior executive grade in January 1920, eventually rising to the rank of staff officer in August 1928. The Foreign Office List shows that he 'resigned' on 30 September 1932.

His work came under the heading of 'communications' which, in effect, meant that he was responsible for '... telegrams, messenger and bag service to and from posts abroad, travelling arrangements', according to the official designation of such employment. The Foreign Office list also shows that from 1934 until 1939 John Herbert King was also in 'communications'.

In 1930 Oldham travelled to Paris for the purpose of providing communications support to a special British trade mission. While there he took some of his cipher material to the Soviet Embassy in the belief that the Soviets would buy it from him. Oldham seemed to be more anti-British Establishment than pro-Soviet or perhaps just short of money. On this occasion, according to most reports, Oldham had no luck at all. Having examined and photocopied the material he gave them, the Soviets returned it to him with the comment that it was all faked, that Oldham was a *provocateur* and that this was yet another clumsy attempt by the British to attack the USSR.

Oldham returned to London, presumably wondering whether the Soviets would disclose his ploy to the British Foreign Office. But the Russians were rather cleverer than that: despite their suspicions that Oldham was a *provocateur*, they sent photocopies of his material to Moscow. There it was decided that the material was not a fake, but in its way quite useful, so Krivitsky, who was then working for the USSR in Amsterdam, was instructed to send a subordinate to London to attempt to make fresh contact with Oldham. The man sent to London made himself known to Oldham as Hans Gallieni, but it is quite possible that this was a cover name for Hans Christian Pieck, a major Soviet Intelligence officer in Holland who concentrated on British affairs. He posed as a Dutch businessman who to travelled around painting as a hobby on holiday.

Hans was evidently able to persuade Oldham to cooperate, probably by manipulating his fear of exposure. In the light of his experience in Paris, Oldham's contempt for communism now equalled his disdain for his Foreign Office masters. Hans reported to Krivitsky that Oldham was unstable and that it seemed unlikely he would observe the strict security rules by which the Soviets operated for this kind of espionage. Krivitsky urged Hans to inquire of Oldham whether he could suggest any of his colleagues who might be enrolled as informants. Oldham then submitted King's name among some others. There is no positive proof as to who those others were.

Introducing himself to the Russians Oldham had given his name as 'Scott', which in no way fooled his interrogator, a GPU man named Vladimir Voynovich. Oldham was followed from the moment he left the Soviet Embassy in Paris. To make matters worse for Oldham Grigori Bessedovsky, the *chargé d'affaires* in the Soviet Embassy in Paris, possibly as a result of his friendly relations with Western businessmen, defected. Having sought French aid on defecting, he happened to tell the story of the man named Scott to a French interrogator. The French alerted the British and as a result information on this case was passed to Guy Liddell for investigation. Bessedovsky had not seen Oldham, so he could give no description of the man, only the name Scott.

There should have been no difficulty in Liddell and the Special Branch tracking down the probable identity of 'Scott' very swiftly, as a check with the Foreign Office would have shown who of their personnel were in Paris at the time of 'Scott's' visit to the Soviet Embassy. Instead all that the Special Branch ordered, presumably under directions from Liddell, was a search for all people named Scott who had moved in and out of the country during this period. There was only one Scott on the Foreign Office List at this time – Sir Oswald Scott, an ambassador who was most certainly not incriminated.

Liddell was the Special Branch's liaison man with both the Foreign Office and the US Embassy in London. The Foreign Office regarded Bessedovsky's information as wholly unreliable. Liddell did nothing to discourage this view and almost made apologies for reporting the matter.

Very little seems to have been made of the fact that the British visitor to the USSR Embassy in Paris had been mysterously referred to as 'B-3' by Bessedovsky. 'Roger' (the code-name of a former member of the pre-War Soviet apparat in Switzerland) told the author 'At that time there were many attempts over a number of years to acquire copies of important papers at Geneva and Paris. This type of espionage was linked to certain people in England and one of them was known as "B-3" to the Russians. They suspected that he still had an informant within their own ranks after he defected. This could explain how he learned about Oldham after 1930.' 'Roger' has long since managed to keep clear of all espionage entanglements to the best of my knowledge and in any case he is now very old indeed, but for his own safety his identity needs to be kept secret.

It was not only Bessedovsky who referred to an agent named 'B-3'. Georgi Agabekov, a GPU operator who had defected from the Soviet Service in 1930, also pointed to a Soviet agent inside the British Foreign Office. Agabekov had fallen in love with an English girl, a Miss Isabel Streater, and in his eagerness to elope and marry, had signed a document in the autumn of 1930, declaring that if arrangements could be made for Miss Streater to leave Stamboul for Brussels by 1 October of that year he would reveal 'in what manner, where and through whom the Bolsheviks receive documents by the [British] Foreign Office, and reply to all questions which shall be put to me which I shall consider myself competent to answer.' Subsequently Agabekov revealed that there was an agent known as 'B-3' who was gathering intelligence from inside the Foreign Office.

It was Krivitsky who provided a few clues as to the identity of 'B-3'. He told the Americans that, when he was stationed in Amsterdam, Moscow had instructed him to send an agent to London to make contact with a man who was engaged in the communications department of the Foreign Office.

'"B-3" had much to do with ciphers and he seemed very willing to supply names of colleagues either in the Foreign Office or in organisations linked to Whitehall,' declared Krivitsky. 'He certainly provided a number of names, but almost always the identities of these were concealed by code-names. I cannot say how many of these names were taken up.'

The significant date which Krivitsky mentioned for the first contact made by 'B-3' was the year 1930. In September of that year Geneva had been the scene of the sensational theft of the keys of Foreign Office dispatch boxes from Mr Philip Noel-Baker, who was then Parliamentary Secretary to the British Foreign Secretary, Arthur Henderson, in Ramsay Macdonald's 1929-31 Labour Government. Noel-Baker was asleep in his hotel bedroom at Geneva when the thief slipped into the room and took the keys from his trousers pocket. He was discovered by Mrs Noel-Baker, but escaped and all trace was lost.

At first there were attempts to deny the incident had ever occurred, and certainly the episode of the theft of the keys was hushed up. But a pertinacious *Daily Mail* correspondent in Geneva, the late H. Challinor James, refused to be browbeaten not only by threats, but by pressure brought to bear on his employers. On 2 October 1930, the *Daily Mail* published a report which stated:

> The recent theft here by a mysterious armed intruder of British Foreign Office dispatch box keys and the consequent fitting of new locks have had a very significant sequel . . . the possibility of its being the work of some foreign power was never lost sight of by the secret service in London . . . The first step was to find if the hand of Moscow had again been at work against Britain . . . A full report is now in the hands of the British Secret Service.

The inquiry left no room for doubt that the thief was a Soviet agent, whose aim was to steal the keys without being discovered, to have them speedily copied and returned to the owner in such a way that a theft would not have been suspected. But Challinor James himself had always considered that it was not just the keys which had been taken, but documents as well:

> He was adamant that the theft was much more serious than a bunch of keys and that the Foreign Office covered up a serious leakage of information. As he said, just to steal the keys did not make sense unless they could be copied and returned without arousing suspicion (no easy task) and unless, of course, they knew that they would have access to other Foreign Office boxes.[3]

There was a strong suggestion that the Geneva affair was linked directly or indirectly to 'B-3'. Agabekov did not live to provide any more intelligence on the matter. The question remains unanswered as to whether he had suddenly become suspicious of the British and feared that someone in their ranks would betray his whereabouts to the Russians. Whatever may be the truth, he suddenly disappeared and sold himself to the Rumanian secret police who provided him with a bodyguard and a house near Bucharest.[4] Despite these precautions he was eventually located by the NKVD and murdered.

All evidence points to the fact that 'B-3' was Oldham and that the authorities had been almost unbelievably slack in failing to track him down very quickly. If Hans could locate the mysterious 'Scott' so easily, how was it that the Foreign Office and the Special Branch failed to do so? Even more curious is the fact that later on when Krivitsky's testimony was produced by the Americans, the British response was merely to refer to 'Scott' and 'B-3', never to Oldham.

By introducing King to the Soviets Oldham probably thought he could pave the way to his opting out of the espionage game. When this ploy did not work he decided to resign from the Foreign Office at the end of 1932, obviously failing to realise that the Soviets would not easily allow a disgruntled agent to retire and thereby constitute a permanent threat to their network.

When I began my research into the mysterious 'EHO', his real identity had never been officially revealed, nor had there been any public suggestion that he was a Soviet agent. After that single notice in *The Times* there was absolute silence in the press. No mention of an inquest, no obituary, no indication as to who the man was, not even in the local press.

A search of wills for 1934 at Somerset House, using the irritatingly slow process of searching for a man with the initials 'EHO' revealed the following: 'OLDHAM, Ernest Holloway, 31 Pembroke Gardens, Kensington, Middlesex, died 28 September 1933. Estate of Pounds 3,600. Administration to Lucy Oldham, widow.' Working back to the London General Register Office for death certificates, I came across the full details, which were slightly different from those reported in *The Times*. Oldham had died from coal gas poisoning, not in the Pembroke Gardens house, but '*on the way to 28 Marloes Road*'! He was described on the death certificate as being 'aged forty-six, formerly a civil servant' and the Coroner had returned a verdict of suicide while of unsound mind.

There are many loose ends to this story of Oldham. On the American side there is considerable evidence that he did more harm to the United States and Canada than even to Britain, not least through his introduction of King to the Soviets.

Oldham's most vital contribution to the USSR was probably his provision of names of prospective agents in key positions in the USA. It is thought that some of these names were provided for him by a mysterious female agent named 'Leonore'. Presumably these names were given to his contact, Feldman.

But did Feldman betray Oldham? The question is apt because in 1932 Feldman was arrested and, despite the fact that his activities in Britain had become known to MI5, he was fined a mere £5 on a trivial charge and ordered out of the country. Was the price for such lenient treatment the betrayal of Oldham and possibly others? For it was just after this that Oldham resigned from the Foreign Office.

Was someone in MI5, or the Special Branch, trying to conceal the fact that Oldham had died in such circumstances by engineering false information to the press? When Sir Percy Sillitoe became chief of MI5 after the war he looked into the case of Oldham and he discovered to his amazement that *Liddell used to meet Oldham in a London public house*.

This fact gives rise to a more sinister possibility – that Oldham did not commit suicide, but that he was the victim of a killing by someone unknown. Not unnaturally, knowing that Soviet death squads were particularly active in this period all over Europe, any such theories point in the direction of the USSR. Peter S. Deriabin, a NKVD officer who defected to the USA in 1954, asked by his American interrogators to confirm that 'murder disguised as suicide' was carried out by the USSR, agreed that this was so, adding that in carrying out such dis-

guised killings 'there is no fixed rule. It depends upon the circumstances, the time, the country, the political situation in the country, the
material, and it depends mostly on the officers responsible for such
kinds of infiltration.'[5]

Another damning indictment of Liddell is a French Intelligence
memorandum. An SR *(Service Renseignement)* report of 1934 raised the
issue as to why, as the French had notified the British of the approach
by a Foreign Office man to the USSR Embassy in Paris in 1930, no
action had been taken to bring charges against the man in question. An
agent known as 'Alexie' was ordered to make inquiries into the case of
'Ernest Holloway Oldham, whose identity as an official of the British
Foreign Office communications division was known to Capt. G. M.
Liddell, of Scotland Yard.'[6]

The French Intelligence view of Oldham's death was that it was
'almost certainly a case of murder and not suicide'. As long as Oldham
was alive, the French felt that he was a security threat to both British
and Russians.

The French report ends with a terse comment that 'Our London inquiries reveal that information on this case was suppressed on orders
from Scotland Yard and that the man who gave these orders was Capt.
G. M. Liddell.'

One final note to this tangled story of Oldham: in October, 1945, on
the understanding that Pieck knew the Oldhams, husband and wife,
MI5 arranged that he should come to London to help Mrs Oldham
identify Hans Gallieni, who had been Oldham's contact man. The day
before this meeting was to take place Mrs Oldham was suddenly taken
ill and died before any identification could be established.

It was Liddell who was responsible for the arrangements for this
meeting with Mrs Oldham. His whole part in the affair from 1930 to
1945 raises many queries.

Baroness B and Mrs S

As MI5 was enlarged under wartime conditions Mr Liddell is credited with holding together the disparate collection of gifted amateurs drafted in from the universities. He offered an 'unbureaucratic, democratic' attitude which appealed to the dons and earned him the nickname of 'Darling Guy' among subordinates.

(The Times, *21 January 1980*)

Liddell's association with MI5 was probably unofficially operative in the late 1920s, but officially it would seem that he came over finally from Scotland Yard about 1934-5 with Hugh Miller and Sanders McCulloch.

When Liddell arrived in MI5 he must have known probably rather more about the service than some members in it. He had had access not only to Special Branch but to Foreign Office reports on matters concerning counter-intelligence. But over and above this he had his own extensive personal contacts which in many respects gave him access to intelligence-gathering as distinct from counter-espionage. In this respect he had an advantage over Kell. It was this advantage as much as anything else which made his entry into the service so smooth and gave him a certain ascendancy over his colleagues.

He had a theory of organisation which endeared him to some of his subordinates: this was that the more important the decision the lower the level at which it should be taken since 'the men on the ground' knew the situation best. It was this carefully developed attitude which helped to earn for him the nickname of 'Darling Guy' among subordinates.

While in the Special Branch Liddell had been in touch with the Foreign Office, MI5, MI6 and the NID (Naval Intelligence Division) as well as the cipher and communications branch of Intelligence. Thus, from the point of view of 'B' Division of MI5 which he joined, he was the ideal man for such work, as this division kept links with

MI6, the Special Branch and, when war came, with various other organisations. The work of 'B' Division extended far and wide from the handling of double agents (in wartime) and enemy analysis to counter-sabotage, Soviet affairs and political subversion.

For a man in his early forties when he joined MI5, Liddell had in some ways aged prematurely. Indeed, some who knew him claimed that he was embarrassed by his appearance – he was balding, short and podgy. By nature he was shy and secretive. By 1935 Calypso Liddell had left her husband and gone to the United States with her children. The next few years were spent in arguments, mutual wrangling and legal battles. Liddell found his high standard of living difficult to maintain after his wife had left him.

In the Chancery Division in 1936 it was recorded that Mrs Liddell,

who was a British subject and the wife of a British subject – both being ordinarily resident in England – took the infant children of the marriage to the United States and was keeping them there without the consent and against the will of her husband. Proceedings were thereupon taken in the Chancery Division to enforce the trusts of a settlement executed by the husband for the benefit of the children, who thereupon became wards of Court; and thereafter an application was made for an injunction restraining Mrs L. from keeping the infants out of the jurisdiction and requiring her to bring them to the country. Notice of this was duly served upon her, and eventually an order was made . . . directing her to bring the infants to England.[1]

An appeal against this order was heard shortly afterwards. Then it was stated that Mrs Liddell had taken 'four infant children of tender years' to the USA in July 1935, 'without the consent and against the will of Mr Liddell.' Lord Justice Romer, in summing up, said:

In my opinion the children of British parents who are wards of Court should not, in the absence of special circumstances, be permanently resident abroad, and it is plainly right and for the benefit of the children in the present case that they should be brought to this country. It has been further contended that even so this order can never be enforced against Mrs Liddell if she chooses to disobey it and that the sequestration of her income would not be for the benefit of the children. It is not the habit of this Court in considering whether or not it will make an order to contemplate the possibility that it will not be obeyed.[2]

Eventually there was a divorce and the Hon. Calypso Liddell married her first cousin, Lorillard, and settled in California. An outraged ex-husband was heard to exclaim 'This is nothing other than incest!'

In the meantime Liddell returned to his bachelor days' existence, often staying with his brothers at a house in Ashley Place, West-minster. It was a period in which he made a number of new friends, all of whom came to play an important part in his life and, not least, in his work. One such was the Baroness Marie Budberg (more usually known as 'Moura'), the third and youngest daughter of Count Ignary Platonovich Zakrevski, the scion of an aristocratic family of Czarist Russia who became a member of the Imperial Council and was noted for his liberal views. Moura had acquired her title following her second brief marriage to Baron Budberg.

Moura Budberg was born in the same year as Liddell, and after being educated at one of St Petersburg's top high schools she spent six months at Newnham College, Cambridge, polishing up her English. In 1911 she married John Benckendorff, who was then a second secretary in the Russian Embassy in Berlin, where she stayed until the out-break of World War I. Exactly how she managed to keep in with almost all sections of Russian society during World War I and after the revolution has puzzled many people. Her husband joined the Russian Army while she went to St Petersburg and became a nurse in a hospital while also functioning as a society hostess. It was in 1918 that she met Sir Robert Bruce Lockhart, who, in his *Memoirs of a British Agent*, described with untypical frankness for those days his love affair with Moura. In the meantime she contacted her husband, who was still in the Army and told him of her affair with Lockhart. Husband and wife agreed to meet at his estate in Estonia, but this plan ended disastrously for both. Benckendorff was killed by his own peasants when he re-turned to his estate and Moura was arrested en route and taken back to Moscow.

It was then that this remarkable woman showed her adaptability. Back in 1914 she had met H. G. Wells when he visited Russia. Now, on an invitation from the Bolsheviks, Wells was to visit Russia again, so Moura volunteered for the job of looking after him and being his inter-preter. After that she also ingratiated herself with the Soviets by obtaining an introduction to Maxim Gorky and became his private secretary. In the autumn of 1921 Gorky left Russia and arranged for Moura to join him in Germany. They lived there for a spell, moving on first to Czechoslovakia and then to Sorrento. In 1933 Gorky returned to the USSR and Moura went to London, bringing her children with her. Through his various Russian acquaintances in London Liddell was introduced to her and soon he became a regular visitor at what Moura called her 'salon'. Sometimes they dined together tête-à-tête. By this time Moura had decided never to marry again. She had briefly been married a second time to Baron Budberg, but he turned out to be a compulsive gambler and was given a divorce on the understanding that he took a one-way ticket across the Atlantic.[3]

Moura Budberg had the talents to play a very clever game in managing to keep close friends with the anti-Bolshevik White Russians in London and Paris while maintaining the closest links with some of the Bolshevik leadership. She continued to visit the USSR at regular intervals, and had a Soviet passport. She even claimed, as we have seen, to have met Reilly in Russia after he had been reported killed.

Evidence suggests that all the time she was a committed Soviet agent, and that Liddell knew this. Certainly she knew exactly what Liddell's job was: 'Our 'cello-playing spy-master' as she used jokingly to refer to him. For a long time she pretended that it was quite impossible for her to visit Russia, making visits there surreptitiously. It was only when H. G. Wells, her lover, went to Moscow in 1934 for a talk with Stalin that he learned Moura had been in that city only a week before. When he expressed disbelief, the Russians changed the subject, saying they must have been mistaken. Eventually she admitted to Wells that she had been to Moscow.

'In 1984,' writes Mr Robin Bruce Lockhart:

he was informed by a senior member of the Russian media that Soviet newsreel material quite clearly showed the Baroness [Budberg] standing beside Stalin at Gorky's funeral ... The same person informed me quite categorically that Moura had been a Soviet agent ... in 1967, when I was writing *Ace of Spies*, I asked for Moura's help over one or two details about Sidney Reilly, whom she had known since 1918. I showed her a draft typescript of the part of the book that covered the events of 1918. The Baroness did her level best to try to persuade me to delete the references I had made to Bolshevik atrocities during the Revolution, claiming that these were lies ... At that time I was unaware that she had known in 1932 that Reilly was still alive. How much more did she know?[4]

Among the most important tasks which Moura Budberg undertook for the USSR was that of 'Trust Number Two', an operation which was just as skilfully exploited as 'Trust Number One'. The Soviet Union's technique in subverting the right-wing was done in two ways: first, through the ploy of doing business with the capitalists; second, by using so-called 'White Russians' as secret agents. In other words, the technique of The Trust was being applied as cleverly in the thirties as it had been in the early twenties.

One of the most skilled of their Russian agents in Britain at this time was a great friend of Moura Budberg, a man who had long lived in London and who, until 1923, was chairman of the Russian emigré Social Democrats in Britain. He was Anatoly Baykalov, a journalist, who, on the pretext of obtaining information, maintained contact with various Soviet citizens. To his British friends – and these were drawn from trade union and newspaper spheres as well as West End clubs and the aristocracy – he always appeared to be a genuine opponent of the Bolshevik regime and a dedicated believer in liberal and demo-cratic government. In the 1930s he acted as a kind of Russian adviser to the General Council of the British Trades Union Congress, analysing publications and reports for them at a guinea a thousand words, pro-viding summaries, translations and occasionally confidential reports on such Soviet officials as Grigori Sokolnikov. It is fair to say that his real motives were never suspected, yet all the time he was a spy in the heart of the TUC.

In 1932-3, however, an Ukrainian named Korostovets reported that Baykalov was holding secret talks with Soviet agents both in London and Paris. As a result of this a Parisian Russian emigré paper claimed he was working for the USSR. It is strange that this information did not reach the British security services, or, if it did, that they kept it to themselves and do not seem to have discouraged anyone from having dealings with Baykalov. This was yet another lapse on the part of British Security which caused the French Intelligence Services to have doubts about the competence of the Special Branch and of Liddell in particular. Meanwhile in London the wily Baykalov was winning favour among British Conservatives and some senior civil servants, in-cluding Sir Edward Marsh and Sir Warren Fisher, head of the Trea-sury. His success with the Duchess of Atholl and Sir Edward Marsh enabled him to supply information to Winston Churchill.

Kitty Atholl, as she was generally known among her friends, was the eldest child of Sir James Ramsay, baronet, of Edinburgh. At one time she envisaged a musical career for herself. Though in many ways a stern, unbending Tory of the old school and a martinet who looked with disfavour on some social reforms, she was not only generous in private, but easily moved to anger by blatant injustices and cruelty, and the enemy of persecution wherever and in whatever form it was to be found. Her husband had been offered the crown of Albania after World War I by Lloyd George, who had the imaginative but quixotic idea that the head of a Scottish clan might make an admirable leader of the mountain tribes of Albania; the Duke refused it. Nevertheless, the Duchess had in her own right made considerable progress both in Scottish social circles and in the political arena. Created a Dame of the British Empire in 1918, she became the first Scottish woman MP, being elected as a Conservative for Kinross and West Perthshire in 1923. From 1924 to 1929 she was Parliamentary Secretary to the Board of Education and, incidentally, a very efficient one.

Some indication as to how far to the right she was in the early thirties may be gathered from her support for Winston Churchill in his opposition to the proposed new constitution for India planned by the Baldwin Government. On this occasion she gave up the party Whip and established cordial relations with Churchill himself, which were strengthened later when the Spanish Civil War broke out. About this time Baykalov had interested the Duchess in his plans to organise a public inquiry into the Soviet judicial and penal system, which, as far as one can gather, was never actually held. Baykalov's ploy gave him a pretext for collecting information on all recent defectors from the USSR, which he passed on to his Soviet masters.

It was on this subject that Baykalov first interested the Duchess. She was much concerned about Soviet persecution, and he took advantage of this to try to convince her that the Russian emigré organisations were working overtime through such bodies as the NTS *(Nacialno Truduvoy Souz)* and others to undermine the Soviet regime and to form a provisional government to take over the country when the Soviets collapsed. And Baykalov, who was as subtle as any 'White Russian' agent of the USSR has ever been, was also able to paint a picture of many communists in Russia who were only too anxious to see the regime made more democratic. 'Democracy in Russia draws nearer every day' was his message. It was Baykalov more than anyone else who helped to swing the Duchess into forthright support for the Spanish Republican cause, though there can be no question but that she would have been horrified if she had learned all that George Orwell saw for himself. With Baykalov, the supposedly mildly liberal White Russian, forever prompting her, guiding her and making sure she met such people as Otto Katz, Kitty Atholl started to oppose the Chamberlain government vigorously on its non-intervention policy. The Whip had been restored to her when the Indian issue was settled, but now she lost it again. She began to appear on platforms with politicians of Labour, Liberal and Communist Parties and so came to be given the altogether ludicrous and inappropriate nickname of the 'Red Duchess'.

Kitty Atholl was no fool and it is a measure of Baykalov's skill and diplomacy that he was able to win her as an unconscious ally of the USSR. She was absolutely right in thinking that the march of fascism needed to be stopped. But, while still appearing to be anti-Soviet, Baykalov was able to persuade the Duchess that the Spanish Civil War would bring Russian communism into contact with liberals and conservatives as well as socialists, and that eventually this must mean that communism would mellow into democracy and Europe would blossom into a garden of lovely democratic design. So he not only obtained visas and various other favours involving the Foreign Office through the Duchess's influence, but he fed her with information and also passed this on to Churchill himself. It was Baykalov who convinced Churchill that his old friend Sidney Reilly had died a dedicated agent of the British Secret Service, faithful to the end.

Baykalov was also responsible for reporting to MI5 that Mrs Wallis Simpson, the mistress of the then Prince of Wales, was a secret agent of the Germans. One of the most observant and calculating of agents, he had noted that Mrs Simpson was frequently at the German Embassy and an extremely close friend of the then German Ambassador, Dr Leopold Gustav Alexander von Hoesch.

This information was passed on to Baldwin via his Secret Service liaison Minister, J. C. C. Davidson (later Lord Davidson). There seems to be no doubt whatsoever that notice was taken of it and that Liddell, who handled this affair, appears to have given no advice that Baykalov might be exaggerating. For while the Russian's picture of Mrs Simpson's links with the German Embassy was unquestionably true, at no time could it be said that she was a German agent. But the Baykalov evidence certainly helped to harden attitudes in the Government against Edward VIII when he came to the throne and seemed intent on making Mrs Simpson his wife.

On 4 February 1936, when Edward VIII had recently succeeded to the throne and was seeing a large number of state and Cabinet papers, J. C. C. Davidson wrote this 'Most Secret' memorandum:

Maurice Jenks [former Lord Mayor of London] came to see S. B.
[Stanley Baldwin] today on a very secret and important matter. It
transpired at the interview that some time ago a man Simpson
came up for admittance to the Masonic Lodge on which Jenks
presides. A message from HRH P of W strongly supporting
Simpson's candidature. Simpson was turned down by the Lodge
and Jenks was sent for by HRH who demanded to know the
reason.

'Do you want to hear the truth?' asked Jenks.

'Yes,' replied the P of W.

'It is because quite obviously we could not admit the husband
of your mistress as it would produce a situation in which the
fundamental law that no Mason may sleep with another Mason's
wife would be broken.'

The P of W denied that there was anything between himself
and Mrs S and gave a pledge to that effect as a Mason. Mr S was
admitted and is now a Mason.

Now Simpson-Mason asks to see Jenks-Mason – the *mari-
complaisant* is now the sorrowing and devoted spouse. He tells
Jenks that the King [Edward VIII had succeeded to the throne on
20 January] wants to marry Mrs S (unbelievable) and that he (S)
would like to leave England, only to do so, that would make
divorce easier – what he really wants is his wife back. S suggested
he should see the PM. S. B. replies to this suggestion with a flat
negative. He is the King's adviser, not Mr Simpson's.

10pm: Clive Wigram, S. B. and I have a frank talk. I am quite
convinced that Blackmail sticks out at every stage. I advocate
most drastic steps if it is true that S is an American . . . [It would
seem that Davidson, with probable security service acquiescence,
was all for getting Simpson sent packing.] The Masonic principle
is very clear. The P of W got S in on a lie and is now living in open
breach of the Masonic laws of chastity because of the lies he first
told . . .

Mrs S is very close to Hoech [*sic* von Hoesch, the German
Ambassador] and has, if she likes to read them, access to all
Secret and Cabinet Papers.[5]

10

Some Very Strange People

Truth or fiction? . . . Sir William Stephenson, Canadian-born entrepreneur, confidant of Churchill, infallible detector of bad eggs . . . Maxwell Knight, known in MI5 as M, who walked his pet bear, sometimes accompanied by his bulldog or baboon, through the streets of Chelsea, attended Aleister Crowley's seances . . . Some wrote their memoirs; others took to imaginative fiction . . . But men called 'Intrepid' [Stephenson] who looked at their colleagues and found them bad eggs in the fullest sense of those words were never the inventions of Dornford Yates.

(Guardian, *29 July 1987*

Liddell had the best of both worlds in MI5, getting along admirably with Kell whom he used to refer to as 'our ageing father figure', while enjoying the company of some of the eccentrics. He found it quite easy to fit into Bohemian circles and to give the impression of what he liked to call 'a professional tolerance'.

What the *Guardian* correspondent wrote in 1987 on the strange people who linked up with MI5 in the 1930s may have seemed unbelievable but it was true. If Himmler, head of the Gestapo, was convinced that the Rosicrucians were a branch of the British Secret Service, one can only point to the fact that he almost certainly knew that Aleister Crowley, the most picturesque and notorious occultist of modern times, worked for MI5. In World War I Crowley had done some pro-German propaganda writing for Vierveck in *The Fatherland* and *The International,* which he edited for about a year. Crowley always claimed that he did this merely to spy on the Germans, and American Intelligence believed his story, despite the fact that his occult temple in London was closed down by the police. Eventually it was established that he had indeed genuinely been trying to help the Allies.

In the inter-war years Crowley spent much time in Berlin where he lived with another notorious spy, Gerald Hamilton, who was most cer-

tainly acting as an agent for the Germans. A strange situation developed with Crowley spying on Hamilton for MI5 and Hamilton spying on
Crowley for the Germans. Living together as supposed friends, they
concocted reports on each other. Hamilton was the model for Christopher Isherwood's Mr Norris in *Goodbye to Berlin.* Crowley and
Hamilton both kept up lengthy correspondence with Tom Driberg,
the former also maintaining links with Guy Liddell whom he called
'the transcendental cellist'. While Hamilton was forever trying to sell
articles to the *Daily Express* via Driberg (and sending lawyers' letters
demanding payment when they did not appear), Crowley's extensive
correspondence touched rather more frequently on occult topics.
'Shall I write to Russia proclaiming myself as The Beast 666?' was one
mysterious question he posed, and he signed some letters to Driberg
'Love is the law, love under will, yours fraternally, Aleister.'[1]

No doubt through such contacts Liddell obtained some intelligence
on pro-German sympathisers. But all evidence on this is curiously
muted. Even today practically all the files on the Right Club, The Link
and the Tyler Kent affair remain classified. Nor do the published
revelations of former MI5 secretary, Joan Miller, throw much light on
these matters.[2]

In the light of the cover-up on all information on the flight to Britain
of Rudolf Hess, this makes one highly suspicious. Who has been
master-minding the cover-up and why. There seems to be little doubt
that, apart from covering up incompetence in handling the matter, one
major reason was the involvement of Britain's royal family and some of
those closely attached to it such as the devious and egotistical Admiral
of the Fleet Lord Mountbatten of Burma, who in his lifetime moved in
a way, which at first seems inconsistent, between supporting in a low-
key manner first, the cause of a Germany in which he could play a part,
and then the USSR. Certainly both just before World War II and in
the first few years of that war American Intelligence was full of doubts
about Mountbatten and even appalled when they learned that he was
to be made Chief of Combined Operations.

It is only recently – after the death of the person in Spandau Prison
alleged to have been Rudolf Hess – that the name of Mountbatten has
been mentioned in British intelligence circles as one of those people
with whom Hess thought a deal might be achieved in the late thirties.
Whether this theory was based on knowledge of some of Mountbatten's indiscretions, his family links with Germany, or even because of
his suspected links to the USSR, is not clear. Until recently the British
answer to American doubts has always been 'how could you possibly

equate Mountbatten with any undercover deal for peace with Germany when he was so gallantly fighting the Germans at sea?' What those who took this view failed to appreciate was the obsession of Mountbatten with his royal connections in Germany and Russia just as much as in Britain and his almost grotesque vanity which sometimes led him to believe that he could achieve far more in international politics than anyone else. Vanity and treachery go together. When Mountbatten boarded the ship of which I was commanding officer in 1943 he asked not only to address the crew, yet, tall as he was, insisted upon my finding a wooden box on which to stand. 'It is essential that they look up at me,' was his excuse for this extraordinary request. When I saw Noel Coward do exactly the same thing in the film, *In Which We Serve,* I knew that he had copied it from his friend, Mountbatten.

Mountbatten's father, Prince Louis of Battenburg, had been hounded out of his office as First Sea Lord in World War I on account of his German ancestry. That Mountbatten never quite overcame the trauma of this harsh and unfair treatment is clear from what he said to General Christison after World War II had ended. Referring to his father having been forced to resign his office as 'that disgraceful episode', he added: 'I have lived determined to get to the top and vindicate his memory. Nothing and no one: I repeat, nothing and no man, will ever be allowed to stand in my way.'

Such ruthlessness was typical of Mountbatten throughout his life. Possibly he visualised himself as emerging as the saviour of a new Germany. While he made no secret of his dislike of the Nazis, he was playing around with various ideas which would have involved him directly in Germany's future both before and after World War II. It is known that at one time he had the idea of making himself King of Rhineland – Westfalen (with Hanover and Hesse thrown in) once the war was ended. This was an idea which had been put forward to him by his friend Peter Murphy in the late 1930s after Murphy had had talks with his German contacts.

Certainly Mountbatten was at times obsessed with the power which his royal connections gave him. For example, he even put forward the proposal before World War II that his great friend, Prince George, Duke of Kent, should be made King of Poland. This extraordinary proposal was confirmed by Baroness Agnes Stoekel in her memoirs, *All is Not Vanity,* published in 1951. There is evidence that even Chancellor Adenauer at one time considered the possibility of asking Mountbatten to preside over a Rhineland state, including Hesse, such a plan even came to the ears of the British Control Mission in Germany. Among the other strange proposals, none of which ever came to fruition were that the Duke of Brunswick should take over Hanover, the aged Crown Prince Rupprecht should rule Bavaria, while Air Marshal de Crespigny, Regional Commissioner for Schleswig-Holstein, put forward his own name as a candidate for constitutional head of that land on account of his popularity with what he called 'my Germans'!

How many of such plans in one form or another were being secretly touted around in talks between Britons wanting to make peace plans with anti-Nazi Germans before or even during the war is a matter of conjecture still. Some of these moves may well have been one of the reasons for the British royal family's hunt for papers in Germany after World War II ended and when Anthony Blunt was sent on this secret mission. Did Mountbatten browbeat King George VI into authorising some such search, making the excuse that it was to rescue the letters of Queen Victoria to the Empress of Germany? This should have been a transparent excuse because the story of Queen Victoria sending Lord Ponsonby to rescue this correspondence had been known for years. Moreover the correspondence would have been totally irrelevant to present day problems.

Mountbatten had been in touch with Blunt for some few years partly through the Duke of Kent and Peter Murphy.

Through his family the Battenburgs he was linked to the Hesse family, and was a close acquaintance of Princess Margaret of the Hesse family. She was the daughter of Lord Geddes and after the war not only took upon herself the title of Princess of the Rhine, but, thanks to Mountbatten's intervention with the Hesse socialist government, was allowed to continue to live in her dilapidated castle.

The Cambridge historian, John Zametica, in a book review recently made the point that 'many powerful members of British society – political, military, commercial, among others, were dedicated to attaining peace [i.e. between 1938 and 1941] and apparently losing the war did not go down well with them. These people faced three problems: Churchill in Britain, Hitler in Germany and a lack of strong leadership within their ranks.' Then Zametica adds:

Halifax was the man in the centre of this intrigue. He was supported maybe by the Duke of Buccleuch. And behind them stood, shall we say, Mountbatten . . . imagine that extremely important negotiations took place between the British peace group and the Germans in, say, County Down, Ireland . . . General Sir

Ian Hamilton ... had been deeply involved in previous peace talks.[3]

Such comments may seem rather in the style of a matador historian who seeks by such means to provoke others into telling the truth. Often it is the only way to get at the truth. Certainly Sir Ian Hamilton invited Rudolf Hess to stay with him at Lennoxlove in Scotland in 1939, the very house which was later occupied by the Duke of Hamilton whom Hess turned up to see in 1941. Mrs O'Mara Vinard, Sir Ian's adopted daughter, became an old friend of Frau Hess after working for the Nazi propaganda machine during the war. There is also evidence in the Dirksen Papers that Halifax asked Fritz Wiedmann, Hitler's secret agent, to inform Hitler that it would be 'the finest moment of his life if the Fuhrer were to drive along the Mall side by side with the King during a state visit to London' as late as 17 July, 1938[4]

Certainly prior to the fall of France Halifax strongly urged the use of Mussolini as an arbiter of Anglo-German differences, which would have been tantamount to surrender. Cabinet Papers in the Public Record Office fully reveal this.

It was his passionate involvement in all things regal, whether in Germany, Russia or Britain, which made the Americans dubious about Mountbatten. They were well aware of his secretive but highly expensive campaign to prove that Anna Anderson, the female who claimed to be the Grand Duchess Anastasia, daughter of Tsar Nicholas II, was a fake. They found this campaign somewhat difficult to explain, even if it was partly connected with Tsarist family money which could still be claimed. Michael Thornton, the author, who once held power of attorney for Anastasia in Britain, and who had secret meetings with Mountbatten (who, incidentally, was Anastasia's first cousin) states that 'Mountbatten spent many thousands trying to prove she was a fake, but mounting forensic evidence in her favour shook him profoundly.'[5]

In the early days of World War II the Americans were worried about Mountbatten on two counts: first, that he might be in the camp of the appeasers and would play a role in a compromise peace with Germany; Mountbatten was certainly a friend of Sir Francis Rose, lover of Ernst Röhm; secondly, that he was also flirting with making a deal with the Russians which might result in secret manoeuvres to persuade the Japanese not to attack Russia, but to seek rewards in the Pacific area. Both views were based on reports coming in from Europe, but consistently denied in London. Yet another report suggested that Mountbatten had plans to play along with some Nazis who disagreed with Hitler in collusion with allies inside the USSR. Only many years later when it was learned that the Soviet Union had infiltrated Rudolf Hess's private intelligence service did this make sense.

It was reported recently that Queen Elizabeth II did not wish to visit Moscow out of respect for the memory of Lord Mountbatten, the argument being that he detested the Bolsheviks because they murdered his uncle and aunt, Tsar Nicholas and the German-born Tsarina. That this is totally wrong may be judged from the fact that in May 1975, Mountbatten eagerly accepted an invitation to visit Moscow to celebrate the thirtieth anniversary of VE Day. It is said that he hoped to conduct and initiate a private Anglo-Russian trade treaty on this occasion. Commenting on this, Kenneth Rose has written: 'In his luggage he had hopefully packed some promotional brochures of the firm of decorators owned by his son-in-law, David Hicks.'[6]

Mountbatten was, of course, never a man to have any sympathies with the extreme Nazis and their tirades against the Jews. His marriage to Edwina Ashley, daughter of Lord Mount Temple and granddaughter of Sir Edward Cassels, Jewish friend of King Edward VII, not only ruled out any such feelings, but was actually given by him as his excuse for sending his two daughters to the USA during World War II. In defending this action, bearing in mind that the King's two daughters remained in the UK, Mountbatten replied: 'With their Jewish blood, they would have been the first for the gas ovens if the Germans had invaded.'

His socialistic views first began to develop when he went to Christ's College, Cambridge, in 1919. Here he struck up a friendship with James Jeremiah Victor Fitzwilliam Murphy, of Magdalene (more usually known as 'Peter' Murphy). The latter had strong left-wing sympathies and until Murphy's death in 1966 Mountbatten relied heavily on him for guidance. Murphy went into the Army after leaving Harrow and was invalided out in 1918, when he joined the Commercial Department of the Foreign Office until just before the Armistice. He then became political secretary to Lord Islington. At Cambridge Murphy read economics until 1921, when he went down without a degree, somewhat to the distress of his tutor, A. S. Ramsey, who, according to the archives of Magdalene College, wrote him a letter saying he hoped 'you will soon find congenial occupation'. In Paris in the 1920s he had talks with prominent Communists. There is a photograph of Murphy taken at a Conference in France along with such British Communists as Harry Pollitt and Arthur McManus.

Murphy then went back to Germany where he had spent eight months in 1913. During which time he first made the acquaintance of Guy Liddell.

Replying to Ramsey, in a lengthy fourteen-page handwritten letter, Murphy said that 'people seem almost more friendly to one than they were before the war!'

Murphy, like so many of Mountbatten's closest associates, was part of the homosexual set which as well as Guy Burgess also included Tom Driberg. Indeed Mountbatten relied on advice from both Murphy and Driberg on both Germany and Russia: all three were frequently in touch with one another, especially after World War II, and Murphy even drafted some of Mountbatten's reports in the Far East, when he became a personal adviser to the head of SEAC. MI5 maintained regular reports on Murphy, but there are suspicions that some of these may have been played down by Liddell.

Another left-wing influence with Mountbatten was P. M. S. Blackett, who was later given important posts by him during World War II. Blackett had been educated at Osborne and Dartmouth and had served at the Battle of Jutland before he was 19. He brought with him to Magdalene College something of the atmosphere of the quarterdeck and was already eagerly turning to the design of a new gun-sight when he went from the Navy to Cambridge in 1919. At Cambridge he suddenly became totally committed to left-wing causes and resigned his Royal Naval commission.

But the strength of Mountbatten's left-wing sympathies did not manifest themselves until the USSR became an ally following the invasion of Russia by Germany in 1941. On the Joint Intelligence Committee he was the only consistent backer of the USSR. Home Office files relating to British fascism and pro-German circles between 1934 and 1948 provide a limited amount of information on such organisations of that period, but a very great deal is still withheld.[7]

There would appear to have been far more instances of distortion and even downright falsification on the part of MI5 in obtaining evidence against pro-German and right wing sympathisers than was the case in investigating communist subversion. Material to be found in the PRO files in the case of John Beckett shows that some allegations made against him were false. Beckett's wife claimed that propaganda alleged to have been made by Beckett was in fact made by an *agent provocateur* in an attempt to elicit information from him. Apart from this, Herbert Morrison, when Minister for Home Security, admitted in 1942 that one Harald Kurtz, an MI5 agent, had given false information leading to the internment of Beckett.[8]

There were other cases as it became evident that false evidence had been manufactured in order to get certain people interned when war came. This unquestionably led to criticism of Maxwell Knight who was responsible for engaging some of these *agents provocateurs*. Clearly, some of the methods employed by MI5 agents were crude, immoral and inefficient and suggestions of a potentially highly dangerous Fifth Column aiding the Germans inside Britain were grossly exaggerated.

This state of affairs can be contrasted to the relatively low-profile treatment by MI5 of communists and left-wing subversives. It is true that the late Joan Miller has told of her role as an MI5 burglar in her posthumously published book, how she was instructed in letter-opening and how to break open a trunk lock before she and an MI5 colleague broke into Palme Dutt's house to find that the trunk contained little more than a copy of his marriage lines. On the other hand it could equally be argued that she had been led into this operation because of false information. Then there was the case in which MI5, by mishandling the arrest of Ethel Chiles, allowed a key Comintern agent, Jacob Kirchstein, to escape in 1928.

One of the worst of such errors, for which Liddell was primarily responsible, was MI5's failure to arrest Theodore Maly, the mastermind behind the network of Cambridge graduates supporting the Soviet cause, and his sinister successor, Willi Brandes. Brandes remains somewhat of a mystery, a man with many aliases and remarkably diverse contacts: for example, it would seem that Tyler Kent was in touch with Brandes after the Nazi-Soviet Pact was negotiated. Brandes was known in London and elsewhere under such diverse names as Bill Stevens, Bill Green, Bill Hoffmann and Bill Nathan. He was controlled from America by another character with a number of aliases, Joseph Feldman, also known as Abraham Seithurway. Feldman was a Russian oilman who operated in Britain under the name of Volardarsky and later started a Soviet network to spy on the USA from Canada. It was information from Krivitsky which led to the breaking of this network which Feldman, originally a GRU agent, was directing from Montreal. In November 1937, Brandes and his wife were allowed to leave the UK because Liddell had decided that it was not a good idea to make arrests as the couple could claim diplomatic immunity. The truth was that not only had the Brandes pair obtained false Canadian papers, but that the RCMP claimed that the British had enough evidence to justify arrest.

If the United States had had a properly organised Secret Service in the 1930s, Liddell might then have been noted as a possible Soviet mole in the British ranks. Lord Vansittart, then a key figure in the British Foreign Office, noted in his papers in March 1938, that 'the American Secret Service which existed during World War I, was more or less liquidated in 1919. It consists of a few agents centred in the Treasury who are concerned firstly with the protection of the President.'[9]

Despite this disadvantage, State Department, FBI and other American archives reveal considerable perceptiveness in this period. For example, they reveal rather more of Liddell's counter-espionage failures in his Special Branch days than are evident in British records. It is abundantly clear that the arrest of Brandes and others who had escaped could have provided much more vital evidence of Soviet activities.

In conversation with Mr L. G. Turrou of the FBI Vansittart was told that 'nearly eighty per cent of the information obtained by the Germans in the USA was being sold by Erich Pfeiffer of the German Intelligence Service to the Japanese at a very high figure.'[10] Pfeiffer ran the German Intelligence Agency in Bremen, but he was also very close to Hess.

There was also the suggestion that Tyler Kent was not the only leaker of information from inside the American Embassy. In February 1940, Guy Liddell wrote to Herschell C. Johnson, the US Embassy Counsellor, warning him:

> that at any rate just prior to the war and possibly still, the German Secret Service has been receiving from the American Embassy reports, at times two a day, which contained practically everything from Ambassador Kennedy's dispatches to President Roosevelt, including reports of his interviews with British statesmen and officials. The source from which the German Secret Service got these documents is not known, but is someone referred to as 'Doctor', and our informant, who is in a position to know, is of opinion that the 'Doctor' is employed in the American Embassy in Berlin.[11]

The mystery of the 'Doctor' remains to some extent to the present day. The late Sir Maurice Oldfield, former head of MI6, declared after his retirement that Rudolf Hess had his own intelligence service and that the head of it was a Soviet agent.[12] Oldfield was not a member of MI6 at that time, but presumably he received this information from colleagues some time after he joined the service. This would make sense in that it is reported that a British Secret Service agent in Berlin told MI6 in September 1939, that Hess's intelligence organisation was regularly receiving diplomatic reports that seemed to have come from a US Embassy either in Berlin or London.

Now this does not tally with Liddell's story of the 'Doctor'. The State Department were soon convinced that any leakage of such information did not come from their Berlin embassy, which seemed to point to the fact that it must come from London.

Was this an attempt by Liddell to cover up on Tyler Kent, who had already served in Moscow as a clerk in the Foreign Service? Certainly Kent's contacts in London had included Willi Brandes. When Kent left Moscow he had asked colleagues to forward to him a briefcase by diplomatic pouch. According to records in the National Archives of the US Department of State, this case contained a hand-gun with ammunition, three photographs (one clothed, two nude) of his Moscow mistress, Tatiana Ilovaiskaya, a photograph of a nude Russian actress and another of an unidentified nude male and female.

One can only pose the question whether the 'Doctor' actually existed, or if he was some kind of a diversion invented by Liddell.

That it could well have been a diversion is strongly suggested by the fact that none of the material held in the London Embassy of the USA was copied to other missions. Thus the viewpoint of Herschell Johnson was that 'somebody in the London Embassy or the State Department is involved. I do not see how else the information could have been leaked.'

At this particular period MI5 knew all about Kent, or at the very least were closely monitoring him, while the Americans had no warning about the mole inside their London Embassy. So why should Liddell have tipped them off about the 'Doctor', but not about Kent at that very early stage in such investigations? A charitable view would be that MI5 had doubts about the reliability of the defeatist views of the US Ambassador, Joseph Kennedy. But who alerted MI5 to the activities of the 'Doctor'? And, much more vital, who was the Soviet spy inside the British Foreign Office in this period? A detailed examination of the evidence suggests that it was not just Herbert King, but that there was someone else supplying material. Despite the fact that the Foreign Office had dismissed Krivitsky's evidence as 'rubbish' and 'totally contradicting our own sources of information', Sir Alexander Cadogan recorded in his diary that the investigators were 'on the track' of others inside the Foreign Office.

Out of these so-called investigations a much more interesting leakage occurs. It is the leakage over a short period between April 1939, and the declaration of war in September of that year, of information emanating from the *British Foreign Office* to the *German Embassy in London.* I have put these two links in italics because it is important not only to separate the Kent case from this affair, but also to stress that this was not a Herbert King-style operation.

It was only after the war, when German diplomatic documents were captured that it was discovered that in this period a number of telegrams from the German Embassy in London to Berlin contained details of the negotiations between the United Kingdom and the USSR on an alliance against German expansion. There was no doubt from an examination of the information given that it must have come from someone inside the British Foreign Office, or with access to its communications.

There was no evidence that such detailed information as this had been given before April 1939. Whoever this informant was, he was never caught, or, if he ever was, his identity was never disclosed by any British authority.

The material from this agent was far from being comprehensive. In fact it was carefully edited and conveyed the impression to latter-day investigators that it only told what the agent himself wished to communicate to the German Embassy. One example of this, cited by D. Cameron Watt, is that one such German Embassy telegram reporting on British-Soviet negotiations in May 1939, was 'quite erroneous in one respect; it alleged that the Soviets wished to defer the question of the inclusion of the Baltic states, Estonia, Latvia and Lithuania, in the scope of the negotiations until basic agreement had been reached on the Soviet proposal for a three-power alliance. The Soviets were in fact insisting that they be included in the negotiations from the beginning.'[13]

The question which now arises is whether this informant to the German Embassy was not a Soviet agent. On many occasions he seems to have edited the contents of the Foreign Office telegrams. As Professor Watt astutely points out: 'One is left with two possibilities: a British source opposed to the idea of negotiations with the Russians, or a Soviet agent in place.'[14]

It is, of course, just possible that the Soviets were using information from Herbert King to pass on through one of their own agents to the German Embassy, but this seems highly unlikely as no such intermediary has ever been named or suggested. The only other candidate for such a spy is the man Liddell named as the 'Doctor', who was never caught or identified. When Tyler Kent died in February 1989, it was stated in his obituary that 'MI5 suspected Kent of espionage soon after his arrival in Britain, but it did not inform Kennedy [Joseph Kennedy, US Ambassador], partly because he too was under surveillance, and partly in the hope that Kent would implicate others.'[15]

It was said that Kent was 'influenced by the strongly anti-British attitude of his Ambassador'.[16] A highly dubious character as Joseph Kennedy was, it would be rather more accurate to describe him as being pro-Irish and at the same time defeatist in attitude than to suggest he was anti-British. After all, one of his daughters married into an English family. Who delayed action being taken against Tyler Kent, for he was not arrested until ten days after Churchill became Prime Minister? It is noteworthy that in his final years Kent devoted much time to denying evidence in declassified FBI files that he had ties with Moscow.

Kennedy waived Kent's diplomatic immunity, which suggests a co-operative attitude towards the British, though pressure may have been put on him from Washington. However, the delays in unmasking Kent are still inexplicable on the British side. A Soviet link in the Kent affair still cannot be ruled out, and it should be noted that Kent was a fluent Russian linguist. Certainly his activities while in Moscow prior to going to London were such that he could easily have been blackmailed into passing information to the USSR. Apart from sexual indiscretions, Kent had also smuggled various Russian Imperial valuables to America.

But it is the undiscovered spy with access to Foreign Office telegrams who remains the mystery. If one analyses his editing of these telegrams in what he passed on to the Germans, the picture which emerges is that this was just the kind of information which the Russians would like to see the Germans receiving. It should be borne in mind that this was the time when attempts were being made to establish a Nazi-Soviet Pact. Was there another mole inside the Foreign Office apart from King? Was this mole someone known to Oldham and a reason why Oldham was silenced by being murdered? Was this mole an informant to Liddell? It is certain that only a highly skilled and remarkably well informed person could have interpreted so supremely well just what passages in the FO telegrams should be passed to the Germans and what should be withheld, if this was the work of a Soviet agent. The normal job of such an agent would be to pass on all material regardless of its value and allow others to assess it.

Shortly after the events of 1940 the entire Communications Department of the Foreign Office was wound up and a new organisation established. American Intelligence in recent years has re-examined this whole question and this view is taken by one of their analysts:

> I am bound not to break any agreements with the British about documents which should not be revealed, but I must say that it would seem that Guy Liddell could very well have been that informant to the German Embassy on behalf of the Russians. We know that he had access to Ultra material during World War II, and this suggests he may well have had access to Foreign Office telegrams before and after declaration of war. I have closely examined what was given to the Germans and, without doubt, this suggests it was the work of a man who was acting in the Russian interests. Probably only a Brit could have done this so effectively. Which raises the question as to whether the story of the 'Doctor' was not a subtle diversion from the truth.

The section dealing with alien subversion in the UK, headed by Maxwell Knight, was comparatively small at the outbreak of war when it was housed in Wormwood Scrubs Prison. Others in the section were William Younger, Philip Brocklebank, Tony Gilson and Richard Darwell. Eventually MI5 moved from the Scrubs and B-5(b) section went to Dolphin Square where Knight prepared three flats, two to be used as offices. Among the staff at Dolphin Square were Joan Miller (who was PA to Knight), John Bingham (later Lord Clanmorris), Rex Land, Norman Himsworth and two women, 'Babe' Holt, who operated the switchboard, and Liz Seale, the typist.

Meanwhile in Liddell's own section of MI5 there were other new case officers. One of these was Dick Goldsmith White, who had been introduced to Guy Liddell in 1936. It was then that he joined MI5, and was asked by Liddell to go to Germany to study what was happening there.

When war came Dick White became Liddell's closest colleague, and his assistant-director of 'B' Division. Certainly Sir Dick White, in retirement and long after Liddell's death, continued to pay tribute to his former chief: 'I knew him very well. He was very industrious, a devoted servant of this country. Throughout the Second World War he hardly ever left his desk. To label him a Soviet spy is a grotesque charge. *Accusing him may have possibly been a way of deflecting accusations against others,*' he told the *Sunday Times*.

The italics are mine. Who were the 'others' Dick White had in mind? He did not say and in view of all that has been suggested about moles inside MI5, this seems to be at the very least an error of judgement on Sir Dick's part, as he only succeeded in creating more of a mystery and more suspicion. It could equally effectively be argued that to accuse Hollis and Graham Mitchell was one means of deflecting attention away from Guy Liddell.

Graham Mitchell joined MI5 in November 1939, and was brought into 'F' Division (Overseas Control) under Major Bertram Ede. This section dealt with security in British colonies, contraband control and a certain amount of surveillance of political parties. Mitchell's job was to keep a watch on the Fascists.

Born at Kenilworth on 4 November 1905, Mitchell was educated at Winchester, where he was an Exhibitioner, and Magdalen College, Oxford. While at school he had contracted poliomyelitis which not only left him with a permanent limp, but also ruled him out for service in the forces in World War II. He always made light of his disability and in fact continued to play both golf and tennis, actually winning the Queen's Club Men's Doubles championship in 1930. For a man with such a disability he was, in fact, quite a remarkable all-round sportsman, for he sailed for Oxford University and was president of the Oxford and Cambridge Sailing Society, later in life becoming Commodore of the Bembridge Sailing Club.

Nevertheless, it was somewhat surprising that Mitchell should have been chosen to enter MI5 in view of his previous employment, first on the *Illustrated London News* (not even a newspaper) and then at the Conservative Party Central Office. Maybe the powers-that-were in MI5 considered Winchester and Magdalen plus the fact that he had played chess for Oxford University sufficient justification for admitting him to the Security Service. Much later he represented Britain at correspondence chess and in this sphere he was at one time ranked fifth in the world. Poor Mitchell, this correspondence chess was one of the reasons brought up against him when he was accused of being a Soviet spy: the suggestion was that in some way he used correspondence chess to pass messages to the USSR which tends to show how ludicrous and paranoic were his accusers.

What does emerge from much of the efforts of MI5 in tackling the problems of the day is that, while they were on the whole tougher on pro-German than pro-Soviet factions, they often seemed too eager to attack minor figures who were marginally or otherwise pro-German, but to cover up on the more important of such culprits. This is particularly true of some in the entourage of the royal family who should have been warned that any encouragement they gave to the appeasers was likely to be misconstrued. In the early days of Winston Churchill's government this was one of the problems they were up against. Since the war this has been to a large extent concealed by directing attention solely to the Duke and Duchess of Windsor, but in fact even with King George VI and Queen Elizabeth there were indications in the 1939-41 period of a desire for a negotiated peace. This was shown originally by George VI's preference for Lord Halifax as Prime Minister rather than Winston Churchill, and by the present Queen Mother of how sad it was that the German commander of the *Graf Spee* should have committed suicide when he scuttled his ship in the entrance to Monte Video harbour in 1940. After all, the *Graf Spee* had set out to sink and destroy innocent and unarmed merchant ships and, quite apart from that, Britain was at war with Germany.

Certainly the people at the head of affairs in Britain at the start of World War II from the monarchy downwards were very odd characters. This applies to the government, the military and military critics. An American Intelligence report states that General Fuller, another of Hess's cronies, told his fellow-members in The Link in 1940 that 'Ironside is with us' (the late Field-Marshal Sir Edmond Ironside was Chief of the General Staff in that period). Ironside, who is credited as being the model for John Buchan's character, Hannay, was very soon dismissed from his post as C-in-C of the anti-invasion forces. Yet General Fuller survived to become a military commentator for both the Beaverbrook press and the *Daily Mirror*.

As to Sir William Stephenson, cited in the quotation at the beginning of this chapter, his geriatrically inspired attacks on colleagues (notably Sir Roger Hollis) must be set against some of his own claims to be the super-Intelligence chief of all time. Intellectually, he would not be on a level with Hollis or Mitchell. The truth is that there is no evidence that he was a close contact of Churchill, or had anything to do with the breaking of *Enigma*, or that he acted as an intermediary between Churchill and Roosevelt. For some years he was regarded as somewhat of a rogue elephant in the Intelligence game not only by the FBI, but the OSS as well. The late Sir John Colville, Churchill's private secretary, declared in his book, *The Churchillians* that he 'never heard Churchill speak of Sir William Stephenson,' and he also described an alleged letter from Churchill to Stephenson, cited in *A Man Called Intrepid*[17] as a 'clear invention', if only 'for obvious reasons Churchill never signed himself "WC".'

Shortly after Stephenson's death in 1989, and following some wildly enthusiastic obituary notices about the man, an article in the *Sunday Telegraph* was headed 'Death of an Intrepid Fraud'. This referred to the comments of Sir David Hunt, another former private secretary to Churchill, who spoke of 'Stephenson's fraudulence'. The article added that 'the French have no record of his alleged *Légion d'Honneur'*, and that nor was there any record of his having been 'amateur light-weight world champion', or 'European light-weight amateur boxing champion', as cited in two of his obituaries. 'Intrepid' was not Stephenson's code-name: it was simply BSC's (British Security Co-ordination in USA) telegraphic address.

As the title of this chapter has already indicated, there were some very strange people in highly responsible jobs during this period in MI5, MI6 and Military Intelligence. Stephenson's close contacts with MI5 will become much more relevant in future chapters.

As a footnote to this chapter one might just mention two other 'strange people'. One was Brian Howard, an old Etonian and Oxonian and a member of the gay fraternity, a friend of both Driberg and Eve-lyn Waugh, who described him as 'mad, bad and dangerous to know'. Howard did not last long in MI5, nor did he have a major job, but he caused a lot of trouble. He was a member of the team responsible for keeping watch on Fascists, eventually being sacked because he was constantly getting drunk in bars and nightclubs and telling people around him that he worked for 'a top secret organisation'. Another Oxonian, Bernard Floud, who had been educated at the same school as Donald Maclean and James Klugmann, Greshams School, Holt, despite having been a member of the Communist Party earlier on, was given a commission in the Intelligence Corps. After Floud, then Labour MP for Acton, was found dead in a gas-filled room at his home in 1967, Mrs Jennifer Hart, wife of Professor Herbert Hart, who also served in MI5 in World War II, and a former history don at St Anne's College, Oxford, declared that she was recruited as a spy by Floud prior to the war. 'I was called a secret member so I never saw a party card and was told not to associate with members of the Communist Party.'[13] She added that her controllers encouraged her to work at a major office of state: 'They said I ought to go into something where I would be useful to them.' She joined the Home Office in the late 1930s, eventually being concerned with the department dealing with telephone tapping and mail intercepts, work which involved her with MI5.

11

The Bentinck Street Set

The *Fuhrer* has high hopes of the peace party in England. Otherwise, he claims, the Hess Affair would not have been so systematically killed by silence.

(*The Goebbels Diaries*, Sphere, London, 1983)

While the vast majority of the British public had no inkling of the dire situation their country was in during the summer of 1940 and were unanimously behind the war effort, those in senior ranks of any of the Establishment services were well aware that defeat was a distinct possibility, even a probability. Indeed, it is likely that Winston Churchill's greatest strength in those days was the fact that he had never grown up, that he still retained a boyish defiance of the facts of life. Immaturity became an asset in his political career.

It was a realisation of probable defeat by maturer figures inside the Establishment that partly caused the swing towards peace moves with Germany on the one hand and overtures to the Soviet Union on the other. In both cases secrecy was essential, particularly as the Nazi-Soviet Pact still existed. There is no doubt that Guy Liddell was already leaning strongly towards an unofficial liaison on behalf of MI5 with Soviet contacts. This idea of an unofficial link with Soviet supporters was, of course, quite separate in his own mind from his private contacts with supporters of the USSR. If ever there was a cautious supporter of a government which was hostile to Western civilisation, Liddell was the perfect model, and he always tried to safeguard his own base. His mentality is not an easy one to explain because it was, like so many of the characters in *Alice Through the Looking Glass,* so hopelessly mixed up. He had this strong hatred of all things German, a romantic liking for Russian music and literature, a love of high society in England and a resentment against that very society's treatment of him and his family, as he saw it in retrospect. Beyond all this had grown within him a feeling that, if he was not the strongest of characters, he could by cunning and caution achieve much more in the way of power than many of his contemporaries. Still suffering from the blow of the loss of his wife, he seems to have found the acquisition of such power and influence a stimulating substitute. There was behind all this the outlook of the man as a musician. The late cellist, Jacqueline du Pré, once said somewhat sadly that until she met her husband, Daniel Barenboim, her only friend had been her 'cello, which she had believed to be human, so much so that she talked to it constantly, and, even at the age of twelve, was unable to relate to other children because she had been made to feel so much apart. Something similar occurred with Liddell, especially after the breakdown of his marriage. On very rare occasions he would tell close friends that he found the same source of inspiration in the 'cello that 'Sherlock Holmes did in his fiddle', adding that when he sought a solution to some difficult problem he often got it right after playing his 'cello in absolute solitude.

A man who shared Liddell's artistic interests and his upper class, Irish connections was Anthony Blunt. Despite the fact that Blunt had been turned down for a job in Military Intelligence after an adverse report, presumably because he had been a communist when at Cambridge, he managed to get into MI5 in August 1940. This was achieved largely through the influence of Guy Liddell after Blunt had previously been turned down as a security risk by Brigadier Harker on information supplied by Brigadier John Shearer and Sir Gerald Templar. This was explained by Liddell's insistence that, as he once put it, 'in a war against Germany, it should not be held against possible recruits that they might have been Soviet sympathisers.'[1]

Liddell's Section B included among its other tasks that of vetting potential recruits not only for MI5, but MI6 as well. He also recommended Philby's move from SOE to MI6. What is more, bearing in mind that he knew all about Blunt's associations with the USSR, he employed him as his personal assistant. Liddell had known Blunt previously both through his Irish friends such as Peter Montgomery, another musically-inclined son of a distinguished Northern Irish family, who had been with Blunt at Trinity College, Cambridge, and 'Peter' Churchill, the left-wing radical of the Churchill family.

During his service in MI5 Liddell had two especially devoted and efficient secretaries: they were more like personal assistants, and later they both became officers. These were Margot Huggins and Jean Findlater. From the very first Miss Huggins took a dislike to Blunt. She felt that her own influence with Liddell was threatened by what she saw as Blunt's increasing authority in the office. It was partly because of this situation that Blunt was transferred to B-1(b), in which section he was concerned with the surveillance of embassies.

Miss Findlater was a native of Tenterden, where she died in 1985. Highly regarded in MI5, she was awarded the MBE when she retired about 1972. Dr Harwood Montgomery Hyde, who knew her well, said that 'she had access to Guy's private diary, as when she first met me she said she knew a lot about me since there were so many references to me in the diary.'[2]

Liddell spent much of his spare time visiting London art galleries with Blunt, who was certainly responsible for advising Liddell as to which pictures he should buy. As Liddell was also very knowledgeable about paintings generally, it seems surprising that the pictures he bought were eventually not worth a lot of money. Maybe Liddell had insufficient funds for really worthwhile purchases. There seems to be little doubt that Liddell was flattered by the attention paid to him by Blunt. Christopher Harmer, another wartime member of 'B' Division, said that Liddell was 'indiscreet and terribly susceptible to flattery'.[3]

Liddell had been appointed as Director of 'B' Division of MI5 in June 1940, and he used the additional authority within the service which this gave him to encourage the entrance of such of his friends as Lord Rothschild and Guy Burgess. He was a frequent visitor to the house in Bentinck Street, London, which was lent for the use of Blunt, Burgess and their friends by Lord Rothschild. This may be one reason why Rothschild would declare after the exposure of Blunt: 'For whom should I put my hand in the fire? I can still name a few, and among them would, undoubtedly, be Guy Liddell.' It may be wondered why suspicion has so readily attached itself to the bluff, hearty Hollis, rather than to Liddell who was a constant companion of Blunt and Burgess (at the time some thought of them as 'the two Guys') and who shared their rather foppish intellectual, aesthetic and social tastes.

Another close friend of Liddell's both before and during the war was Tomás Harris, whose parties in his Mayfair home he, along with Blunt and Philby, regularly attended. The world of art in the late 1930s seems to have led to a number of recruits into the world of Intelligence, and Harris, the art collector, like Peter Wilson of Sothebys, was one of these. Born in 1908, the son of an English father and a Spanish mother, Harris was brought up in an atmosphere which was redolent of the artistic and Bohemian world. His father, Lionel Harris, founded the Spanish Art Gallery and brought to Britain many Spanish works of art. Tomás carried on this task, though his own inclinations were towards being an artist rather than a dealer. When, in 1923, he was awarded the Trevelyan-Goodall scholarship at the Slade his examiners learned to their amazement that, as he was only fifteen, he was too young to be eligible. He was versatile, too, being a competent practitioner in the arts of sculpture, ceramics, stained glass and tapestry as well as painting. He never completely stopped either art dealing, collecting or painting even in the war years.

After leaving the Slade School, Harris studied painting and sculpture at the British Academy in Rome. Then in 1930 he decided to become an art dealer. It was in Rome that he was first recruited into the Soviet Secret Service through an Italian underground communist who was also an art dealer. 'His recruiter was, in fact, one of our INSA linkmen in Italy,' says 'Roger', the code-name of a member of the pre-war Soviet apparat in Switzerland. When Harris started art dealing seriously this involved much travelling in Spain. Some of this dealing was done on his own behalf, but much more was done on behalf of the Soviet government through secret channels in Paris, Brussels and Rome. By this time Harris had become friends with Georgi Agabekov-Arutyunov, who was short of funds and, though still hunted by the NKVD and therefore anxious to remain outside Russia, he tried desperately to get back into the Soviet Intelligence network. Somehow he was lured into an operation connected with the looting of Spanish art treasures during the Civil War. The Russians had developed a plan by which churches, monasteries, castles and even nunneries which came into Republican hands should be robbed of all the art treasures and valuables which would fetch a good price on the international market. An NKVD agent named Zelinsky organised the sales in Belgium, where Agabekov-Arutyunov had many contacts, and Harris ran the London and Paris end of the business. According to Mark Oliver, the picture dealer, large numbers of these works were in Harris's possession during and after the war.

The late Ellen Wilkinson, MP (a former communist who had long since been disillusioned about communism and become an opponent of it) knew all about Agabekov-Arutyunov and she learned much later that, shortly after being seen talking to Harris in an inn on the Spanish-French border in 1937, he had disappeared completely. Later he was said to have been killed by NKVD agents.

Harris's entry into British Intelligence after the outbreak of war was curious to say the least. It was largely through the influence of Liddell that he was brought into MI5, where his intimate knowledge of Spain and all the complex political ramifications in both the Franco administration and the underground was considered invaluable. Before Harris joined MI5 he was, together with Philby, at the SOE training school at Brickendonbury Hall, near Hertford: Philby himself described Harris as 'our outstanding personality . . . taken on, at Guy's [Burgess] suggestion as a sort of glorified housekeeper, largely because he and his wife were inspired cooks . . . The work was altogether unworthy of his untaught, but brilliantly intuitive mind.'[4]

Harris's very close friendship with Philby, which extended over many years, began at that period, though they may have met before in Spain. In any case the Russians had by this time realised that Harris was a shrewd and ruthless operator who had all the makings of a highly professional counter-espionage officer. Then, quite suddenly, he was brought into MI5. A handsome, swashbuckling man, gregarious and charming, providing all the indications of considerable wealth, an admirable, generous host, Harris's magnificent home in Chesterfield Gardens was almost a museum in itself. The Harris parties, even in the midst of wartime rationing, were noted for the quality of the liquor and the skilled and imaginative cooking. In MI5 the Harris party circle was known as the 'Chesterfield Gardens Mafia'.

It was Harris who made overtures to lure Philby away from his isolated work in SOE to a much more important job, which called for a special knowledge of Franco Spain, in Section V of the SIS (its counter-espionage section) which was linked to MI5 and particularly concerned with the Iberian Peninsula. Its chief task was to obtain information of espionage operations planned against the British from abroad. Most of these were being mounted by the Germans from Spain and Portugal. It was a job which suited Philby and the Russians perfectly: Philby was brought into Harris's orbit in MI5, while Section V was not only a vital part of MI6, but had links with the Foreign Office and various Service Intelligence departments. And it was at Chesterfield Gardens that Harris introduced Philby to Dick Brooman-White of Section V. Kenneth Benton, who in the spring of 1941, was sent out to Madrid as head of counter-espionage, with the rank of Second Secretary in the embassy, explained the function of Section V:

> Our job was to recruit the spies recruited by the *Abwehr* for work in Britain and the Americas. A great number of these had to travel through Spain because of the naval blockade in more northern waters. If we could spot the spies our authorities could arrest them either on landing in England, or by means of the Royal Navy's control of trans-Atlantic shipping. Alternatively, instead of having them arrested, tried and – usually – shot, we could 'turn' them and use them against their former masters.[5]

Often London would know a great deal about these spies before they had even arrived in Spain or Portugal, their normal staging-points. Nevertheless they were known only by their code-names and these did not always indicate the sex of the spy or give any physical description. This presented great problems of detective work for both MI6 and MI5 and a good deal of surveillance before an agent was finally identified. But it had the advantage, as far as the Soviet side of Harris's work was concerned, of enabling some Russian agents to be slipped in with the German agents. Sometimes the former posed as the latter with Harris's full knowledge. How many of these Soviet agents were smuggled into Britain may never be known. Many arrived as refugees from concentration camps and parts of Nazi-occupied Europe, a few were brought in on the SOE network (of which both Harris and Philby had a good deal of inside knowledge), but it is certain that the most effective of them came in under the cover of the 'Double-Cross' set-up, the organisation which 'turned' enemy agents to pass back by radio or otherwise false information to their German employers.

One of the ablest of these triple-agents was merely listed in Sir John Masterman's account of Double-Cross as 'Treasure', 'A French citizen of Russian origin . . . an intelligent but temperamental woman who was controlled by Kliemann, of *I Luft*, Paris.'[6] Her real name was Lily Sergueiev, a strikingly attractive, auburn-haired girl, daughter of a Russian father and French mother. She told many people that she had a romantic passion for the game of espionage and had always wanted to be a secret agent. Sometimes she gave friends the impression that she would become an agent for whichever nation first offered her such work. In Paris she posed as a White Russian, while in Vienna she was mainly to be found with left-wing friends. She had relatives in Cambridge and friends in Bristol, not to mention having known Richard Sorge. By the mid-thirties her uncle, Nicolai Vladimirovich Skoblin, had brought her into the Soviet network. When war came in 1939 Lily was contacted by Hans van Meegeren, the Dutch painter and forger of Vermeers, who indicated that the Russians wanted Lily to obtain a job as a German agent and then make her way into Britain. So it was that when the Germans entered Paris in 1940 Lily contacted an *Abwehr* officer whom she had known for some time. Eventually she was enrolled as a German agent. When the Germans wanted to send her to Lisbon, she protested that she would be much more useful in England where she had friends. Her plan was to get into Britain so that she could turn and work against the Germans.

After some delays the Germans acceded to her requests. Meanwhile the British side made checks on this determined young woman. No doubt Harris had to await instructions from his Soviet contact before he could give the go-ahead for an entry visa. For Lily had gone straight to the British Consulate in Madrid and it was on a British visa that she was flown to London via Gibraltar in August, 1943. 'I knew this young woman had been brought into the *Abwehr* network as far back as the end of 1940,' said the late Major Donald Darling, of MI9 (the war-time escape organisation) who was stationed in Gibraltar for most of the war:

> What struck me as odd was that nothing had been done about launching her into the espionage orbit for the best part of three years. It didn't quite make sense. I gathered London approved her trip and that she had friends and relatives at Cambridge and Bristol and, so she had said, in Banbury, too. But what had she been doing in the meantime? It was unlike the Germans to keep an agent on ice, as it were, for so long. From what I have gathered since she must have been feeding them false information from Soviet sources in the interim. Long afterwards I recalled that story about friends in Banbury. That was where Klaus Fuchs handed over material to his Soviet contact, Ruth Kuczynski. It is rather odd that she should have mentioned Banbury to me, because she made no reference about this place to the Consulate in Madrid. I do remember one very odd thing, looking back on it all. I asked for the names of her Banbury friends (we had the details about the other people she was supposed to be seeing) and she was slightly evasive. She just said, 'You know Tomás Harris? – he has all the details on Banbury. If you check with him –'. Well, of course, I did know Tommy Harris from long before the war when I was running a travel agency in Spain. But I was very surprised indeed that she should already seem to know the man who was to be her case-officer in London.[7]

So Lily Sergueiev went to London and was given the code-name of 'Treasure' (in the *Abwehr* she was known as 'Tramp'). The visits to relatives in Cambridge and to friends in Bristol were all checked out by the authorities. But on the Banbury end of her story there is a blank. She was used by B-1(a) to feed back false information to the Germans, especially regarding plans for the invasion of the continent. Kenneth Benton has described her as 'one of our best double agents', while Sir John Masterman said that she did not belie her code-name:

in March of 1944 she was sent to Lisbon in the hope that she might be given a wireless transmitter. The hope was fulfilled and on her return wireless communication was established. Later it became necessary to operate the transmitter in her name using our own operator, partly because she was in poor health and partly because she proved exceptionally temperamental and troublesome.[8]

This latter statement seems to diverge from the popular view that 'Treasure' was indeed a treasure. Nevertheless Lily was allowed to return to Paris when it was liberated and, as a result, her German case officer was arrested and brought back to Britain. She had been the only woman in the *Abwehr*'s service to have been trusted to operate a clandestine radio in enemy territory, for the Germans regarded her just as highly as the British. One reason why she may have been allowed back into France so soon was that she was slowly dying of an incurable disease, but there was another reason for her going: she needed to report to her Soviet control officer in Paris. Norman Holmes Pearson, professor of American literature at Yale University, who served in London with the American OSS and was closely linked to the 'Double-Cross' organisation, said: 'We had reports long after the war was over that one of our agents who liaised with the Russians was told that Lily Sergueiev had given the Soviet Union the most detailed plans of American-British operations in the closing stages of the war.'[9]

Harris's supreme feat in the war and the one in which he brought all his artistry to bear was that of the agent 'Garbo', perhaps the most brilliant hoax ever perpetrated in military operations. Harris was really the creator of 'Garbo'. His idea was to build up a completely fictitious espionage network for the Germans inside Britain – just to keep them quiet and mislead them. But the linchpin in this scheme, which naturally fitted in splendidly with the underlying motive of providing a realistic network for the Russians, was the conception of 'Garbo'. Harris was neither an academic, nor an intellectual, but he had a fast-thinking brain and astonishing intuition. Anthony Blunt told how 'Operation Garbo':

misled the Germans about Allied plans for the invasion of France. The success of the operation was mainly due to the extraordinary imaginative power with which Tomás directed it. In fact, he 'lived' the deception to the extent that, when he was talking in the small circle of people concerned, it was difficult to

tell whether he was talking about real events or one of the fantas-
tic stories which he had just put across to the Nazi Intelligence
Service. One of the highest soldiers said of 'Garbo', 'it was worth
an armoured division.'[10]

Harris left MI5 at the end of the war, but he did not divorce himself
completely from intelligence work with the British. Major Donald
Darling told the author that after World War II:

> Philby used to sub or borrow from Harris in Madrid to settle his
> drink bills and other matters which cost him a lot of money. Har-
> ris was Philby's paymaster in Spain for years after the war. He was
> also a key figure in planning the escape of Donald Maclean's
> wife, Melinda. You may recall that just before she fled to Switzer-
> land to join her husband in Russia, Melinda Maclean was to have
> gone on a visit to Majorca. After the war Harris set up a home and
> studio for himself at Camp de Mar, Majorca. Well, someone in
> London got to hear of Melinda's proposed visit to Majorca and
> suggested that a watch might be kept on Tommy Harris. The
> grapevine then suggested that Melinda's visit was cancelled on
> account of this. Tommy, of course, continued to have his own
> spies in MI5, the principal of whom was Guy Liddell.
>   As to the ramifications of the Philby-Harris-Maclean-Burgess
> set-up, I remember a man named Farmer, who turned up in São
> Paulo at the time of the Burgess-Maclean scandal. He had been a
> close friend of Maclean's family and told me, after some whis-
> kies, that he had just had a cable from Maclean from Helsinki,
> saying 'All well, don't worry'. I soon saw that was a plant, pre-
> viously arranged by Maclean with Farmer, otherwise how could
> he have known where to find Farmer in Brazil? I reported it at the
> time to PCO, Rio [Passport Control, British Embassy], who
> seemed quite uninterested. Farmer was a painter, quite pleasant
> and beardy and I thought from Fitzrovia [that area of northern
> Soho the Bohemian life of which centred around the Fitzroy
> Tavern].[11]

There is some confirmation from 'Roger' concerning the Majorca
connection with Melinda Maclean's escape:

> The whole affair was very carefully planned long in advance. First
> of all, just to test reactions not merely of MI5, but also of the

press, there was Melinda Maclean's trip to the South of France at Grimaud in 1951. MI5 had always opposed this, but reluctantly gave way. There was not much else they could do. The publicity surrounding that trip was largely due to the fact that there was a rumour that she was secretly to meet her husband there. That *canard* was put around by a Soviet agent. Then there was her stay in Geneva and, when things seemed fairly quiet, there was the plan to stay in Majorca with an American friend. But it was always understood over here that a get-away from Majorca was cancelled because of an MI5 watch. Where the British officials slipped up was not to suspect something was amiss when, for no very good reason, Mrs Maclean cancelled that trip. I learned this from an ex-PAKBO man who was a frequent traveller between Majorca and Geneva.[12]

PAKBO was the organisation created out of INSA by Otto Puenter, a native of Zurich, to provide intelligence on Nazi and Fascist activities during the Spanish Civil War. PAKBO was composed of the first letters of the main contact points of the organisation – Pontresina, Arth-Goldau, Kreuzlingen, Berne and Orselina.

After the war Harris gave up his commitments as an art dealer, concentrating more on painting and collecting. He spent much more time in Spain, first in Malaga and Madrid and later in Majorca where he built himself a house and studio.

In January 1964, Harris was driving his wife along the Lluchmayor Road from Palma, Majorca, when the car skidded for several yards, knocked down a telephone pole, then went off the road and crashed into an almond tree. Mrs Harris escaped with minor injuries, but Tomás suffered a fractured skull which proved fatal.

The accident puzzled everyone, both in Majorca and London, though it was noted that this came about shortly after Philby's defection to Russia and the consequent interrogation of various other suspects in London. There was no question of Harris being drunk. Some thought there could have been foul play and that his car had been tampered with before he drove it. A telephone call was received by a top executive in MI5 suggesting that somebody should be sent to Majorca to investigate the whole affair and also, so he added ominously, 'to make sure nothing incriminating is left behind at the studio'. But, as far as can be ascertained, no action was taken.

One of Harris's wartime colleagues, a senior Army officer who had maintained a liaison with the 'Double-Cross' organisation, said:

When Philby finally defected I began to feel sure that Harris was probably a Soviet agent, too. When I heard of Harris's death I was certain it was no accident. He was a driver *par excellence.* But which side killed him? That is anybody's guess. His wife cracked up badly after this tragedy and I am sure she felt her husband had been murdered. Poor woman, she didn't live long afterwards.[13]

Perhaps one of the most damning comments on how the Russians acquired intelligence from the British through illicit sources was this statement made by Colonel T. A. Robertson, a key figure in the 'Double-Cross' organisation. He was recalling a talk with Blunt as the war drew to a close, saying:

I think we were talking about what would happen after the war and how we would react to the Russians. Then he [Blunt] said something like this: 'it has given me great pleasure to have been able to pass the names of every MI5 officer to the Russians.' Or whatever he called them. I was taken aback. I thought: why should he tell me this? It was an electrifying remark. I couldn't keep it under my hat. I suppose I must have told Guy Liddell.[14]

Certainly if he did, Liddell took no action regarding this.

By this time wartime activities had put him under great stress. He had become a chain-smoker and his secretaries noticed his black moods, even if these were hidden from many of his colleagues. These were tense days, especially for someone like Liddell who was still involved in sorting out reports from two schools of thought – those who wanted to see Britain opt out of the war and let Germany and Russia fight it out, believing that the Nazi-Soviet Pact was totally insincere, and those who were all for making a deal with the Russians against Germany.

Kenneth de Courcy, who now goes by the name of the Duc de Grantmesnil, had at that time been taking soundings in Europe and had made reports to the effect that the French would not continue to fight Germany. In an issue of his newsletter *Special Office Brief,* 2 April 1987, de Courcy presented an account of some events in 1940 and, in particular, of the role of the former Conservative Cabinet Minister, the late R. A. Butler, then an Under-Secretary at the Foreign Office. Following information which Butler received from de Courcy, he conveyed these doubts about the French to Lord Halifax, his chief, and an envoy was sent to sound out Joseph Kennedy, the US Ambassador.

De Courcy certainly was an informant to Sir Stewart Menzies, then
head of MI6, as well as to Chamberlain and Butler, and such advice as
he gave was highly relevant and in relation to French attitudes was fully
borne out by subsequent events. Yet one of the most vehement of
opponents of de Courcy was Guy Liddell who expressed the view
loudly and clearly that he should be silenced, as should the Imperial
Policy Group which he represented. In putting forward this view Liddell had the support of at least two other prominent people in MI5.
The suggestion was – and it was even put to Churchill as Prime Minister – that de Courcy should be interned, one excuse being that the
Russians were pressing for this.

Hugh Dalton, originally the Minister responsible for SOE,
recorded in his wartime diaries for February 1943, on a trip to Moscow, that 'Stalin . . . referred to the publications of de Courcy . . . he
was told by Clark Kerr [later Lord Inverchapel and at that time British
Ambassador to Russia] that they were of no importance whatever . . .
he [Stalin] did not believe us . . . "Which of your departments," he
asked, "is encouraging them?"'[15]

One of the major criticisms that can be levelled against Liddell
during the war, and one which once again suggests his allegiance to the
Soviet Union, concerns his handling of the double-agent, Dusko
Popov. As has been seen, the 'Double-Cross' system was infiltrated by
Soviet agents and in some cases partially Soviet-controlled without the
British being aware of this, though some insiders in MI5 must have
known what the score was. As Dusko Popov himself revealed 'some of
the agents tried to triple-cross us'.[16]

Popov was one of the most astute and intelligent of all 'Double-
Cross' agents. It was he who obtained details through his German
contacts about a Japanese request to the Germans for full information
on the torpedo bomber attack by the British on the Italians at Taranto
in 1940. Popov also managed to get hold of Japanese questionnaire
which was clearly indicating plans for an attack on Pearl Harbor, as it
specifically asked for details on defences in this area, including ammunition dumps, aerodromes, naval installations, submarine depots,
mine depots and torpedo protection nets.

Colonel T. A. Robertson told the late David Mure that:

Tricycle [Popov's code-name in 'Double-Cross'], his questionnaire and his information about Pearl Harbor and his proposal
for a bogus spy ring in the States were all sent to Hoover [head of
the FBI] on the advice of Guy Liddell. Liddell, as the head of 'B'

Division, was one of three who could from time to time be consulted on Double-Cross matters.[17]

The question is whether Liddell was consulted internally by the
'Double-Cross' Committee as the head of 'B' Division and if, after
this, the Committee took a unilateral decision to pass on all the material to the FBI alone. Lt-Commander Ewen Montagu, of the Naval
Intelligence Division, who was the link man with the War Board, as
well as being a member of the 'Double-Cross' Committee, claimed
that he would not necessarily be informed of any decision taken as to
the passing on of Popov's information. Nevertheless he agreed with
Colonel Robertson's view that it was Liddell's decision simply to pass
on the intelligence to Hoover, arguing that Liddell was the right person to deal with this and so was Hoover. Yet this was a matter of such
importance that it was surely the duty of any British authority to ensure
that Popov's news went first to the American Naval Intelligence (a
first-class and long-standing US intelligence service) and probably to
the President of the USA.

What made matters worse was that Liddell denigrated Popov in his
messages to Hoover, implying that he was merely a double-agent and
that his information needed to be checked. The result was that Hoover
took an immediate dislike to 'Tricycle' and seems to have completely
failed to pass on any of his vital testimony either to the American ONI
(Office of Naval Intelligence) or to the White House. Hoover alleged
that Popov had been given the code-name of 'Tricycle' because he
liked to go to bed with two girls at once! Did Liddell tell him this story?

Popov was left in no doubt whatsoever that Hoover did not trust him
and that in some ways he was in more danger in the USA than when
conducting his 'Double-Cross' activities in Europe. He complained
that he had to wait weeks before Hoover would see him. When the
meeting took place the two men clashed. Popov suggested he should
be allowed to go to Hawaii to set up a 'Double-Cross' network there,
but this proposal was totally rejected. Long afterwards he wrote that
because of the neglect of his vital questionnaire, Hoover ' was the man
responsible for the disaster of Pearl Harbor'.[18]

In 1946 Hoover published an article in *Reader's Digest* in which he
said 'One day in August, 1941, we met a youngish traveller from the
Balkans on his arrival in the USA. We knew he was the playboy son of a
millionaire. There was reason to believe he was a German agent.' [NB:
no mention of his being a British agent!] This again makes one wonder
just what Liddell had told him. Everything points to the fact that Lid-

dell had no particular desire to stress the urgency of this whole matter, and that he even went so far as to suggest that anything Popov might have to say was either false or of little consequence. Yet this very same information was passed on to the Russians in great detail, as they have since acknowledged.

The USSR, then facing the full might of the German armies on their western front, were in serious trouble. The news which Popov had provided was an unexpected bonus for them: it meant that the Japanese would not be attacking Russia, but would concentrate their forces against the USA and Britain. Having had confirmation of all this from their man in Tokyo, Richard Sorge, Stalin was able to withdraw his eastern army from the Soviet's Pacific defences and bring it back to assist in the defence of Moscow and Leningrad. If the USA had had detailed news of Japanese plans for Pearl Harbor, not only could the Americans have been fully prepared against such an eventuality, but it is just possible that by confronting the Japanese with their knowledge of the plot, they might have been able to stop it and even change Japanese minds about the wisdom of such action. Among those close to the Emperor were still some who opposed the idea of a war against the USA and Britain and favoured an attack on Russia. This would, of course, have been a blow for the USSR.

It is at this point that Liddell, as a Soviet agent, may have materially affected the whole course of the war. Stalin himself thought it vital that Japan attack the USA, and the evidence suggests that Guy Liddell was acting according to his wishes.

In late 1942 Soviet intelligence on German plans began to improve. Until then such intelligence had been incomplete, if not negligible. By the spring of 1943 Marshal Zhukov was able to give Stalin a detailed assessment of German military plans for the summer campaign of 1943.[19] Some of this may have been due to the capture of German Enigma machines during the Stalingrad campaign, but even this would not have meant that signals traffic could be read, certainly not without considerable hard work being put in first by cryptanalysts. By this time, however, Soviet Intelligence was being given an ever-increasing amount of material from their moles inside both MI5 and MI6. This has never been directly admitted by the Russians, but there is a clue in comments made by Marshal I. S. Konev, commander of Steppe Front, who recorded in April 1943, that 'all types of intelligence and including those from external sources were concentrated on disclosing enemy plans and intentions, including external radio intelligence.'[20]

That by this period the USSR were getting all they wanted in the way of such intelligence on the Germans from their own espionage network is shown to some extent by their increasing indifference to the official help in this respect they were receiving from the British. The Russians became much less co-operative towards their allies. They closed down an intercept station which they had allowed the British Admiralty to set up near Murmansk and actually ignored 'a final British *démarche* which threatened them with an end to Sigint assistance unless they showed a genuine interest in co-operation.'[21]

12

A Mysterious Telephone Call

If then, it were in the writer's power to direct his country's destiny, he would accept, for the time being, the general structure of capitalism – but he would modify it gradually . . . with the deliberate purpose of diminishing the glaring inequalities of fortune and opportunity which deface our present civilisation. He would take a leaf from the book of Soviet Russia . . .

(Professor Arthur Pigou)[1]

This quotation from the works of Professor Pigou of King's College, Cambridge, is not only relevant to the current chapter, but to the thinking of a number of people high up in the Establishment of the 1930s and 1940s, and, as Liddell was one of Pigou's occasional contacts, to some extent it applies to him, though no doubt he would have worded such thoughts much more ambiguously. Possibly Pigou's main contribution to the Soviet cause, apart from his occasional cautious incursions into espionage before World War II, was his training of economists in the direction of Marxist practice.

Outwardly Pigou seemed to approve Chamberlain's Munich settlement, despite his opposition to the National Government. In December 1939, a distinguished group of intellectuals, including Beatrice and Sidney Webb, Bernard Shaw, Charles Trevelyan, Peter Chalmers Mitchell, the Dean of Canterbury, Sir Richard Acland and the actress, Sibyl Thorndike, made a joint statement to the press that 'certain circles would gladly divert the so-called war effort against Russia and that such a diversion would be interpreted by the working-class as an assault on socialism'. Pigou was asked to sign this, but, cautious man as he was, he declined.

Pigou, an astonishingly deceptive character, attended the first congress held in London by the Russian Social Democrats in 1905. It would seem that from then on (and this was the only occasion on which he is positively known to have been present at a Russian-sponsored political meeting) he took a decision to keep his role as an informant to the Russians in exile a closely guarded secret, for a diary of that year was kept by him entirely in code and with references solely to links with the Social Democratic Party of Russia.

Born at Ryde, Isle of Wight, in 1877, Pigou was the son of a retired Army officer from a family with Huguenot ancestry and associations with China and India. He won a scholarship to Harrow where his father had also been educated and among his contemporaries were Winston Churchill, Leo Amery and George Trevelyan. His coded comments for 1905 suggest that he was already committed to giving the revolutionaries illegal aid, if necessary. 'Advised Tchaikovsky [this must have been Nikolas Tchaikovsky, a relative of the composer] on financial routes for payment of arms shipments to Riga' and again another entry stated : 'Established communications with Piatnitsky via George Flemwell in Switzerland : this is permanent link by Verlet in Geneva.'[2]

Pigou's cryptic references to making financial arrangements for payments for 'arms shipments to Riga' indicates that a few Britons were aiding the revolutionaries in obtaining arms supplies. Maxim Litvinov, who had early associations with Britain, was himself in charge of gun-running in 1904, and undoubtedly he must have developed a British network to assist him in this. But it was the sprucely attired intellectual, Nikolas Tchaikovsky, who spoke perfect English, who was the recruiter of agents in Britain and the key man in the subterranean arms traffic. He was a welcome visitor to many London drawing-rooms and salons and was doubtless able to weigh up potential recruits on these occasions. Samuel Hobson tells how he himself was lured into the illicit arms traffic by Tchaikovsky :

> in the later winter of 1904 Tchaikovsky came to see me. He had something on his mind, but was slow, even cautious, to open it. Gradually I realised that he wanted me to cooperate in shipping arms into Russia. They had bought 6000 Browning revolvers in Boston, USA, and the serious job was to get them shipped, first to England, where they must be packed in a special way, and thereafter to Riga.[3]

One of Pigou's more important contacts in the early years of World War II was a young Dutch student, a member of the communist underground in Holland, who had been imprisoned briefly in Germany with David Haden Guest for pro-communist activities. Haden Guest, the son of a Labour Member of Parliament, had been a confirmed communist supporter since his days at Trinity College, Cambridge. He was never the type who would make a Soviet agent: temperamentally he was quite unsuited to such a role. But, while briefly held under arrest in Germany in the 1930s, he had linked up with two Dutch youths who were being groomed as Comintern agents. To one of these he gave important contacts in Cambridge, later to be used to establish the identity of a wartime spy.

According to 'Roger', one of these Dutch students was 'chosen to establish a clandestine radio station in Britain and another, if possible, in Ireland. So much vital intelligence was already being obtained from Britain at this time that it was considered necessary to have this retransmitted direct in the event of war. Cambridge was chosen as a centre because we had contacts there'.[4]

There have been frequent denials that any clandestine radio could have been operated from Britain during the war without either detection or connivance, as all wave-lengths were monitored. But even an amateur, using a transmitter-receiver apparatus of only 10 watts output, could work undetected with a reasonable degree of luck, provided he moved his set from one area to another within a given perimeter, kept the periods of transmission very short and varied his times of operating. 'The Soviet transmission centre in Cambridge was set up shortly before the war,' says 'Roger', who was extremely active in the whole field of communications, having a cover that was never blown:

> It was largely controlled by Dutch communist agents working independently of, but guided and advised on problems of locations by Pigou, who knew the terrain intimately. Sometimes the transmitter was moved out as far as Duxford, Trumpington, or even Great Shelford, but at others it was in the heart of Cambridge. This Soviet communications system inside the UK became much more extensive in 1942-3, when it was developed by a married woman agent who came from Geneva. They must have used at least twenty different locations.[5]

The 'married woman agent who came from Geneva' must have been Ruth Kuczynski, who had master-minded the Soviet spy network in Switzerland from shortly before World War II until she went to England in December 1940 – as we have seen, she was an alleged contact of Hollis's, though there is no evidence for this. Her code-name was 'Sonia', and she was also known as Ruth Werner, Ruth Brewer and Ursula Beurton. She was the daughter of a well-known Berlin

economist, Professor René Kuczynski, who arrived in Britain in 1935.
In 1935-6 she visited the USSR and was received there 'with great enthusiasm' – her own description. 'During my stay in Moscow I
attended the *"Funkerschule"* [the Wireless Communication School].'[6]
Following her service as a Soviet agent in China, as previously
described, and then in Switzerland, she was given swift promotion for
a woman in the ranks of Soviet Intelligence : 'In China I was a captain
and then a major . . . After a few years I was promoted again by two
steps, first to Lieutenant-Colonel and then to Colonel, although this
was not communicated to me officially.'[7]

Donald Darling of MI9 was always puzzled as to how Ruth Kuczynski managed to get into Britain so easily : 'there must have been
some fiddling among officialdom for this to happen and she did not
come in through my organisation'. Ruth herself says she made a marriage of convenience with a man she calls 'Len':

> we wanted to select a good date for our marriage and selected the
> 23rd of February, the birthday of the Red Army. The British
> Consulate in Geneva received me rather unfriendlily when I
> applied for a British passport after our marriage. On 2 May 1940,
> envied by other German refugees, the British passport was in my
> hands.[8]

Eventually she settled in the Banbury area not far from Oxford. One of
the main criticisms against Liddell has always been his failure to investigate various reports of alleged radio transmissions in the Oxford
area. Nor was Kuczynski even put under surveillance as far as can be
ascertained. That she conducted radio transmissions she has since
admitted herself : writing of the period after December 1940, she has
stated:

> I have used the transmitter twice during the week. Twice in each
> month I travelled to London to speak with my father and Jurgen.
> Jurgen prepared economic analyses for the Soviet Union – four
> to six intelligence reports per month were sent . . . After I suc-
> ceeded in establishing contacts with the military I received in-
> telligence material which could not be sent by the transmitter.
> During a meeting with Comrade Sergey I received a small parcel
> containing a small transmitter. I was transmitting from Britain for
> five or six years where the amateur radio traffic, as in Switzerland
> during the war, had not been permitted.[9]

This admission by Kuczynski makes 'Roger's' claims about other such transmissions much more plausible. 'Transmission from Cambridge,' he said 'was confined to very occasional short messages, mainly consisting of a series of five-digit numbers delivered by voice transmission. The Soviets, of course, maintained their own radio link with Moscow for the duration of the war and in fact the equipment at their embassy in London was replaced by British-made apparatus in 1941.'

Anglo-Dutch co-operation both through the SIS and the SOE during World War II was a disaster from the beginning. Not only did it result in Britain being landed with George Blake who was eventually to betray his adopted country in every possible way, but the Germans infiltrated the Dutch SOE network and, through H. J. Giskes, of the *Abwehr*, largely controlled it by his operation, *Nordpol*. False radio messages from carefully planted Nazi operators resulted in 47 out of 54 SOE agents being picked up and shot at the Mauthausen concentration camp. That was bad enough, but what has never been told before is how the Soviet Intelligence infiltrated the Dutch network, sometimes slipping in an agent or two through the SOE and SIS, without this being discovered.

During the first years of the German occupation of Holland a net of five secret radio-receiving and transmitting installations was set up in Holland by one Daan Goulooze. Through these he contacted Moscow. The Soviet-controlled Dutch radio operators were more effective in staying undetected for long periods than were those of either the SOE or the Germans themselves. According to Professor Ger Harmsen, his biographer, Goulooze was responsible for organising the codes, and his operators were in ignorance of the contents of the messages sent and received: 'he was a most careful operator and highly regarded by the Centre [Moscow HQ]. His organisation was broken up by the Germans in 1943. Goulooze himself was arrested and sent to the concentration camp of Sachsenhausen. He survived the war.'[10]

One of the great myths perpetuated by Soviet disinformation has been that of *Rote Kapelle*, the organisation led by Leopold Trepper, which was never the outstanding intelligence agency that the Russians have suggested. But it has served their purposes to cover up some highly successful communications operations which have remained undetected. The Cambridge station and the equally mobile one operated from inside Germany were two of these. There was also an espionage group built up in Belgium with Dutch leaders, notably Anton Winterink in Arnhem and a certain 'Velo' whose real name is unknown.

'Roger' has indicated that some carefully selected items of Enigma material from Bletchley were passed on to the Russians, but that some of this came unofficially from undercover British sources in Switzerland. The material from Cambridge, he insists, was largely on airfields, dispositions of squadrons and addresses of top secret stations. I asked him if he could give me any examples of material received direct from Cambridge:

> We did not get all of this material. Some of it was sent to Holland, some was even sent from Cambridge to the agents we had in Oxford [Kuczynski ?], which was always somewhat of a joke. But what we did get I remember was information about aircraft being used for clandestine operations in Europe. Pigou himself through his ex-pupil, Wilfred Noyce, secured intelligence on squadrons formed on Newmarket racecourse (he told me as much after the war when we all three met), and a year later we had news of the setting-up of a very hush-hush, camouflaged air base at Tempsford, not far from Bedford.

Soviet-British cooperation in intelligence matters, though generally poor, was more marked with regard to the Dutch agents than with any others. In 1942 no fewer than three Soviet agents, all of Dutch nationality, were parachuted into Belgium and Holland in a joint Anglo-Soviet Secret Service operation. All three had been trained in Moscow.

Best known of these was a middle-aged Dutch communist and former clergyman, J. W. Kruyt. After having worked for the International Workers' Help organisation, Kruyt had joined the Russian trade delegation in Berlin and in 1937 became a librarian in Moscow. Together with his son, Kruyt had volunteered for the job of a secret agent. Eventually the two went to London. When Kruyt senior was parachuted into Belgium from a British aircraft in July 1942, he broke a leg on landing. A few days later he was arrested by the Gestapo, but refused to talk and swallowed a poison capsule. The Germans discovered this in time to save his life, but he still remained silent and was executed. Nico Kruyt, his son, jumped from a British aircraft on 21 June 1942, near Hulshorst in Holland. The plan was for him to link up with the Daan Goulooze network. He landed safely and made his way to the rendezvous in Amsterdam. The third agent, Bruno Kuehn, a German communist, arrived shortly afterwards, but he was eventually caught by the Germans in Amsterdam.

Roger Hollis

Guy Liddell

Joyce Whyte in the Girton Tennis team of 1917 (standing, left)

Baroness Moura Budburg (centre)

Lieutenant, the Lord Louis Mountbatten and the Hon. Edwina Cynthia Annette Ashley, on the occasion of their engagement in 1922

Above: Guy Liddell
playing the 'cello

Left: Tom Driberg with a
'R'Bab', a Russian musical
instrument, 1956

The base of this plane tree in Duchess of Bedford Walk, Kensington, was used by Soviet informers for passing messages to their KGB controllers.

Right: One of a number of enquiries by Liddell answered from Washington, 1940

DEPARTMENT OF STATE
WASHINGTON

26 MAR 1940

CONFIDENTIAL

No. 91

4/3 - Letter to Capt. Liddell

MAR 12 1940

MEMORANDUM

Reference is made to H.V.J. memorandum no. 63 of July 6, 1938 in which information was requested with regard to Fritz Max Cahen also known as Ferdinand Max Cahen.

It is understood that Mr. Cahen is now residing at Greenwich, Connecticut, and that he is a close friend of Wythe Williams who publishes the Greenwich Times and who was formerly a well-known foreign correspondent in Europe. No information has been developed to show that he is pro-Soviet, but he has been reported to be decidedly anti-Nazi. Conflicting information has been received with regard to him personally. Some consider him to be very egotistical and likely to exaggerate his important. Mr. Williams, however, is said to believe in him, and it is his interest which is said to have

given

James Jesus Angleton, the CIA counter-intelligence chief who has
long suspected Liddell

Admiral of the Fleet, Earl Mountbatten of Burma at the time when
he was passing secret messages to the Soviets

The Kruyts had their own Soviet contacts in Britain quite apart from official links permitted by the SIS and SOE. The Dutch communist network with which they were associated had the task of collecting and transmitting military and economic intelligence to Moscow, and some of this they obtained through the Cambridge transmitter. Their story was that they maintained contact with the Russian Embassy in London via the RVV (Dutch Council of Resistance), but in fact it was via Cambridge that permission was requested for a number of underground Dutch communists to travel clandestinely to London and from there on to Moscow. But when the reply came through it was mutilated and undecipherable.

The fact was that Moscow still found it hard to believe that the British were genuinely cooperating with the USSR on intelligence matters. 'Roger' states that:

> the more some of the British tried to help the USSR in this way, the more we began to realise that Moscow regarded all such moves as a trap. That explains the mutilated message : it was a deliberate sabotaging of the proposed visit via London. Two Russian pilots from Belgium were passed through our network on to Gibraltar. From there they were sent to London where, at first, the Soviet Embassy refused to see them, but reluctantly did so after three months. It was thought in London that they had been liquidated at the Embassy, as they were suspected of being 'British plants'.
>
> Yet, despite this, we enabled 14 Soviet agents to be smuggled through to Britain during the war. Three of these were German women who were all undercover communists sought by the Gestapo. One young communist and a potential sleeper-agent we helped on his escape route to Britain was George Behar, who was smuggled out of Holland into Belgium disguised as a Trappist monk. Later, as you know, he changed his name to George Blake.

Surprisingly, the closely-knit Cambridge network operating in the Soviet interest during the war managed to survive more or less intact and apparently without being detected by the British. An ex-OSS and later CIA agent, whose code-name for the purposes of this book must be 'Poe', insists : 'We [the Americans] had it on good authority from two defectors that this network carried on until just after the war. We found it hard to believe that MI5 did not know all about this.'

'Roger', however, maintains that this is only partly correct. 'There was a lengthy period in the spring of 1941 until much later in the summer of that year when all was silent on the Cambridge front. As a result one of our group was withdrawn from operations in Switzerland to make special inquiries.'

The reason for this period of silence seems to lie in the discovery in an air-raid shelter on Christ's Pieces at Cambridge on 2 April 1941, of a 27-year-old Dutchman believed to be Jan Willen ter Braak. In fact, that was not his real name, and he was a Soviet spy masquerading as a refugee from Nazi-controlled Holland. British officialdom has subsequently allowed it to be thought that he was a German spy.

The death certificate for ter Braak states that he committed suicide 'by shooting himself through the head with a revolver, causing haemorrhage and laceration of the brain'. The probability is, however, that he was murdered by an NKVD agent to stop him talking in the event of arrest. For this reason the whole story of Jan Willen ter Braak will probably never be known. It has been suggested that he was parachuted into Britain early in October 1940, when a German parachute was found in a field near Amersham. But there is no evidence whatsoever of his having arrived in the country in this way, or of his having contacted the Germans. Sir John Masterman, who somewhat ruefully wished ter Braak could have been secured for the 'Double-Cross' system, expressed the opinion that he was the only agent who escaped capture, but that he was never able to establish contact with the Germans. He suggested that ter Braak 'perished when his stock of money was exhausted'.[11]

But Sir John's statements about ter Braak raise more questions than they supply answers. If he spent six months in this country without being captured and had in his possession a radio-transmitting set (like other spies sent over here), how was it he never once established contact with the Germans? Or, for that matter, how was it that he did not fall into the orbit of the XX ('Double-Cross') Committee to be turned against the enemy? But what is even more baffling is the total silence concerning ter Braak from both the Dutch and German authorities. Dr Louis de Jong, director of the Dutch Institute for War Documentation, who devoted his life to compiling books on the history of the German occupation of Holland, stated 'he cannot be traced over here. As far as I know he entered England during the war under a false name.'[12]

Practically all other German spies who entered Britain during the war have been traced and documented by the Germans themselves. Even Ladislas Farago, who had access to German records, could only

describe ter Braak as 'the mystery man of the team' in his own comprehensive work on German espionage in Britain during the war.[13] Later
he told me that he thought ter Braak might well have been a Soviet
agent for a brief period and that he had been liquidated because he had
wished to opt out.

British official sources are silent on ter Braak. The inquest on him
was held in secret and the Coroner's records for the period are conveniently missing, while, according to the Cambridgeshire Constabul-
ary, police records concerning the case have long since been destroyed. MI5 moved into the area immediately the Dutchman's body
was found and the next day copies of the *Cambridge News* containing
details of this discovery were withdrawn after an urgent call from
London made by the Ministry of Information (no doubt alerted by
MI5).

No copy of this edition of the paper is now available. But Mr F.A.
Reeve, of Woodlark Road, Cambridge, recalled that, according to the
original report, 'murder was suspected'. This theory becomes even
more probable when one learns that Mrs Alice Stutley, the air-raid
shelter marshal for the area, who inspected the shelter on Christ's
Pieces after a small boy had reported finding a body there, discovered
'the body of a man dressed in a dark overcoat, horn-rim glasses and
black homburg hat, wedged tightly underneath one of the fixed slatted
seats . . . she could see no pistol, but it was evident he had been shot in
the head.'[14]

After the war it was suggested that MI5 knew all about ter Braak,
that they had followed him everywhere after his arrival in England and
that no action had been taken because they wished to find out what
people he contacted. If so, how was it the authorities allowed him to
commit suicide? Yet in recent years a very different story has been told
by officialdom. An Intelligence officer who actually investigated the ter
Braak affair states that 'he was not important, he had no radio set and
had only been here briefly. All that was of interest found on him were
various bus tickets showing he might have been visiting airfields in this
country.'[15]

This statement I totally reject. There is abundant evidence from
many people in Cambridge that ter Braak had been in the city for
several months. The only conflict of opinion was that some believed he
had been there even longer – a whole year longer. If the 'Double-
Cross' organisation could have rounded up anyone, Jan Willen ter
Braak was their obvious target over a long period. Not only was he
registered with the Cambridge police, but known to a number of inha-

bitants of that city (he moved his lodgings frequently) and some of the local people had even reported him to the police as being a suspicious character. And if indeed he was running out of funds, as Sir John Masterman suggested, here was their chance to intervene and 'turn' him.

For a while he stayed with a Mr and Mrs Alfred Sennett in St Barnabas Road, Cambridge, and, according to Miss Rosina Greenwood, for the last three months of his life he lodged with her in Montague Road. From all accounts he was very much liked by those who met him and he gave expensive presents to the people with whom he stayed. There is evidence that he had an office in Rose Crescent and some suspect that he used this for his transmitting. How many addresses he used is anyone's guess, for his bogus passport is said to have given one in Oxford Street (this should have read 'Road'), Cambridge, and it is known that he also stayed in Chesterton Road and had yet another address in Sidney Street, where he sold second-hand books.

Ter Braak conducted his second-hand book business quite openly. At the local police station he was known as 'Dr' ter Braak, a Dutch scientist and author who was engaged in writing a book on the medicinal properties of plants grown in Dutch territories overseas. He had visited various university college libraries, notably King's and Clare, and had spent a great deal of his time in the Botanic Garden. Professor Pigou was in the habit of taking walks over to Coton many days of the week and someone noticed that he met ter Braak there regularly. But when he was questiond after the Dutchman's death he shed no light on the matter.

There is a good deal of independent evidence that ter Braak made visits to Coventry, Bletchley, Banbury and London. In his possession were said to be a number of Red Cross letters intercepted by the *Abwehr* and intended for use as blackmail. Professor Kurt Lipstein, a Fellow of Clare College, Cambridge, and the son of Dr Alfred Lipstein of Frankfurt, stated that he was once summoned to Cambridge Police Station:

> I was told that there was a message from the German Government for me. Upon my amused reply, 'what do they want with me?', I was shown a Red Cross letter (the officially authorised channel of communications between residents in the UK and enemy countries) signed by my father. Having identified the letter I was left alone with it for a long while. Then I was told I was free to reply by the same means, and the interview was concluded.

The incongruity of the argument (Red Cross letters were usually handled by the Red Cross and not the police) and the fact that a man was found dead in an air-raid shelter, led me to connect the spy with the arrival of the letter. This was confirmed by the fact that, upon leaving the police station, I found another person of German origin waiting to be interviewed. In later years, having learned of the adventures of the spy in Cambridge, I concluded (without further proof) that the Red Cross letter was found on the man and may have been used in order to put pressure on me.[16]

In the late forties snippets of unofficial information about ter Braak began to emerge from the shadowy depths of Whitehall, though none was ever formally put on record. It was said that on his visits to London ter Braak showed an unusual interest in buildings in Whitehall, Downing Street and the highly guarded areas behind the Admiralty and Storey's Gate; and that:

> he had shown a great interest in Winston Churchill's movements and on other occasions was followed to war factories which the Prime Minister was visiting . . . ter Braak's lodgings, searched by the Security Service whilst he was out, contained a wireless transmitter, detonators, a Luger pistol, a file on Mr Churchill's movements and three crudely forged Dutch passports. Coded notes revealed that one of his tasks was to assassinate Allied war leaders as the opportunity arose.[17]

Why, if he was suspected of being a would-be assassin, was he allowed such freedom to operate for so long ? And, most puzzling of all, why did officialdom pretend that he was so unimportant and hadn't been in the country for more than a few days? When he was found his pockets were empty and all name tags had been removed, and Mrs Rosina Greenwood, his last landlady, said that when two detectives came to search his room 'all they found was a suit of clothing'.

To try to solve the riddle of ter Braak I sent a letter, appealing for information, to *Het Parool*, one of the largest daily newspapers in Holland. Under a prominent headline, 'Who was J. W. ter Braak?' it was duly published on 24 January 1978. The first reply from one K. J. ter Braak stated that his father, who had died a few years previously, was named Dr Jan Willen Gijsbertus ter Braak. In the autumn of 1938, when Dr ter Braak was staying at a *pension* in Scheveningen, his passport was stolen and he suspected the thief was a German chambermaid. He felt sure that this passport must have been used for the ter Braak who went to Cambridge.

Finally, there came this letter from The Hague:

> although I have not gone through the Second World War, it plays an important role in my life emotionally. I cannot risk going into this right now, as it could have unpleasant consequences for me . . . the ter Braak you mention was Dutch and not German, though his name was not ter Braak . . . he had studied at the Agricultural University at Wageringen, specialising in tropical agriculture . . . he was most certainly not a Nazi spy, though he posed as one to find out what the *Abwehr* were plotting in England. He was acting solely in the interests of the USSR and Holland . . . I should like to have details of his burial place. I do not wish to say any more except to provide one item of information which may enable you to assess the accuracy of what I say. It has been said that ter Braak was looking for Churchill's secret hide-out to kill him. This is wrong. What he was interested in was the secret government headquarters at Dollis Hill in London. Ter Braak provided many details of this and, if you can make checks in official records in London, you will find what he told us was correct: (1) the code-name for the research station was 'Paddock', named after its address which was Paddock Road, Dollis Hill, close to the old Post Office research station; (2) you will find that there was an air raid close to the station late in 1940; (3) ter Braak was protected by a Cambridge professor who had a very close colleague in the Cabinet Office in London.[18]

'Paddock' was the code-name for the Dollis Hill station and it was mentioned in a memorandum of Sir Edward Bridges in Cabinet papers, dated 14 December 1940, expressing concern about the possible discovery of this location by the enemy as three high explosive bombs had been dropped on Dollis Hill. All this fits in with the narratives of 'Roger' and 'Poe' to a considerable extent, though neither had any information on ter Braak.

There were still a number of unanswered questions. If, as the correspondent from The Hague suggested, he had posed as a German spy, this was either a very stupid or most certainly a brave thing to do in a country at war with Germany. This is borne out to some extent by the mysterious incident of the Red Cross letters. If ter Braak had been given these by the Germans in order to blackmail Jewish refugees into cooperating with the enemy under threat of harming their relatives still in Germany, all one can say is that he never acted on this. 'Roger', however, takes the view that evidence of association with the Germans may have been planted in one of his various lodgings in order deliberately to mislead the authorities:

> I should say that someone felt that ter Braak was in danger of compromising a Soviet network, that he knew too much and might break down under interrogation, so he was murdered. This could have been done by the NKVD, or even by one of the controllers of the Double-Cross system who was himself involved in Soviet espionage. I am certain that ter Braak must have had a rendezvous with someone in that air-raid shelter.

The position in which ter Braak's body was found as described earlier lends some credence to murder rather than suicide as the cause of death. Having personally investigated the air-raid shelter, I can only suggest that murder seems the likeliest answer and that the body was tucked away beneath the seats in the hope that it would not be spotted too quickly.

For some years I followed what turned out to be a false trail on this quest for the truth about ter Braak. The letter from The Hague had mentioned ter Braak being protected by a Cambridge professor. I thought this might have been Pigou, but neither 'Roger', nor 'Poe' was able to throw any light on this. I decided that this was much too vague a trail to explore, and that the answer lay with MI5 who had immediately sent a senior officer to Cambridge to investigate the case. Three years later I tried to establish contact with the anonymous writer from The Hague via the accommodation address he had given me. Two weeks later I received a telephone call, not from Holland but from somewhere in the UK. This was a terse acknowlegement of my letter in a slightly German accent, begging me not to write again as there was not much which could be added to his original letter and he did not wish to be 'drawn into any kind of publicity'. Then came this surprise revelation:

> I cannot help you regarding the name of the Cambridge professor who protected ter Braak. I can say that ter Braak was badly let down and was almost certainly murdered on instructions from someone inside British Security. The truth was that ter Braak had had enough of espionage and he wanted to give it up and

escape from the Soviet controller and settle down to a normal citizen's life in Britain. The British found out about this and they were afraid that, in order to protect himself, ter Braak might give away to the police details of Soviet agents inside the British Security and Intelligence Services. The man they wanted to protect was a former member of the Special Branch and at that time an officer in MI5, Guy Maynard Liddell. Liddell had been ter Braak's controller and protector up till that time, knowing full well he was a Soviet agent.

Suddenly everything began to come much clearer. I had thought that it seemed incredible that a man who was, as far as one could ascertain, a fairly low-grade spy should be able to track down with such facility such places as the 'Paddock' research station and keep tabs on places the Prime Minister was visiting. For security reasons such matters were kept secret and never published in the press, at least not until afterwards. Ter Braak must have got his information from someone inside the British Establishment who had knowledge of all this. Liddell, of course, would have had such knowledge.

Contact with the mysterious informant from The Hague ceased after this. But his last words were interesting:

The USSR were always disbelieving of any evidence coming from British sources, even from such agents secretly informing them. They would wish everything to be checked. Liddell was able to give sufficient information for ter Braak to go around and check its authenticity for himself. That was where he was valuable. Liddell fully understood this. It would be only fair to say that he was a British patriot, but that he was equally an ardent supporter of the USSR. For him Germany was the enemy. But he could be ruthless and when ter Braak was liquidated, he agreed to this because he knew that his own future was in jeopardy. It must have been the only occasion on which he felt this, for from all accounts he was a very cautious manipulator of people and events to help the USSR.

13

'Something Russian in His Background'

> A spy is above all a man of politics who must be able to grasp, ana-
> lyse and connect in his mind events which seemingly have no
> connection . . . Espionage is a continuous and demanding labour
> which never ceases.
>
> *(Pravda)*

Following the failure of the Arcos raid, the murder of Ernest Oldham
and other misdeeds in which Liddell was implicated, there was very
nearly another disaster over the Gouzenko defection just after the war
ended. Igor Gouzenko was a 26-year-old cipher clerk working for the
GRU (Soviet Military Intelligence), stationed in the USSR Embassy
in Ottawa. In September 1945, he left the Embassy with documents,
intending to pass on information of a spy network in Canada to the
Canadian authorities. It must have come as a considerable shock to
him when he began to realise that nobody seemed to want to know
about these things or to take any interest in him. Mackenzie King, the
Canadian Premier, disliked anything to do with espionage and, above
all, he did not want to disturb relations with either the Soviet Embassy
in Ottawa, or with the USSR. Fortunately, Norman Robertson, the
Canadian Permanent Secretary for External Affairs, took a somewhat
different view of the situation and in arriving at this he was helped by
the fact that William Stephenson, the head of the British Security
Coordination (BSC) in America, was in Ottawa at that time. As a result
the RCMP were called in and they took Gouzenko, his pregnant wife
and small son into protective custody.

Not surprisingly after the almost grudging reception he was at first
accorded, Gouzenko remained almost permanently suspicious and
worried about the possibility of attempts being made on his life. It was
decided that the safest place for him and his family was in an old farm-
house within the precincts of Camp 'X', the carefully guarded establishment on the Canadian shore of Lake Ontario set up to teach the
Americans and others the arts of secret warfare. It was a positive and

constructive link between the SOE and the newly created OSS. Eventually Gouzenko and his family settled down under a new identity at Mississauga on the outskirts of Toronto. Here he died in 1982.

No copy of the report by the British Security Coordination organisation on the Gouzenko affair has been made available to the public. While it is not surprising that any such copy has not been found in the drastically weeded SOE archives, it is perhaps strange that no copy has appeared anywhere in the USA. Among the first people to talk to Gouzenko on an official level were Peter Dwyer, head of the counter-espionage section of BSC and a former MI6 officer, and Superintendent George McLellan, of the RCMP. But it would seem that at first interrogations were carried out entirely by RCMP officers and only many months later by judges and other officials in connection with the report of the Royal Commission appointed by Mackenzie King to investigate the activities of the Soviet spy ring which had been operating in Canada for some time. In connection with this Gouzenko had named Fred Rose, a Canadian MP; Sam Carr (national organiser of the Canadian Labour-Progressive Party); David Gordon Lunan, editor of *Canadian Affairs*; and Kathleen Willsher, assistant registrar of the Office of the United Kingdom High Commissioner in Ottawa. In addition Gouzenko's information led to not only the arrest of these people, but other Soviet agents such as P. Furnford Pemberton Smith, of the National Research Council in Ottawa; and Edward Marsarall, of the National Research Council. It was a formidable list, comprising 22 local agents and a team of 15 Soviet specialists, the latter all being given cover as members of the Russian Mission in Ottawa. How productive this team of agents was may be gathered from the fact that Professor Tamond Boyer, of McGill University, provided the information that a plant for the production of uranium was being set up at Chalk River and that experiments had proved that uranium could be used for making a new type of bomb. The Royal Commission's report stated that:

Canadian citizenship documents such as passports, naturalisation certificates and marriage or birth certificates were sought for illegal purposes and in some cases obtained. Such documents were sought not only for use in Canada, but also, as illustrated for example in the Witczak passport case . . . for use in the United States . . . Such planted agents could in time be used not only for espionage but for sabotage, leadership of subversive political groups and other purposes.[1]

Yet despite all these preliminary probes and interrogations of Gouzenko four months passed by and no arrests were made by the Canadians. It was then that Sir William Stephenson decided to take action on his own account to force the hand of the reluctant Mackenzie King. He engineered the release of the Gouzenko story to the press via Drew Pearson. Prior to this there had even been a story to the effect that 'Prime Minister Mackenzie King wanted quietly to return the documents on espionage in Canada taken from the Soviet Embassy by cipher clerk Igor Gouzenko to avoid controversy.'[2]

There has been some considerable dispute as to whether or not Sir Roger Hollis interviewed Gouzenko shortly after the latter's defection. Certainly Hollis was in Ottawa about this time, and he is said to have been sent there with Liddell's approval. One of the major points in Chapman Pincher's case against Hollis concerned his alleged behaviour over the Gouzenko case. In his book, *Their Trade is Treachery*, Pincher states that Hollis had been sent out to Ottawa to deal 'with the MI5 aspects of the Gouzenko revelations . . . The records show that Hollis reported the minimum amount of information from Gouzenko.'[3] The implication was that Hollis had failed to report Gouzenko's allegations that the Russians had a spy inside MI5. This allegation is not borne out by the facts. In the first place it was not until further cross-examination of Gouzenko a few years later by the RCMP that allegations of a mole inside MI5 were made. Secondly, Norman Robertson, the Canadian Permanent Secretary for External Affairs, came to London after Gouzenko's defection and gave a report on the Russian's revelations both to the head of MI6 and the director-general of MI5, so Hollis would have been in no position to withhold information without exposing himself immediately. Finally, Hollis did not speak Russian and he would have had to rely largely on what he was told by Nicholson of the RCMP who did speak that language.

To some extent it was Sir William Stephenson who stirred up the controversy surrounding Hollis. Stephenson had this to say:

When Hollis arrived in New York en route to Ottawa to take an unwanted part in the Gouzenko debriefing I ordered him to fly back to London on a bomber which was ready to depart for Britain. I had my own men, including Peter Dwyer and others, including Nicholson of the RCMP, who was fluent in Russian.

On one of my many visits to London Guy Liddell, whom I considered to be the most solidly intelligent officer of [MI]5, warned me to be wary of Hollis as he was rabidly anti-American. Coming from Guy, I took it that he was warning me that Hollis was un-trustworthy. Therefore I decided not to allow him to trespass in the Gouzenko case. I agreed to a representative of MI5 appearing – Mills of the Circus family [Cyril Mills]. Gouzenko was one of the most important Russian defectors of all time and I count it as one of my successes to have rescued him from the KGB.[4]

As far as can be ascertained Cyril Mills did not interview Gou-zenko. He was in mid-Atlantic at the time and did not turn back.

One of the problems with defectors is that, though their instant revela-tions at the time of defection are usually invaluable, their later state-ments, especially as the years go by, tend to be not merely inaccurate, but even add up to disinformation. That is not to say that the disin-formation is deliberate, but that there is an almost subconscious feel-ing that more information must be produced even if it means using the imagination. I am not saying that this was the case with Gouzenko, but pressure by his interrogators later on may have caused him to embel-lish what he knew.

Liddell's alleged warning to Sir William Stephenson about Sir Roger Hollis being anti-American is puzzling in the extreme unless it was a deliberate attempt to keep Hollis away from seeing Gouzenko or learning too much from the RCMP. There is no evidence that Hollis was in any way anti-American except that he was critical of American cooking, according to letters to his mother! He had been on suffi-ciently good terms with the allegedly anti-British Hoover to be given a signed photograph of the FBI chief and a set of golf clubs. As Liddell claimed to be a close friend of Hoover, which he almost certainly was not, it may be that Liddell was jealously guarding his own somewhat tenuous relationship with the head of the FBI.

Did someone inside MI5, or even in the Canadian counter-espion-age organisation, intervene to prevent further investigation of what Gouzenko later described in these words:

The case of the member of MI5 [Gouzenko has been variously reported as describing this as both MI5 and '1 of Five' which could be translated in a number of different ways] was, in my opinion, much stronger [than those of Rose or Hiss] and there was more to go on . . . In the first place I was not told by some-body, but saw the telegram myself concerning this person. And then, as a second confirmation, I was told by Lieutenant Lubimov [in Moscow]. With these two pieces of evidence there is not the

slightest doubt in my mind that there was a Soviet agent inside
MI5 during the period 1942-43 and possibly later on . . . This
man had something Russian in his background.[5]

The last phrase might mean almost anything from a family connection
with Russia to close associations with Russian people. In the latter
sense it could refer to Liddell on account of his close friendships with
people like Moura Budberg, Baykaloff and others. This, admittedly, is
mere guesswork. It has also been suggested that what Gouzenko
meant was not MI5, but 'one of a group of five'. Another puzzle is the
code-name which Gouzenko, under interrogation, mentioned for the
man in MI5 : it was 'Elli'. Now 'Elli' was the code-name of Kathleen
Willsher. Despite this, Gouzenko still appeared to insist that sometimes the same code-name was used for two different people and that a
female name was occasionally given to a male agent. There has also
been some divergence of opinion as to whether the code-name in
question was spelt 'Elli' or 'Ellie'. An analysis of Soviet code-names
has shown that sometimes, though not always, the code-name is taken
from some of the letters of the real name of the person, this being considered useful in checking against records. While this would not apply
in the case of Hollis, 'Elli' could apply with Liddell's surname.

But there was another defector who also pointed towards a Soviet
agent inside MI5 and this somewhat strengthens Gouzenko's theory
that 'the mistake in my opinion in dealing with this matter was that the
task of finding the agent was given to MI5 itself . . . The results, even
beforehand, could be expected as nil.' However, in the light of this
statement, it is surely ironic that when Constantin Volkov, the vice-
consul attached to the Soviet Consul-General in Istanbul, asked the
British Consul for asylum, his case was handed to MI6 to deal with! He
promised to reveal details of various Soviet networks and claimed to
know the names of three Soviet agents working in Britain – two in the
Foreign Office and one 'the head of a counter-espionage organisation
in London'. The task of interviewing Volkov was given to Kim Philby
who flew to Turkey with dire results: Volkov was liquidated before he
could make his revelations.

Certainly, according to John Best in Ottawa and Peter Hennessy in
London, material in declassified papers in Ottawa in 1981 confirmed
that Gouzenko told his interrogators that he knew of two British officials using the code-name of 'Elli', one being Miss Willsher, and the
other 'whose name he did not know, was in Britain'.[6] This seemed to
confirm that the original code-name was 'Elli', but that it had been

changed to the more feminine 'Ellie' by some of the media only after it was established that it referred to Miss Willsher.

Ilya Dzhirkvelov, a fairly recent defector from the USSR, says that he is 'inclined to doubt whether Igor Gouzenko, the cipher clerk who defected in Canada in 1945, could have any real knowledge about the KGB's [here he means NKVD, of course] agents in Britain, particularly among members of the Intelligence Service, because the KGB never used the GRU's communications system.'[7]

On the other hand he would know about GRU contacts inside other services which, although probably much rarer, did exist even then. Towards the end of his life Gouzenko suffered from diabetes and to some extent had a drinking problem, the latter probably due to the strain of living in hiding all those years (he was never photographed without a hood over his head). For this reason some of his latter-day statements may not always be as accurate as were the answers he gave to much earlier interrogations. For example he stated in 1981 that '"Elli's" controller in Britain had made contact with "Elli" using a *dubok* [hiding place] for messages in a crack in a tombstone.' He added that it was for this reason that he feared he might be betrayed by this same 'mole'. Peter Hennessy, of *The Times*, who interviewed Gouzenko towards the end of his life, stated that the Russian 'asked his wife, Svetlana, to memorise the Elli story and tell the RCMP, if he was seized by the Russians.' The suggestion was that belatedly he felt he had not been asked sufficient questions about 'Elli' by his original interrogators.

Many of the answers to all these puzzles might have been obtained long ago if certain documents in the Canadian Government's archives had not been missing. These documents include not only Privy Council files on the Gouzenko case, but a diary written by Mackenzie King, who died in 1950. It has never been satisfactorily established whether these records were discarded by mistake or deliberately. The discovery that the documents were missing was made by Professor Jack L. Granatstein, an historian who was writing a book about the late Norman Robertson. As to whether or not Hollis interviewed Gouzenko there is a divergence of evidence. Gouzenko himself said he could not confirm that Hollis interrogated him, but whoever the 'Englishman' was, the interview was 'very short . . . he just listened, he didn't write one word. Maybe he asked one or two questions.' Sir William Stephenson insisted that Hollis did not interview Gouzenko, but against this one must set the fact that in the last years of his life Sir William was far from being an accurate observer of events and his memory sometimes lapsed. Gouzenko's use of English improved enormously over the years he was in Canada : it is possible that later he was able to express in English details of evidence which originally had been given in much less fluent terms.

The last few years of the war were marked by a sudden speed-up of Soviet successes in intelligence gained from agents in the UK. Official (or at least semi-official) versions of British Intelligence code-breaking successes in World War II have always tended to present an exaggerated view of the importance of the British capturing of Enigma, particularly in view of the fact that the French and the Poles played a great part in this. They have also constantly asserted that Soviet cryptography was of negligible value and that the British never told the USSR anything about Enigma. But there is increasing evidence that, not only did the Russians manage to crack the German M3 code machine by the end of 1942, but that a Russian naval mission was given one such machine by the British in about the middle of 1943. One of my informants insists that this was done unofficially 'having been cleared by an officer in the NID [Naval Intelligence Division] and an officer in the counter-espionage section of MI5 [Liddell was, of course, head of that section].'

For a long time I sought for some further confirmation of this story. Only this year came the claim that an Enigma machine was given to a Russian naval mission in June 1943. 'The items were insufficient to crack codes yet were assumed to be somehow too embarrassing for the official record.' The report adds that 'the Royal Naval Submarine Museum now tells me that the three-rotor machine must have originated from the German U-boat 205, sunk off Derna on the North African coast in February 1943, in shallow water. The boat was attacked suddenly, which probably explains why the decrypting machine, which should have been thrown overboard immediately, was recovered.'[8]

There is alleged to be in existence what is called the Swedish List of Eight Primary Soviet Collaborators in Britain, based on reports gathered by Swedish Intelligence during World War II. This list has never been disclosed officially, though it is said to have been given to British Intelligence. Names on that List are said to include Liddell, Mountbatten and the man who gave the order for General Sikorski to be murdered when his plane crashed at Gibraltar in 1943. The nearest one can get to any such revelation of collaborators' names is that of the List of Seven supplied by Comstantin Volkov in which he stated in a typed document in Russian that 'there are at present seven such agents [i.e. important agents]: five in British Intelligence and two in the Foreign Office'. He described one of the agents as '*ispolnyayushchiy nachalnik*', in other words someone 'head of a counter-espionage department'.

14

Liddell Writes To A Comrade

There are emerging indications of high-level moles in Great Britain who have never been caught, including a former senior officer in the British Security Service.
(Tennant Bageley, former deputy chief counter-espionage officer of the CIA's Russian division)

Further evidence of Liddell's helping of the Soviets emerges in his intervention in the question of the repatriation by compulsion of Russian emigrés from the USSR.

It should be noted that at that time the Home Office, to its credit, was gravely disturbed at the widespread Foreign Office cynicism on the subject. John Galsworthy, then a third secretary at the Foreign Office, wrote a minute stating:

At the meeting [with a Home Office official] . . . it was, I thought, agreed that when a Soviet deserter [*sic*] came into the hands of the civil police the latter should more or less assume, or pretend that the man in question was willing to return voluntarily to his camp and hand him over to the local military authority accordingly. Any misunderstanding about the man's real wishes was, I thought, to be attributed to 'language difficulties', etc. . . . If the deserter makes it abundantly clear that he is not willing to return, the civil police are to release him more or less into the arms of a military escort who will then bundle him away to the nearest Soviet camp.[1]

The hypocrisy of this iniquitous game played by the British was almost incredible. One protagonist was Sir Christopher Frederick Ashton Warner, who died in 1957. He played a leading role in Operation Keelhaul (the repatriation plan) as head of the Northern Department of the Foreign Office. With the full knowledge of Sir Orme Sargent, then Deputy Under Secretary of State, he maintained a close liaison with Colonel Ivan Chichaev, the NKVD officer in London who operated from his flat in Palace Gate. He took the same unrelenting line. Apart from Chichaev the key men in London, operating quite independently of the Soviet Embassy, were the secret agent, Anatoly Baykaloff, and Sabline, the renegade Russian who lived in great style at Brechin Place, Gloucester Road. On his writing paper he made great play with the fact that he was 'former Imperial *Chargé d'Affaires* for Russia in London' and claimed to be representative of the Russian Refugees Community in the UK. But he was all the time working with the Soviets to obtain the maximum repatriation. Both Sabline and Baykaloff were on friendly terms with Liddell and the Baykaloff archives record that in July 1944, a communication from Liddell to Baykaloff stated : 'N. and F. have been returned to Paris, ostensibly for further duties, but Soldatenkov [Captain Soldatenkov, liaison officer between the Soviet Embassy and the War Office] has been informed of this move and doubtless he will advise his people to pick them up in Paris.'[2]

This would appear to be one of the very rare occasions on which Liddell committed himself rather too rashly to paper. But it shows how some people at the FO, the WO and even MI5 were working along with the Russians in the most nefarious schemes. Obviously, N. and F. were either prisoners or personnel utilised in the SOE or the SIS and, at the request of Baykaloff or Sabline, or both, were being repatriated by a particularly shabby trick. Contact between Liddell and Baykaloff was being maintained as late as early 1950, for on 15 February of that year there is a note from Liddell to Lord Vansittart stating : 'We have now seen Baikaloff [sic]. For your information there are two rather large gaps in his story, so there is no real evidence to implicate Radukovic.'[3] This note was addressed from Room 055 of the War Office, so it was official.

With the end of the war the new Prime Minister, Clement Attlee, decided that it was time for a change at the head of MI5. Quiet and modest as he was, Attlee had a remarkably cool, shrewd and strong character. In this respect he was perhaps a far abler Prime Minster than has generally been suggested. He was quick to size up a situation and equally prompt in acting on whatever decision he arrived at with the minimum of fuss.

Rumours had reached his desk that all was not well in MI5, that some of the personnel needed sorting out and that it required a chief who would bring some degree of order into a service which needed to be groomed for peace-time work. From inside the service the Prime

Minister was confronted with strong pleas for the appointment of Liddell as the new director. He consulted the Home Secretary, Herbert Morrison, and learned of some objections to this proposal, following the coming retirement of Sir David Petrie. Ellen Wilkinson, as Parliamentary Secretary to the Minister for Home Security in the National Government of 1940, had taken a keen interest in the fate of many of her ex-communist friends who were being hounded down by the Stalinist hard-liners. She had personally recommended many of these for services to various British-sponsored Resistance groups and it was rarely that her judgement was wrong. According to Julian Amery, in 1942-3 it was suggested that some ex-communists who had proved their value as guerrilla fighters in the Spanish Civil War might usefully be employed in Yugoslavia. Being on very friendly terms with Ellen Wilkinson, Amery asked her to provide a list of likely names. She drew one up and Amery showed it to Kim Philby, whom he had met in Spain while both were correspondents during the Civil War. As Philby was by now in the Iberian Section of MI6, he was asked to vet the names. He pooh-poohed the whole idea, firmly advised against it, and made the comment : 'Once a communist, always a communist. Don't take any notice of the word "ex".' So the plan was dropped. Unquestionably Philby did not want any anti-Soviets being sent to Yugoslavia.

One of Ellen Wilkinson's favourites had been Willi Muenzenberg, who had been marked down by the NKVD for elimination. It was Muenzenberg, apparently, who warned Ellen that he had an enemy in British counter-espionage who made mischief for him among his colleagues, and, he hinted, was also 'trying to trap Arthur Koestler'.[4] It was a vague kind of warning and Ellen thought no more about it until she was given the news of Muenzenberg's death. In the summer of 1940 Muenzenberg was one of the refugees let out of an internment camp in France as the Germans came in. He had been anticipating attempts on his life by NKVD agents for some time. Muenzenberg went off with two unknown 'refugees' and was later found hanged in a forest near Grenoble. It was clearly not a case of suicide and almost certainly the 'refugees' were Soviet assassins. Whether Ellen Wilkinson linked the Muenzenberg comments with Guy Liddell is not clear, but she certainly remembered Muenzenberg's warning and as a result expressed her doubts about him. Morrison concurred and it was then that Attlee decided to bring an outsider in as chief of MI5.

The man he chose, Sir Percy Sillitoe, was from 1946 until 1953 Director-General of MI5. At the age of 20 he had gone abroad to serve in the British South Africa Police. When war broke out in 1914 he had been gazetted in the Northern Rhodesia Police, but after British forces had occupied a considerable part of German East Africa he was one of the officers sent to administer it. Returning to Britain, his progress in police service was steadily upward. At the age of 35 he became Chief Constable of Chesterfield and three years later was made Chief Constable of Sheffield. In the late 1920s Sheffield was troubled by large gangs of gamblers and ruffians and in certain areas of the city the public were in such dread of them that it was hard to get witnesses when arrests were made. It was Sillitoe's personal influence which gave the police the confidence to break up the gangs. In 1931 he was sent to Glasgow where he was up against many similar, but in some ways much worse problems. There was corruption in both the corporation and magistrates of the city as well as the problem of gangs on a far worse level than in Sheffield.

The outcome of all this was that Sillitoe not only cleaned up the gangs, but even managed to track down such associates of the gangs as the chairman of the Glasgow Police Committee, and such successes brought his name before the public. At the same time he was no mere gang-buster, but one who sought to improve police techniques. He was always one to concern himself with the welfare of the men under his control, while at the same time being a pioneer in new techniques for the police. In 1943 he was appointed to be Chief Constable of Kent, a county which was then in the front line of British defences against German aggression. Little has been said about his work in this period, but there is no doubt that he coped in a highly efficient manner with many matters which were more concerned with counter-espionage than ordinary crime. It was reports of his handling of these matters which brought him to the attention of Clem Attlee and which led to his appointment as chief of MI5.

His appointment caused alarm throughout MI5, not only because some of its members feared he would bring orthodox police methods into the service, but because some of them wondered just how he would regard them as colleagues. Apart from this there was among the hierarchy of MI5 a large degree of snobbery and contempt for those they regarded as 'policemen'.

When he left MI5 Sillitoe wrote that:

> since its earliest beginnings MI5 has alternately intrigued and in-
> furiated the public by the aura of 'hush-hush' with which it has
> seemed to be surrounded, and when I joined it I found it so ex-
> tremely difficult to find out precisely what everyone was doing

that I began to feel that its popular reputation was in no way exaggerated. Some of the blame for my early puzzlement rests no doubt with me. I was among men of a different type from those who had previously worked under me, and, instead of a force or team from whom I could expect unquestioning obedience to rules and a scrupulous respect of discipline, I had to attempt to direct a number of highly intelligent, but somewhat introspective individuals who gave me an initial impression that they were working in a rather withdrawn isolation, each concentrating on his own especial problem . . . I found myself wondering what precisely my role was to be.[5]

Sillitoe felt that MI5 had become far too élitist and very much of a clique and that it desperately needed to be disciplined. He also felt that the passion for secrecy about the service's very existence was overdone and in *Who's Who* he had no hesitation in giving his room number at the War Office, then used as MI5's cover. He had no time whatsoever for the ultra-tolerant attitude of the intelligentsia in MI5 for pro-Soviet Union views. He had himself had experience of communist mobs in Glasgow in the 1930s, when they attacked a number of his police in plain clothes at a rally, causing extensive injuries. One was crippled for life, and from then on Sillitoe took tough measures against them, insisting on processions under strict police control.

It was Herbert Morrison, the Home Secretary, who made Sillitoe Chief Constable of Kent, and it was from Sir Alexander Maxwell, then Permanent Under-Secretary of State at the Home Office, that Sillitoe received a letter asking him if he would agree to be considered for the MI5 post. After various interviews Attlee personally confirmed the appointment which dated from 1 May 1946, the very day on which Alan Nunn May was charged at the Old Bailey.

From the very beginning of his appointment the pro-Liddell faction in MI5 ganged up against Sillitoe in a variety of ways. He was made to feel that he was an outsider and that his presence was resented. This was shown in a variety of ways, one example being that some of his most senior colleagues, declared his son, 'irritated my father by going out of their way constantly to make lengthy Latin quotations to one another in his presence.'[6]

Much of quite vital information was never passed on to him, as he later discovered and he soon found that many of the staff were, in his own opinion, useless bums. He sometimes mentioned that he found the influence of some of the female secretaries much greater than it should have been. He also felt that information from the public, which he regarded as invaluable (while admitting that there were some eccentrics), was taken much too indifferently and in many cases neglected.[7]

It is noteworthy that Attlee, unlike some Prime Ministers who followed him, took a close personal interest in MI5 and one can only deduce from this that the Prime Minister was not altogether happy with the Security Service. Every Thursday Sillitoe had an appointment with Attlee for a one-hour talk. Harold Macmillan might have saved himself a great deal of trouble over the Profumo case if he had followed this practice. In this connection Attlee's foreword to Sillitoe's book, *Cloak Without Dagger*, published after he retired from MI5, is particularly relevant. 'MI5, though technically a branch of the War Office, is under the direct control of the Prime Minister,' wrote Attlee. 'When it fell to me to make this appointment I was fortunate in finding Sir Percy Sillitoe,' adding that the reader of Sir Percy's book 'will find much of absorbing interest, but is sure to wish that the obligations of secrecy had not prevented Sir Percy from lifting the veil from his activities in his last post.'[8]

Anyone who knew Attlee and talked with him on occasions, as this author has done, should realise that this was Attlee's oblique but subtle way of saying that he rather wished more could have been told about MI5 in this period. The picture which has most unfortunately been portrayed since Sillitoe's departure from MI5 has been that of a policeman totally out of place in a service which called for highly intellectual talents. This is total balderdash: someone like Sillitoe was desperately needed to put MI5 back on to the right track and to get rid of the devious amateurs who held power. Nobody could have had a more difficult term of office because it was during this period that the errors and the treachery of the past came home to roost with a vengeance. The pro-Liddell faction in MI5 were, of course, only too happy that Sillitoe, as chief of the service, should take all the blame for cases such as Fuchs, Pontecorvo, Burgess, Maclean, Philby and Blunt, which dated back to long before his entry into the service.

Sillitoe worked at MI5 from 10 a.m. to 5 p.m. each day, while living in Putney. A newcomer to the world of state security and intelligence he may have been, but he was very quick to sum up accurately the intelligence and counter-espionage services of other countries. He thought the USSR had easily the best of such services, with the French second and, remarkably, the Italians third, while expressing the view that the Americans were fast and keen learners, but that they still had a long way to go in catching up in both these spheres.

As to his allegation that he was not always kept informed of quite important developments, one example of this is the case of Alexander Foote, one of the most remarkable wartime agents of the USSR, the Briton who later defected back to his own country and wrote that classic, *Handbook for Spies*. Foote had this to say about his recruitment: 'The man in charge of the formation of the battalion [i.e. the British Battalion of the International Brigade in the Spanish Civil War in which he served] was Wilfred Macartney. The political commissar was Douglas Springhall, who played a more vital part in my life later when he recruited me for the Red Army Intelligence.'[9] As MI5 had been closely interested in both these characters they should have been very much concerned with every scrap of information that Foote could give them, or at least equally as concerned as MI6. Foote served in the Soviet network in Switzerland with which Ruth Kuczynski was associated, being principally employed as a radio-operator. But Foote's story is perhaps best told not by his book, which was obviously to some extent censored by the British, but by a statement which he signed and passed on to a British MP in the hope that someone on high would follow it up with appropriate action. It reads as follows:

I was recruited into the Razvedka, the Intelligence Service of the Red Army, towards the end of 1938, on my return to this country and after almost two years service in the International Brigade in Spain. Until the outbreak of World War II I was active in Germany, subsequently operating from Switzerland against Axis powers until my arrest by the Swiss Federal Police towards the end of November 1943. Because of the geographical situation of Switzerland, entirely surrounded by the Axis powers, it was not possible for the Soviets to reinforce their agents in the Swiss anti-Axis network, and I had swift promotion, being at the time of my arrest in charge of the sole remaining communications between the Soviet General Staff in Russia and its sources of information 'in the heart of the German High Command'.

I was subsequently released by the Swiss and arrived in Moscow in January 1945. Owing to a peculiar set of circumstances it then appeared to the Soviets that I had in fact been 'got at' by the British Intelligence Service, and that certain actions on my part *since* my release by the Swiss in September 1944, were construed in Moscow to be British-inspired with the object of 'retarding the advance of the Red Army'. I was cleared of this suspicion only after a lengthy scientific interrogation and a check-up on the spot in West Europe after the end of the war.

At the beginning of 1947 (still in Moscow) I was informed that I was to be entrusted with the rebuilding of a Razvedka network in the USA from a HQ which I was to establish in Mexico. I was told that all Resident Directors of Soviet Espionage had been withdrawn from activity in the territory of Russia's co-belligerents in June 1941, and that numerous dormant sources of information in the USA were to be re-activated.

My arrest by the Swiss as a Soviet agent had made it impossible for me to work again while living under my own name and I left for East Berlin to establish a German background for a new identity.[10]

In this statement Foote makes no reference to what changed his mind as to his future conduct, but he goes on to say:

In mid-July 1947, I announced myself to a British Intelligence HQ in West Berlin and subsequently in Hanover made a report to a certain Mr — — who, I understood, had flown from London to interview me.

Mr — — adopted a rather unfriendly and sceptical attitude towards me and more or less limited himself to taking down notes of statements that I volunteered. Although I had for the previous two years been in regular contact with high officers of one of the Soviet Union's most important agencies, little interest was evinced in what I had to say or what I had learned . . . He then informed me that I should not take it for granted that I should be allowed to return to England. In short, my impression was that Mr — — wished to antagonise me into saying as little as possible.

During the interview I reported the names of two of my former colleagues, 'John' and 'Sonia' [Sonia was, of course, Ruth Kuczynski] who had, since 1941, been living in England. I mentioned that although I had been told in Moscow that they had been dormant during the war, it was obvious that some contact between them and the Centre had been made, for it was known that the couple had recently had a child. Also towards the end of 1941 I had sent 'Sonia' (by means of a Post Office jargon telegram) to see the London Soviet military attaché on organisational matters.

I spent a total of about ten weeks incommunicado as 'guest' of

MI5, one month in Germany and six weeks in a flat in Hammersmith, London. My release coincided with my trial '*in absentia*' before a Swiss Military Tribunal, where I was sentenced to three years' imprisonment, 15 years' expulsion, 8000 francs fine and the confiscation of my property.[11]

Later Foote learned that 'John' and 'Sonia' had fled to East Berlin and he implied that someone had tipped them off that MI5 would shortly be on their track. Then came the most significant part of his testimony:

I would point out that if I, at the time of my defection, had been persuaded to continue my work with the Soviets, with the secret cognizance of British Intelligence, very possibly the latter would now be in possession of facts and information about *Razvedka* activities which at present they do not have. Also, if the couple, 'John' and 'Sonia', had been put under lengthy surveillance instead of being alerted by precipitate police action, their contacts with sources of information in this country would ultimately have been disclosed.

I am deeply conscious that in affairs of espionage and counterespionage what superficially may appear to be blunders or worse can have a totally different aspect when assessed in the light of the full facts of the case, and for this reason I have until now rejected all offers to publish the story of the treatment of my affair by the M.I.5 office responsible. However, in view of recent events in this country, it appears to me to be in the interests of security that the reason for the apparent failure of our Intelligence to draw any benefits from my defection should now be studied by the Committee of Privy Councillors set up by the Prime Minister.

Alexander Foote also compared the thoroughness of his interrogation by the Swiss and the detailed notes they made of what he said with the perfunctory interrogation by Mr — — , 'who did not appear to have very profound knowledge of the Soviet espionage system. Questions, if any, were sketchy and unplanned.'

His successor in the Hammersmith flat as a 'guest' of MI5 was:

a certain defecting Soviet colonel. This individual after only a short stay preferred the risk of death by deciding to return to the Soviet Union. To obtain his repatriation he left the flat and created public scandal in Olympia. It is reasonable to suppose that this colonel was in the hands of the same people and had been subject to the same cynical treatment that had been accorded to me.

There is no evidence that Foote's plea was heeded, or that his criticisms were followed up. For a while he settled down as a minor civil servant in the quiet bureaucratic backwater of the Ministry of Agriculture and Fisheries. When he left the Soviet Secret Service he still had a fair amount of money in a Swiss bank. Then, strangely almost three years after he had left the country, he was tried in his absence and lost all his worldly goods in effect. Previously the Swiss had treated him leniently, at least to the extent of showing some kindness to him during his imprisonment and eventually releasing him on bail. Was some subtle pressure brought on the Swiss by the British? Did someone in Intelligence circles – possibly Kim Philby, then in charge of the section of MI6 concentrating on Russia – plant on the Swiss false evidence against Foote? 'Roger' is quite sure that this is what happened. 'Smears against Foote were being passed around in diplomatic circles shortly after he returned to Britain. Somebody in London was damning Foote. Philby in conjunction with Liddell is almost certainly the answer, as it is for the extraordinary way in which "Sonia" was allowed to escape to East Germany.'

When Foote decided to write his book, *Handbook for Spies*, all about his work for the Soviets, he was forced to accept that his story should be written and published under MI5 supervision. Foote's version of events would have been embarrassing to the pro-Soviets in both MI5 and MI6. He died on 1 August 1956, in University College Hospital, London. He had swung over from being pro-Soviet to supporting any Conservative MP who would listen to his case and pleas. Alas, there were too few of these around at that time. He maintained to the end of his days that there was treachery in high places in Britain and that he was constantly frustrated in bringing this to the attention of the authorities. His estate amounted to a mere £1756.

Long afterwards Sir Percy Sillitoe learned from a British MP who had tried to take up Foote's case much important information which had never been passed on to him when he was head of MI5. By this time Sir Percy had long since left the service and there was not much he could do about it. 'I blame Liddell mostly,' he confided afterwards. 'He would certainly have had all the answers to many things which were puzzling me at the time. As for Foote, I would have welcomed a long talk with him.'

As to the 'defecting Soviet colonel' to whom Foote referred, this was Colonel J. D. Tasoev, who had been head of the Soviet Reparations Mission in Bremen. He had been welcomed by MI6 who had helped him to come over to London in May 1948, but changed his mind after being installed at Hammersmith (largely because he suspected that at least one person who had interrogated him was not to be trusted). Here again Sillitoe suspected that somebody in his own service had caused Tasoev to be suspicious, but he was never able to get at the truth. Tasoev was returned to the Russians, though the extraordinary allegation has been made that prior to this 'a lengthy debate was held in Broadway [Intelligence headquarters in those days] about the relative merits of dumping the recalcitrant Soviet into the North Sea from a height of 20,000 feet.'[12]

Almost the whole of his period in office at MI5 Sir Percy was made to feel an outsider – 'an African policeman', said one colleague in a foolish and derogatory reference to his earlier career in Africa. He had the feeling that some of these same senior colleagues deliberately stayed behind after he had left the office in order to discuss things among themselves without reference to their chief. Long afterwards *The Times* commented that 'the qualities that make an outstanding policeman do not necessarily fit him to direct counter-espionage and military security, and there were not wanting those who thought MI5 at fault in the cases of Fuchs, Pontecorvo and Burgess and Maclean.'[13]

As will be seen in the next chapter, to link the name of Sillitoe with failure to deal with Fuchs *et al* is totally unjust. But the denigration of Sillitoe continued for many years, nearly always inspired, whether to politicians or the media, by his own colleagues.

More than any other chief of MI5 he travelled widely during his term of office, paying particular heed to MI5's overseas links in British colonies. He went to the USA, Canada, Egypt, Kenya, Malaya (as it then was) and Palestine, Australia and New Zealand. All this was very much in line with the Attlee policy of involving Commonwealth countries in any problems which seemed to affect them as much as Britain. That this policy brought results is unquestionable: Sillitoe himself recorded that 'as a result of my 1948 trip' the Australian Secret Intelligence Organisation was set up after 'a rewarding talk with J. B. Chifley' (then the Prime Minister).[14]

On this occasion Sir Percy was accompanied by Sir Roger Hollis specifically to advise the Australian government on security needs. Three years later he again visited Australia and talked with the new Prime Minister, Sir Robert Menzies. About the same time Sir Percy was particularly effective in advising the authorities in Kenya about how to tackle the Mau Mau terrorist problem. Here his experience in Africa stood him in good stead, and his advice produced almost instant results.

15

Five Run For Cover

I would not dream of denying that MI5 was mistaken about
Fuchs, and that it would have been much more laudable had the
department been able to establish – or merely to suspect – in 1942
that Fuchs was passing information to the Russians
(Sir Percy Sillitoe)[1]

Though in no way can this be attributed to the new chief of the service,
Sir Percy Sillitoe, if MI5 ever went through a really disastrous period it
was in the years 1946 to 1951, as I shall continue to argue. Again and
again vital information was not passed on to him.

He should particularly have been given details of Anthony Blunt's
mission to Germany in the spring of 1945 to obtain papers alleged to
have been the property of Britain's royal family. From every point of
view – possible blackmail, undesirable communications prior to or
during the war – MI5 should have been in full possession of the facts.
The royal family should never have had any special protection in such
circumstances. Nobody has ever been completely truthful about this
Blunt mission.

In *Spycatcher*, Peter Wright keeps almost totally silent on this topic.
All we read is that Sir Michael Adeane, then private secretary to the
Queen and Keeper of the Queen's Archives, told him that, when he
interrogated Blunt, he was on no account to question Blunt on this
particular mission. Bearing in mind that Blunt was then not merely
under suspicion but more or less proved to have been a Soviet agent,
this was an outrageous demand by Adeane. Only by keeping MI5 fully
informed could the threat of blackmail of the royal family and others be
avoided. How was it that Wright failed to press this point, or, assuming
that he was not high enough ranking to do so, that he did not press the
point on his superiors? After all, if there was incriminating material in
the Hesse or any other archives that Blunt was delving into, any of it
could have been passed on to the Russians. Probably it was and this
may provide some answers to the various mysteries surrounding both

the identity and death (deaths?) of Rudolf Hess and the man alleged to
have impersonated him. Hesse or Hess are equally important from a
security viewpoint.

Wright was, of course, quite the wrong person to have been interrogating Blunt either on this or any other questions. He was basically a
technician, one better trained in the techniques of 'bugging', 'debug-
ging' and phone-tapping than with the subtleties of interrogation.
How he came to be allowed to interrogate such key people as Blunt is
one of those imponderables which the hidden files of MI5 are unlikely
to reveal.

Nevertheless the question needs to be posed: did MI5 probe into
the Blunt mission to Germany, despite the quite arrogant edict of
Adeane (assuming Wright's allegation to be correct)? If not, one can
only say that the service allowed itself to be dangerously manipulated
by outsiders. Secondly, did they look into the allegations of Madame
Suzanne Blum, the Duchess of Windsor's lawyer, that secret agents of
Buckingham Palace took papers from the Duke's Paris home after his
death without the Duchess's authority. Both 10 Downing Street and
the Royal Librarian at Windsor Castle have denied this, but a member
of the French DST (Counter-espionage service) told the author that
'we were convinced that something like this happened. One suggestion is that the papers were taken while the Duchess was away in
Britain for the Duke's funeral. Another report we had was that Lord
Mountbatten planned a further raid on the Duchess's home a few
years later. Even the French Treasury were apprehensive about this.'

Certainly Mountbatten's official biographer confirms Mountbatten's visits to Paris in quest of papers and his failure to make much pro-
gress with Madame Blum. The Duke de Grantmesnil, better known as
Kenneth de Courcy, having heard that documents from the Windsors'
Paris home were to be sent to Windsor Castle Library, wrote to the
Duchess suggesting that his own papers concerning the former King
might be added to the collection. He said he was surprised when he received a letter from Madame Blum, dated 24 March 1979, stating :
'How can you still believe what you read in the newspapers? The
Duchess did not give away the Duke's files: they were taken away with-
out her knowledge.'

Another blunder in MI5 was undoubtedly the whole handling of the
Fuchs case. Fuchs should have been constantly watched and monitored after his arrival in Britain. It was known from the moment he
arrived that he was a member of the German Communist Party.

True, MI5 was not helped by the devious and evasive Foreign

Office (traits of which this section of the British Establishment seems never to have shaken off). In November 1943, Hollis asked the Foreign Office to license a non-Communist German trade union paper because it was 'not in Britain's interests for the Communists and Russians to control everything.' Back came the FO's comment : 'MI5 exaggerates the danger . . . of Communist influence . . . and suffers from many delusions . . . that the Foreign Office will have to educate them.'[2]

It was, of course, the Foreign Office and the Soviet-infatuated Anthony Eden who needed the 'education'.

In all this Guy Liddell duly concurred, always giving the benefit of the doubt to the Soviet side.

In 1941 Fuchs had been released from internment in Canada and, having learned in Canada something about the Tube Alloys project, he applied to join it. Wing-Commander Arnold, who was then in charge of a section in MI5, was given the application for vetting. It was handed to a man whose name for the purpose of this book had best be coded as 'Treacle': this officer made a strong recommendation that on no account should Fuchs be allowed access to secret information. Not only was this officer aware of Fuchs' membership of the Communist Party in Germany, but he had the impression that someone had told Fuchs that his application was certain to be accepted, as he seemed extremely confident. This file ruling against Fuchs was not only removed, but altered to a security clearance. This much Wing-Commander Arnold afterwards discovered, but by then it was too late.

The cover-up by Liddell and his friends has been to put the blame on Hollis. It has been alleged that Hollis 'repeatedly cleared Fuchs for secret work'. This is totally untrue: he was not involved in this.

Neither Fuchs, nor Nunn May should ever have been given absolute security clearance to work on the nuclear-bomb project.

What was worrying Liddell at this time was the fact that Wing-Commander Henry Arnold, a security officer linked to MI5, knew that certain files on Fuchs had been removed and that at least two members of MI5 had cleared this immigrant scientist, despite his known membership of the Communist Party in Germany. Wing-Commander Arnold had served in the Royal Flying Corps in World War I and in the Intelligence Service of the RAF between the wars. Before joining MI5 he had been senior security officer to the Bank of England. When Fuchs applied to join the Tube Alloys project (the code-name for the British atomic energy scheme) that application was sent to Arnold's section for security assessment. It was dealt with by Mr Brian Grimston who, after reading his file and noting his communist background, recommended that under no circumstances should Fuchs be allowed access to secret information. The file was intercepted by another member of MI5 who altered the recommendation to a security clearance. It has since been suggested that Sir Roger Hollis 'repeatedly cleared Fuchs for secret work'. Sir Roger was not involved: Fuchs had at least two protectors inside MI5 and one of these was Guy Liddell.

When Fuchs was eventually caught Sillitoe was appalled by such blunders. He read the riot act to the whole of MI5's staff, including Sir Dick White, then director of 'B' Division, at whom much of the criticism was directed. Nevertheless, Liddell and Roger Hollis both persuaded Sir Percy into concealing from the Prime Minister how the Fuchs' file had been ignored. This was something he deeply regretted later in his life. At the same time it was concealed from him that 'Sonia' (Ruth Kuczynski) had been confirmed as a KGB agent by Alexander Foote.

The next major blunder and the one which hit the headlines was the sudden and secret departure from Britain to the USSR of Burgess and Maclean. It was this event which marked the end of Guy Liddell's career in the service. By this time Liddell was beginning to realise that his days were numbered and that he desperately needed allies. His constant nervous chain-smoking had already injured his health, affecting his heart.

Though an unsuspecting Hollis had backed Liddell, Liddell himself had no qualms about denigrating Hollis. Here he was subtle, as always, causing the denigration to come from outside MI5 rather than from within it. Liddell had an unerring instinct as to just how to smear people so that the effect would be immediate. One choice he made was the late Sir William Stephenson, who in 1982 sent me a cable from his Bermuda home stating that 'I was warned about Roger by Guy [Liddell], who was the most capable of all Five people.'[3]

But the pressure on Liddell undoubtedly increased about the time that Burgess and Maclean fled the country. By then MI5 had been alerted to put both men under supervision, and Liddell had reason to be especially worried in that Gouzenko had also named Fuchs as a spy in the Soviet cause some years earlier; much later Gouzenko himself asked: 'Why did it take them as long as five years before they arrested him?' But what must have made life even more difficult for Liddell was the fact that he had been a close friend of Burgess as well as being an occasional party-goer with Maclean.

Much has been made of the question as to who tipped off Maclean and Burgess that they were in danger of being interrogated and were already under surveillance. This is almost irrelevant as so many people could have given them such information – not only Liddell, but Philby, Blunt and others with MI5 contacts. Not least Tom Driberg (later to be created a life peer as Lord Bradwell in the last Wilson government) who still maintained links with MI5. I have often recalled a curious incident concerning Driberg in the summer of 1944. I was ferrying a landing-craft backwards and forwards to the Normandy beaches when I seized the chance to go to Bayeux, at last under Allied control. In a bar in that city I saw Driberg in the uniform of a war correspondent. Less than an hour later I saw him in another much less conspicuous bar, out of uniform and wearing a beret, with two men who, I was told, were secret members of the Spanish Communist Resistance.

Who allowed Burgess and Maclean to escape? Sir Percy Sillitoe in his book, despite what he may have felt personally, said 'In so far as the disappearance of the two Foreign Office officials themselves was concerned, I can only emphasise the inescapable truth that no shred of legal evidence had ever been available against either of them which could have served as grounds for the issuing of a warrant for their arrest.'[4]

This is true enough, but two points need to be made: first, that much of the evidence which was available was kept away from Sillitoe himself, and, second, that there were quite unnecessary delays in having Burgess and Maclean interrogated. Under such interrogation it is almost certain that Maclean would have cracked, a factor which was fully recognised by Liddell. For more than two years MI5 had been asked to find out who was the mysterious agent code-named 'Homer' in their own ranks and this investigation had been conducted in a desultory fashion without any kind of attempt at cooperation with the FBI, even though this agent was supposed to be in the USA. Any careful study of Maclean's early days at Cambridge University should have indicated that he was a prominent suspect. In March 1934, he had himself condemned 'the capitalist, dictatorial character of the University' in a letter he wrote to *Granta*, at the same time urging student representation on the Appointments Board, and student control of college magazines without interference by the authorities. Yet the names put forward by MI5 as suspects in the early days of the quest for 'Homer' were of the most unlikely Foreign Office characters, none of whom was ever found guilty of treachery. In all this MI5 received 'guidance' from Kim Philby in Washington, where he was then stationed as liaison officer with American Intelligence.

Rather more significant is the virulent campaign waged against the late Morgan Goronwy Rees regarding his attempt to alert the authorities about the Burgess-Maclean disappearance. Goronwy Rees told me that shortly before Burgess left to go to his post in the USA he went to a farewell party at Burgess' flat. Among those present were James Pope-Hennessy, Liddell, Hector McNeil, then Secretary of State for Scotland, Blunt and David Footman (of MI6). According to Goronwy Rees, Burgess once asked him whether he would be 'willing to help', the suggestion being the Russian cause. To add emphasis to this appeal, Burgess gave the name of Anthony Blunt as one who was already working for the Russians:

> I don't suppose he could have named a person who carried more weight with me [said Rees]. He was someone whom I both liked and respected greatly, and with whom I would have gladly joined in any enterprise. Nor was I alone in my admiration: there was no one I knew who did not praise his intelligence, his uprightness and his integrity. Indeed, he possessed all those virtues which Guy did not. All they had in common, except friendship, was that both were homosexuals. But it now appeared that they were both also Comintern agents.[5]

Long after Burgess and Maclean disappeared behind the Iron Curtain officialdom tried to give the impression that neither of them could provide any really valuable information to the Russians. This was not the case. Maclean, when he was posted to Washington at the end of the war, was joint British secretary on the Combined Policy Committee on Atomic Energy. This alone made him privy to a wide variety of secrets, including all secret Anglo-American exchanges on NATO and the Korean War. Security in the British Embassy was in some respects non-existent at this time. For example Maclean as a member of Chancery was allowed to import two Jamaican female servants to Washington. A few months later one of these women was identified by the FBI as a communist and promptly deported. Burgess, despite all attempts to downgrade his sources of information, was by reason of his wide social contacts an invaluable agent. In some respects he was superior to either Maclean or Philby because he had the knack of endearing himself to people in the highest poisitions. He had been welcomed to Churchill's home in 1938 and it was Burgess who was detailed to show Anthony Eden around Washington in 1950. Eden was then hostile to Churchill's support for German rearmament and Burgess may have played a part in this. Despite his lowly position in the Foreign Office, he was on first-name terms with a number of top ambassadors. He was close to Hector McNeil, Ernest Bevin's number two in the Foreign Office at one time, and therefore a close confidant in many matters, including a long secret conference between McNeil and Spaak, the Belgian Premier.

General MacArthur was quite certain that Burgess and Maclean had told the Russians before they defected that the USA would not bomb Chinese bases if the Chinese entered the Korean War, with the result that China invaded in 1950. 'The British traitors, Burgess and Maclean, defected to the Soviet Union during the Korean War with full top secret information on the war plans and intentions of the United States – plans and intentions which, in so far as they related to our reaction to formal acts of war against us by Red China, were not communicated to me as commander in the field.'[6]

There is some confirmation of this from the British side. Mr Robert Cecil, who succeeded to Maclean's post as head of the American Department in the Foreign Office, states that 'after he had absconded ... I found in the filing cabinet reserved for the Head of the Department a numbered copy of the Cabinet paper containing Prime Minister Attlee's account of his hasty visit to President Truman in December 1950, the aim of which was to ensure that General MacArthur should not be permitted to use the atom bomb in the Korean War.'[7]

Goronwy Rees was one of the first to suspect that when Burgess suddenly left his apartment without giving any plausible story as to his plans that he had decided to defect to Russia. He telephoned David Footman of MI6, saying he feared Burgess had gone to Moscow and urged him to alert MI5. Next he telephoned Blunt with the same warning. This may seem odd in view of the fact that Rees had already been told by Burgess that Blunt was, if not a spy, at least a supporter of the Soviet cause. But Rees knew that Blunt still had contacts with MI5 and he probably wanted to test his reactions. Rees also reported a curious incident, confirmed by his wife, of one Sunday morning when Burgess took them to Limehouse for a Chinese meal. 'Burgess stopped outside a ships' chandler's shop and pushed something through the letter-box,' said Rees. 'From what I learned later this letter-box was also used by Blunt.'[8]

The man who interviewed Rees regarding his information was Guy Liddell, and Rees found him 'discouraging, dismissive and even mildly threatening in the sense that he kept indicating that all this not only wasted MI5 time, but could be considered "mischievous to the cause of national security". That was his exact phrase.' Later it was discovered that a worker engaged in nuclear research who had been missing from his South Wales home some time before had been found dead in a flat above the ships' chandler's.[9]

This story by Goronwy Rees was also confirmed by my ex-CIA informant, 'Poe', who says that 'we were certain that both Blunt and Burgess used this Limehouse dead-letter box'. But from this very moment Liddell and Blunt ganged up against Rees, actively dissuading him from making any statement to MI5, and actually suggesting that any such statement could in effect be interpreted as 'a confession' by Rees which might harm his future career. Rees, referring to the fact that Burgess disappeared with Maclean on 25 May 1951, said that:

> Not until the end of the following week was a move initiated – and then in the most peculiar circumstances. Guy Liddell asked me out to lunch. I was taken aback to see that he came accompanied by Anthony Blunt . . . They did their level best to convince me that I'd be wasting everyone's time if I went along and submitted the kind of nebulous evidence against Guy Burgess that I seemed determined to offer . . . Where Burgess might have gone was no concern of theirs.[10]

For Liddell to bring Blunt along with him to such a lunch was a significant move. Undoubtedly both Liddell and Blunt guessed that he had been told by Burgess that Blunt was in the ring of pro-Soviet supporters: there was, Rees felt, a veiled and unspoken hint that whatever else he did, he had better not mention Blunt's name. Nor did he, and perhaps this was Rees' only mistake, though one must bear in mind that in the first place he had only Burgess' word for this story and, secondly, that he had been a friend of Blunt. However, Rees insisted on talking to someone else inside MI5. In fact he was grilled by two people:

> I was soon summoned for a second and longer interrogation which proved a gruelling business. They treated me as if I were a spy and a traitor with lots to hide . . . My interrogators took me back through the tortuous byways of my friendship with Burgess. I held nothing back this time. I revealed the name of Blunt as the only other conspirator given to me by Burgess when I'd asked for one.[11]

Express Newspapers had been insistent in their editorial columns that the inside story of the disappearance of Burgess and Maclean should be revealed. Lord Beaverbrook, who had taken a personal interest in this, commissioned Colonel O. Pinto to conduct a full investigation into the affair, paying particular attention to the escape route through France. But somehow or other pressure was brought to bear on Beaverbrook. Suddenly he cancelled the project and told Pinto to make no further inquiries. Pinto, however, refused to be silenced and he gave a certain amount of information to Kenneth de Courcy, who records that following up on this 'we sent an experienced man to France. But the late Roger Hollis was ahead of us. He sent two officials of MI5 to France to ask the French police to frame our man with a currency offence and to arrest him. The French police came to us and told us. In fact our man was travelling on an official Bank of England currency allowance.'[12]

My sources in the security services show that in fact it was not Hollis who was responsible for this, but more undercover intrigues by Guy Liddell. But by this time the smear campaign against Hollis had already started.

Goronwy Rees found in the latter years of his life that there had been a constant intrigue, which he felt was not only devoted to barring him from various worthwhile posts, but even smearing him with publishers. I came to know him well during the last three years of his life, something for which I am most grateful but sad. By that time he was suffering from the terrible disease of cancer which in the end killed him. Yet, somehow it never seemed to matter. He himself never allowed his suffering to dim his zest for life, nor to impinge upon friends or acquaintances. I cannot recall anyone who died with more dignity and gaiety, and who even in the last year of his life could take great delight in an impromptu party. There was never anything vindictive or paranoic about Goronwy's desire to see the whole subject of infiltration by the USSR thoroughly ventilated, though he certainly did not disguise his contempt for those who wanted to have it both ways, not merely betraying their country, but accepting honours from it and making the most of the British way of life.[13]

It is interesting to note that the Committee of Inquiry set up by the Home Office in July 1951 confined itself solely to the issue of the security clearance of Foreign Office employees, resulting in the recommendation of positive vetting. Quite clearly the wider issues had either been hidden from the Committee or totally ignored by them. The cover-up on Anthony Blunt was continued, and this in no way helped Anglo-American intelligence and security contacts. Demands for information on the Maclean-Burgess scandal from the FBI were fobbed off with lies from Liddell and a cover-up by MI5. The FBI wanted to know the precise date on which MI5 had targeted Maclean for surveillance : MI5's response was to put back the date by 14 days in an effort to show that their inquiries had never produced any suspicions against Maclean which might provide evidence for action. This proposal was put to Sillitoe who was extremely angry about what he saw as an attempt to deceive Britain's allies. He reprimanded his subordinates, particularly Dick White and Liddell, and, most reluctantly, went to the USA to see Hoover to try to make what amounted to excuses. This was a task which went right against the grain for a man of Sillitoe's calibre and it did him no good at all. The FBI were convinced that MI5 were covering up and even two years later when they asked for permission to interrogate Blunt they were refused by the British.

Is it conceivable that Liddell was just an appalling incompetent with vague Soviet sympathies, unfortunate in his friends and unjustly smeared by his enemies? Or was he the top Russian agent in MI5? Sillitoe had his suspicions even at that time, but when he raised these with senior members of the service his subordinates tended to cover up on Liddell and point in the direction of Roger Hollis. He was himself at first almost persuaded that Hollis was the villain. What at the time Hollis did not know was that Liddell had in the words of Rees 'done his utmost, with Blunt at his side, to persuade me not to report my suspicions about Burgess officially for at least ten days after the disappearance of him and Maclean. I wanted to take my case direct to the Director-General of MI5, but Liddell insisted that there were good reasons for not doing this.'[14]

By this time, however, even the ultra-cautious Liddell found that events had moved much too fast for him. A possible spy emerged inside No. 10 Downing Street in the person of Phillip Jordan, the Prime Minister's recently appointed press officer. Jordan had been a close friend of Donald Maclean in Washington and as a result he suddenly became involved in the question of his disappearance. Within a few days he suddenly died of a heart attack. Only belatedly was Attlee warned of the security risk regarding Jordan, even then not by MI5, but by someone outside the Intelligence and Security Services, Lieutenant-General Mason Macfarlane, formerly head of the British Services Mission to the USSR and Governor of Gibraltar, but then a Labour Member of Parliament.

At last many of Liddell's indiscreet friendships had come to the knowledge of Sillitoe, not least his regular meetings with Philby and Burgess not only at the Bentinck Street flat but earlier on at the Moore Arms in Chelsea, and later meetings with Blunt at another hostelry, as well as Friday nights at another well-known haunt of homosexuals in Chelsea. It is interesting that Liddell seemed to prefer the company of homosexuals even though he claimed not to be one himself.

The infiltration of Soviet agents into Britain's nuclear projects reached out to Canada in World War II. Blanche Clayton, the daughter of a colonel who retired from the Army and settled in British Columbia, had two brothers: Henry, who became head of the Nuclear Physics Division at Chalk River, and George, who was a senior executive at a uranium mine in the Yellow River region. Blanche had been a governess for a while and one of her pupils subsequently married the Number Two in the Nuclear Physics Division at Chalk River. She had been at the University of British Columbia and later went to Montreal to do a PhD course. While in Montreal she did a vacation job in the Medical Division at Chalk River and while there found evidence that Bruno Pontecorvo, (who, later defected to Russia) had been a Soviet agent at the time he was at Chalk River. He had left incriminating papers in a library book that she looked at while browsing around the library. On this occasion she talked freely about what she had found in both the medical and nuclear physics department, but did not tell the security officers. Obviously someone decided that Blanche Clayton was a major threat to Soviet agents inside Chalk River. Just how they set about discrediting her is not clear, but shortly afterwards she was put into a mental hospital. She was not released until the consultant concerned returned from his holiday and found that she had been admitted in his absence. He not only discharged her, but said that there 'had been no clinical reason for Blanche to be admitted to the hospital'.[15]

Miss Clayton returned to Britain, working first in the Zoology Department at Oxford (she had a degree in this subject) and later in Edinburgh. After a while her acutely perceptive mind identified a group of distinguished academics and scientists in the United Kingdom who, she alleged, were linked to both Pontecorvo and Fuchs. Attempts were made to discourage her, but when she was persuaded to report her suspicions to Wing-Commander Arnold, he found that much of what she said fitted in with his own conclusions. Among the names which Miss Clayton gave Arnold were two of the most distinguished names in the world of science, one of them being a close friend of Liddell. There is no doubt that from this time onwards she was subject to a subtle form of harassment and became a very frightened woman. She was scared to talk to almost anyone in case once again somebody sent her to a mental home. Eventually she was found hanging from a wardrobe without projections and which was shorter than herself: the technical difficulty of that method of suicide should have left her time to think better of it and having only recently become a convert to Roman Catholicism, this also made her highly unlikely to attempt suicide. Her doctor, Dr. A. M. Sweet, when called to her home said that what he saw 'was consistent with murder, but could have been suicide'. He left the detailed examination of the body to the pathologist who performed the post mortem.[16]

The FBI's response to their own discovery of Soviet agents in MI5 was to press their findings on Sillitoe. They made it quite clear that they were not prepared to work with either Philby, who had maintained links with them in Washington, or with Liddell.

Liddell was quietly and without any fuss allowed to leave MI5 to take up the post of Security Consultant to the Atomic Energy Authority as a replacement for Kenneth Morton Evans. In 1953 Liddell, who already had the CBE, was awarded the honour of Commander of the Order of the Bath.

Liddell, to sum up his time at MI5, used all his influence to cover up the failures of MI5 and to smear and destroy anyone who attempted to reveal the presence of Soviet agents inside the service, while always playing along with anyone who would direct attention to other innocent people. He was still being protected by the Establishment, the Conservative Government of Winston Churchill, in which he had a number of friends.

Liddell had already managed to ingratiate himself with the Churchill family, having been requested to arrange a cover-up of minor scandal concerning Sir Winston. The way he managed to do this is in itself a tribute to his powers of manipulation extending even to other countries. As long ago as the late 1970s I was told that 'you will never be able to expose Guy Liddell. His contacts with the Conservative Government of 1951 onwards and the fact that he saved the Prime Minister, Churchill, from a rather nasty situation.'

This information I then very much doubted. However, having been told somewhat esoterically that the clue to all this lay somewhere in Switzerland, I was astonished to find in the diaries of Sir Alexander Cadogan, a major Foreign Office adviser to Churchill in World War II, that on 8 September 1951:

we passed another beautiful old chateau – is it called Beauregard, belonging to a family of the same name? Anyhow, the son of the house was a godson of Winston, and when the latter was staying on the Lake of Geneva in, I think, 1947, he felt he ought to give his godson a present. So he sent him a captured German radio (the son being aged about fifteen). The boy plugged it in and turned it on. But it was not a radio, but a booby-trap and it went off and killed the boy. A terrible story, and the father has not returned to the chateau since.[17]

16

Cover-Ups in High Places

I have no doubt that nothing has been learned from the Vassall case, just as nothing was learned from the case of Burgess and Maclean. The first necessary step is to take security out of the hands of 'amateurs' and put it into the hands of men with security training and experience.

(Major A.W. Sansom, a former security officer)[1]

When Burgess and Maclean defected to Russia in 1951 the American FBI mounted a full-scale investigation of their own. They were convinced of Philby's guilt and the part he played in trying to cover up for the two traitors. At the same time that the British government was still pretending that there was no firm evidence that the pair had fled to Moscow, the FBI had in their possession this curious anonymous letter delivered to the US Embassy in London:

This is the deposition which Maclean made to me on 24 May: I am haunted and burdened by what I know of official secrets, especially by the content of high-level Anglo-American conversations. The British Government, whom I served, have betrayed the realm to Americans. I wish to enable my beloved country to escape from the snare which faithless politicians have set. I deeply admire the example of patriotism shown by these men and women – Johnstone, Bidwell, Dagleish, Rides and especially John Peet – who chose voluntary exile because they could not countenance, but had to expose, the criminal instructions of the Foreign Office to conduct subversive activities within the People's Democracies . . . I have decided that I can discharge my duty to my country only through prompt disclosure of this material to Stalin, whom I shall beg to release it at once, so that it may alert the British people. . . .

The existence of this document was not made public until November

1977, through the US Freedom of Information Act. Why was its text not revealed – at least in the United States – in 1951? Did pressure from British sources prevent this? Or did J. Edgar Hoover of the FBI believe that in keeping quiet he might be able to track down the third, fourth and fifth men he had always suspected must exist? Curiously, no comment was attached to the files, which was unusual for FBI dossiers. Obviously this was one of a number of carefully contrived anonymous messages (there were telegrams to the mothers of Maclean and Burgess from Paris and Rome respectively to say all was well) to ensure that the news was circulated. Maybe the intention was to stir up trouble between the US and Britain.

Not all the names in this diatribe are readily identifiable. Johnstone was a former *News Chronicle* correspondent who defected to Russia in 1948, while Peet had been Reuter Correspondent on Berlin after World War II, then went to East Germany to edit the English language *German Democratic Report*. 'Poe', the former CIA officer, has this to say about the anonymous letter: 'We were absolutely certain that the intermediary for the letter was another Soviet agent of British nationality. Our first suspect was Blunt, but later we even suspected that it was an attempt by Liddell to give Maclean a mischievous image in this country. Maybe he thought the Americans would release the story. If so, he erred, because pressure from outside his service for us to keep quiet came from London.'

When Sir Percy Sillitoe retired from his post at the head of MI5 his services were immediately snapped up by Sir Ernest Oppenheimer and the De Beers company to tackle the problems of diamond smuggling. At MI5 Sir Dick White was put in charge, with Hollis as his deputy until 1956, when Sir Dick was appointed head of MI6 and Hollis, on Sir Dick's recommendation, was made head of MI5. At the same time Graham Mitchell was promoted to the office of Deputy Director-General.

The nine years in which Hollis was Director-General were among the most successful periods in MI5's history. It has been said by some of Hollis's carping critics that most of the successes were the result of CIA tip-offs, but it was MI5, not the CIA, which initiated the arrests. There were no fewer than nine major espionage cases which resulted in convictions, including the Portland Naval Spy Ring (Konon Molody, Houghton, Gee); George Blake; John Vassall; the Krogers; the instrument engineer Brian Linney, jailed for 14 years for communicating defence secrets; Frank Bossard, the missile research worker jailed for 21 years for selling secrets; Peter Dorschel, jailed for seven years for trying to buy secrets of US Polaris submarines based in Britain.

Apart from an impressive list of convictions of spies during his term of office as chief of MI5, Hollis also found time, like Sir Percy Sillitoe, to visit various parts of the Commonwealth to advise on intelligence. He was, as we have seen, instrumental in helping the Australians to create their own Security and Intelligence Organisation (ASIO).

This was something which was held against him by his critics after his retirement when they alleged that he arranged for the Soviet Embassy in Canberra to be tipped off that Vladimir Petrov, one of their MVD agents, was about to defect. These criticisms have since been firmly refuted by Colonel Sir Charles Spry, who was Director-General of ASIO in 1954 when Petrov defected. Sir Charles oversaw every aspect of the case of Petrov's defection and he had known Hollis ever since the late 1940s. 'One key point about Hollis is worth stressing and I think it is crucial. Hollis knew about Petrov several months *before* Petrov defected. If Hollis had been working for the Russians, to have let the defection take place would have been unthinkable. My memory of Hollis is that he was a stickler for formality and the rules and would never dream of sharp practice.'[2]

Furthermore Sir Charles Spry, referring to the story that the Soviets had sent out two 'strong-arm men' to Australia to prevent Petrov's defection, declared that 'the two Soviet couriers sent out in fact did not arrive in Australia until *twelve* days after Petrov's defection.'

It is true that Hollis did not enjoy easy personal relations with ordinary members of the service who tended to find him aloof and reserved. He stuck rigidly to the rules. Some of his own colleagues called him 'Mr Inertia' just because of this. Others, rather more sympathetic to his problems, were impressed by the way in which he faced up to the treachery by which he was himself surrounded. He made a habit of working late in the office, long after most other key people had left, and he depended very much on his highly efficient secretary of some 18 years, Miss Edith Valentine Hammond.

Nobody could have failed to come under criticism in the circumstances faced by Hollis during his term of office as chief of MI5. It was evident from the number of convictions being achieved that Britain was facing an extension of Soviet infiltration in the postwar period. On top of this Hollis had to deal with one of the most incompetent of Prime Ministers regarding the handling of intelligence and security matters of the past half century. Macmillan's cynical attitude to this whole business was (a) that it 'is only the nuts and bolts that matter', implying that the only problem was the obtaining of highly technical top secret information; and (b) that catching spies only caused a lot of unnecessary trouble and that it was much better to keep quiet and keep track of them. Certainly he gave the impression of turning a deaf ear to all intelligence questions, almost implying that the less he heard of them the better.

It is not altogether surprising that, according to his brother, Marcus (himself a member of MI6), Hollis declared that 'the best Prime Minister he had to deal with was Harold Wilson'. But, for Harold Wilson read George Wigg, Wilson's highly efficient intelligence liaison officer. Macmillan neither had, nor seemed to wish to have any such officer, while Wigg and Hollis had an admiration for each other.

There was a case in 1963 when Hollis is said to have dismissed a memorandum urging him to warn the then War Minister, John Profumo, about the latter's association with call-girl Christine Keeler. It was this scandal which nearly brought down Macmillan's government on account of Keeler's concurrent association with Ivanov, an attaché at the Soviet Embassy. Much has been written about the Profumo case and the dubious role played in it by the unhappy Stephen Ward. Lord Denning, Master of the Rolls, who was appointed to undertake an inquiry into this whole affair, probably summed it all up when he declared in his final report that once the security service had come to the conclusion that there was no security interest in the matter, but only the moral misbehaviour of a minister, they were under no duty to report it to anyone. Later in his memoirs Lord Denning commented on the confidence he felt in Hollis during the inquiry.

Nevertheless the Profumo case and the trial of Stephen Ward for living wholly or in part on the earnings of prostitution, a highly controversial proceeding especially as Ward had been used as a contact man by an MI6 officer, had repercussions far and wide. These were mainly due to the other people in both what was known as the Cliveden set (so-called because they met at Cliveden, the home of Lord Astor) and those in Ward's own circle. Mountbatten as well as a number of MPs had been present one weekend at Cliveden when Eugene Ivanov, the Soviet intelligence officer, challenged Profumo to a race across the swimming pool. Both Mountbatten and his close relative, David, then Marquis of Milford Haven, were friends of Ward, as, too, was Countess de Rohan who at one time lived at the house of Sir Francis Rose.

Following this case Hollis had two other problems. One was the possibility that there had been in addition to John Vassall at least one, if not two dangerous informants to the USSR inside the Admiralty. Suspicion rested on two senior British naval officers who had worked under NATO, one an admiral, the other a captain; information was coming in from American sources as well as British that some of the documents photocopied for the Russians were such that Vassall could not have had access to them. MI5 had found the Admiralty singularly unhelpful in trying to track down these leaks and security within that service had been lamentable. Indeed, the delay in uncovering Vassall was not due to incompetence on Hollis's part but to constant insistence from the Admiralty that there was no real evidence of a spy in their ranks, despite the fact this had already been confirmed to the Americans by the defector, Anatoli Golitsin, who claimed that he had seen photocopies of three extremely secret British naval plans.

I am told by 'Poe' that:

'in the CIA we had considerable evidence pointing to a senior officer in the Royal Navy who had passed information to the Russians. We feared this had been going on for a long time, possibly since the end of World War II, but the complaint was that we never had any help from the British side. That may well be because there was also some firm evidence that Lord Mountbatten was himself mixed up in all this and that he was instrumental in playing down the idea of spies inside the Admiralty. He kept dismissing our pleas as "American hysteria" and it would seem that some in MI5 fell for his anti-Americanism. We had heard rumours of his pro-Soviet sympathies. Remember that he was not only an influential figure in the highest circles in your land, but First Sea Lord in the years from 1955-59 and then Chief of the UK Defence Staff. Certainly the man suspected by the Americans and one who was later closely monitored by MI5 had been on Mountbatten's staff. Our information was that this high level spy was operating at least until 1964. What we could never understand was how Mountbatten, a known homosexual and therefore a security risk, managed to achieve the kind of promotion and jobs he got. Was he ever positively vetted?'

This is an apt comment. His biographers have stressed that Mountbatten had many female friends during his lifetime, and the homosexual factor has always been played down. Yet it was known inside the Navy long before World War II that he was homosexual, sometimes even risking such conduct in his cabin when at sea. It cannot be denied that he was a security risk.

As to the question of the spy inside the Admiralty, MI5 definitely looked into this question, but Hollis, not getting any real help from the Admiralty, and fully realising that any mention of the name Mountbatten could create a great scandal, played this close to the chest. It is said that Hollis declined to have one senior officer interviewed by MI5.

My own inquiries into this puzzle, while definitely not suggesting that Mountbatten himself was the informant in question (though he may well have been aware of the matter and, as I will show, personally sent other secret messages to the Soviets), narrowed the list of probable culprits down to three, all of whom had at some time or other worked for Mountbatten. In each case there was, one way or another, evidence of what Soviet defectors have referred to before as 'a strong Russian connection'.

As to Mountbatten himself, his left-wing views have already been noted, and in connection with this the continuing influence of Peter Murphy. This had been most marked in the Far East when Mountbatten was made Supreme Allied Commander South-East Asia. After the war Mountbatten's backing of the extreme left-wing Malayan People's Anti-Japanese Union proved not only to be a disastrous mistake, but to some extent paved the way for the Communist terrorist campaign in Malaya in the early 1950s. Not only Murphy, but Driberg, too, were involved in giving Mountbatten advice and this proved to be as unwise as regards Vietnam and Indonesia as it was in Malaya. Driberg was certainly not an authority on this part of the world, yet on 4 October, 1945, there is this remarkable letter from Mountbatten at SEAC HQ to Driberg: 'Your offer to mediate with the Viet Nahm [*sic*] Republic only reached us on the Friday evening . . . I have instructed Gracey to accept your offer with thanks, if you were still available. If only the French will be reasonable and come forward with an imaginative offer, the war in French Indo-China can be over.'[3]

Then he went on to complain that 'the Dutch are even worse. They have been reviling Christison and Van der Plas for meeting the Indonesian leaders, Sukarno in particular.' It was the same Sukarno who later became President and caused untold damage in South-East Asia. Not until 1966-67 did General Suharto take over as President and the Communist Party in Indonesia was outlawed and dissolved. It is interesting that Mountbatten asked for this letter 'to be destroyed as I presume it is improper to write either to a journalist or an MP in the above strain.'[4]

In 1946 Driberg gave Mountbatten a memorandum on the Dutch East Indies, while on 22 October SEAC's Supremo replied that 'The

Dutch are quite incredible about Java in their attitudes towards Sukarno. If only I had a free hand in French Indo-China and the Netherlands East Indies I feel I could settle both problems as easily as Burma.' It was his handling of the Burma problem which led to Burma not joining the Commonwealth.

Mountbatten seems to have had a complete disregard for all our allies except for the USSR at this time. Even Churchill warned him about his anti-Americanism, as Mountbatten himself recorded in his own papers – 'I think you should be careful about your anti-American attitude' – as cited by Philip Ziegler, his biographer. His hostility to the French can be judged by the fact that he backed the Vietcong (he called them the Annamites) and said they were 'trying to liberate their country'. His aim in the Dutch East Indies was to keep the Dutch Army out of Java while backing Sukarno's liberation movement, and his Java policies were at this time severely criticised on Australian radio programmes.

In correspondence with Driberg on 3 December, 1986, Mountbatten referred to a report which he had made to the Combined Chiefs of Staff shortly after the war which 'was originally suppressed by Ernie Bevin as being likely to offend the French and Dutch governments too much'. A malevolent influence on Mountbatten at this time was Peter Murphy who was hostile to Bevin, then British Foreign Minister. Murphy called the latter 'Mr Ramsay MacBevin', commenting in one letter to Mountbatten that 'everyone out here [presumably in South-East Asia where he then was] is very critical of the Labour Government except the right-wing extremists who are cock-a-whoop about the extent to which Mr Ramsay MacBevin has managed to discredit socialist leadership. I am not really utopian enough to imagine we can get any socialism out of the Foreign Office. The only people who seem at this distance to come out well are John Strachey, Nye Bevan and someone called Blackburn'.[5]

In the light of Murphy's views it is worth noting the extent to which Mountbatten relied on his friend as recorded in this letter to Driberg after he became Viceroy of India on 3 August, 1947: 'I should be interested to see what you think of my Report to the Combined Chiefs of Staff, which is now finished and within the next two or three weeks will be submitted to London and Washington. Peter Murphy has helped to re-write and re-arrange it in such a way that the ordinary layman can understand what we are after.' It is not surprising that this close friendship with Murphy in these circumstances resulted in the latter coming under a renewed surveillance by MI5 after the war.

Mountbatten had always taken a keen interest in 'The Trust' and its history, and personally visualised a re-creation of 'The Trust' as being one way of coming to an accommodation with the USSR. Stalin had been suspicious of the technique of 'The Trust': being a cautious peasant in his outlook, he disliked the idea of trying to be too clever and risking the use of liberals, businessmen and others to form a pro-Soviet under-cover group. But once he died there were those in the Soviet hierarchy who welcomed the idea of re-creating 'The Trust' as a means of seeking support for the Soviet Union in the Western World. Sometimes Politburo members tried to be too clever after Stalin's death and used 'Trust-style' tactics as much to increase their own power and influence as to help the cause.

The most disastrous attempt of this nature was that of Lavrenti Beria who paid for it by being arrested and executed in 1953. As head of the NKVD and chairman of the Ministry of Internal Affairs (MVD), Beria was in a powerful position and in his earlier days had sometimes posed as a moderate socialist intellectual opposed to the Soviet regime when he met White Russians and other anti-Soviet Europeans. That this ploy was to some extent successful was evident to me even in 1948 when, on a visit to Spain, I was told by a Spanish diplomat of the Franco regime: 'Beria is the man to do business with in Russia. He is a splendid fellow and actually on our side. Once Stalin has gone we may see big changes in our favour. He is an admirer of your Mountbatten.' Highly improbable as this seemed at the time, the recent disclosure by Lt.-General Nikolai Pavlenko that in October 1941, Beria negotiated with Hitler through a Bulgarian intermediary, makes the Spaniard's comment more understandable. The aim was for a peace deal.

But if Beria failed, there were others in the Soviet hierarchy who re-created what in effect was Trust Number Three once Stalin was dead. The aim was to carry on with the cold war quite ruthlessly while seeking friends and contacts in the non-Soviet world, with special emphasis on trade, industry and science. Already the Russians had acquired valuable allies in the USA among such people as Averill Harriman, who had been Ambassador to the the USSR from 1943 to 1946. Harriman not only had extensive business interests, but was Director of Foreign Aid under the Mutual Security Act from 1951 to 1953. As long ago as 1920 Harriman, through his business connections, had granted a loan to Lenin and in 1928 was the chief organiser of the engineering undertaking which put heavy Soviet industry on its feet. Two others who fitted in admirably with Trust Number Two were Harry Hopkins, one of the most powerful men in the White House under Roosevelt, and James Conant, who from 1941 to 1946 was chairman of the National Defence Research Committee charged with, among other things, the question of producing atomic weapons.

Yet probably the USSR's most valuable asset in terms of influence in the USA was and still is Dr Armand Hammer, the redoubtable chairman of Occidental Petroleum. The grandson of a Russian emigré to America, he brought off something of a minor coup in the field of pharmaceuticals in the early 1920s. Then in 1921, learning of the famine problem in post-revolutionary Russia, he went to that country and took over a field hospital which he bought from the American Government. Soon afterwards he met Lenin and organised the first trade deal between USSR and the USA. This largely involved the exchange of American wheat for Soviet furs, caviar and some other luxuries. As a result Hammer acquired the agency for 38 American firms and the right to open Russia's first pencil factory.

Ever since then Hammer has been a supremely important figure, not only in his world-wide oil interests, but in the joint construction of huge chemical fertiliser plants near the town of Kuybyshev on the Volga and the barter of American superphosphates for Soviet urea and potash in 1973. He also lent his support to the development of Siberian natural gas for shipment to the United States. In terms of extending relations between the USSR and the West the work and influence of Hammer run parallel. If those policies can be summed up in a single phrase they amount to what is now called 'One Worldism', the theory that countries can slowly be merged into a vague conglomerate. This has to some extent already been achieved, first through business and banking deals such as those initiated by Hammer and others, but also by infiltrating agents of the USSR into the EEC bureaucracy with the aim of winning backing in membership countries. This does not necessarily mean it is done through communist influence, but more usually through socialists in the EEC and, in some cases, Conservatives committed to the idea of European unity at any cost.

Though he never allowed himself to be dragged into political discussion, the One Worldism theme very much attracted Guy Liddell as well as Lord Mountbatten. Liddell has been described by members of his family as being in effect 'somewhat of a left-wing Tory',[6] but that in itself was just as useful a mask for his real feelings as was Kim Philby's pretence of being a liberal when in the Middle East as a newspaper correspondent after he left MI6.

Mountbatten tended to take somewhat of an anti-American viewpoint regarding the USSR in the post-war period, though this was to some extent disguised by his friendship with Armand Hammer, something which developed out of Mountbatten's interest in another form of 'All-Worldism', the development of the United World Colleges, aimed at bringing together young people from all over the world. This idea was conceived by Mountbatten, who persuaded Hammer to establish one such college in the USA. The tradition has been carried on by the Prince of Wales, who has been depicted in glowing terms in Hammer's autobiography: 'Whatever Prince Charles does, I am sure there is a purpose behind it. He has such an inquiring mind, he is so inquisitive. He is always seeking learning . . . Charles has found himself now. He is completely at home with himself and well prepared, if and when the moment arrives, to become King. I think he will make a very successful King, and one of the best and most popular Britain has ever had . . .'[7]

The Mountbatten influence on the Prince of Wales has frequently been commented on, and indeed as time has passed his influence on the whole of the Royal family has grown. What is particularly interesting is that as long ago as 1954-55 he was sending confidential messages from himself personally to the Soviet Defence chief indicating his fondness for Russia and the Russian people. The gist of one such message was that he regarded that his connections by birth with the family of the late Tsar gave him every reason to extend the goodwill he felt for the Russian people to those ruling the USSR at the present moment. That part of the message was relatively harmless, but Mountbatten went on to say that he had 'a highly critical opinion of current American foreign policies' and that in any showdown in the 'Cold War' in which the USA used aggressive tactics, 'I should be on the side of the USSR.' That such personal messages were passed secretly to the Soviet Ministry of Defence, presumably through diplomatic bags, was reluctantly confirmed to me by the late Captain Geoffrey Martin Bennett, who was naval attaché in Moscow, Warsaw and Helsinki after he was promoted to the rank of captain in 1953. He begged me to make no reference to the Mountbatten messages in his lifetime, but he confirmed what I had also been told from another naval source that no copies of this and other similar messages were allowed to be taken and that even carbon copies relating to the typewritten copies were destroyed. Original messages from Mountbatten while at the Admiralty were in green-ribbon typing and his signature was also in green ink, I was told. Certainly the correspondence in the Driberg Papers confirms this.

In addition to such high up leaks from the Navy, Hollis had further cause for exasperation over the question of immunity for Anthony Blunt. The task of interrogating Blunt had been given to minor figures in MI5 who were no match for Blunt's admittedly superb intellect. In short, there was still no real proof of guilt against Blunt and on 2 March 1964, Hollis saw Henry Brooke (Home Secretary) and told him what the situation was.

What of Guy Liddell during this period? He had left MI5 in the early 1950s, so how was it that Peter Wright, a technician in the service, apparently came to know him so well? Did they meet on occasions? For one of the most remarkable oddities of *Spycatcher* is the high regard which Wright goes out of his way to show for Liddell. He writes that after he read Liddell's office diary he decided 'the accusation against Guy Liddell was palpably absurd'. He claimed that Liddell's office diary was considered so secret that it was code-named 'Wallflowers'. Wright said he had listened to Liddell's taped historical memories of MI5 and thought him 'a tragic figure' who had been 'undone by unwise friendships'.[8]

But it is impossible to see Liddell as merely a victim. Following their interview, for example, Liddell set out to destroy Goronwy Rees and his character: I am repeatedly coming up against people who have listened to Liddell's diatribes against Goronwy and who say to me 'But Goronwy was mixed up in all this as a Soviet agent himself.' When one asks them for evidence it always turns out that this came either from Liddell or one of his pals. Similarly when the late Major Donald Darling suspected that Philby and Harris were part of a Soviet network of spies from information he had received during his wartime service in MI9, the escape organisation, he tried to infiltrate the movement to learn more. This ended in Darling being grilled by a Foreign Office man and later by Liddell himself who accused Darling of being 'a Red agent'. His life was also made a misery.

Liddell died suddenly at his home on 2 December 1958, at the age of 66. Obituaries were terse: even that in *The Times* said little more than that 'but for his war service 1914-18, which interrupted his 'cello studies in Germany, he might well have become an accomplished professional musician.' He had 'a clear mind, sound judgement and mastery of detail,' it added.   Sometimes the lists of mourners at funerals can be especially illuminating with regard rather to those who were not present than those who were. It is interesting to note that Sir Roger Hollis did not attend the funeral service for Liddell, though he was meticulous as a rule in attending all such services for former or present colleagues. Liddell's funeral service was held at St Michael's, Chester Square, in London, a perfectly convenient venue for Sir Roger Hollis, who lived nearby. He had been knighted in 1960.

Among those present at the funeral service were Sir Stewart Menzies, ex-chief of MI6; Anthony Blunt, Tomás Harris, Lord and Lady Rothschild, Dick Brooman-White, MP and Major Stephen Alley. Not only was Hollis absent, but so, too, was another former head of MI5, Sir Dick Goldsmith White.

Liddell was dead, but the Liddell story had not yet begun to emerge, and, in the smear campaign against Hollis, it continues to this day.

Perhaps one of the most percipient summaries of Liddell's life and career was that given to me by Andrew Gow, a former Fellow of Trinity: 'An inhibited person, Liddell tried not to be as conspicuous as other power-hungry people, assuming a wait-and-see attitude. He kept his love of power to himself. But by trying to achieve too much behind the scenes he always ran the risk of losing everything, which he very nearly did.'

In 1961 news came from the USA based on reports given to the CIA by Major Anatoli Golitsin, a senior KGB officer who defected to the Americans in December of that year. Not only did he point in the direction of Kim Philby as a Soviet agent, but he indicated that there were a number of others inside both MI5 and MI6. The emphasis was on MI5, and Golitsin's evidence in this respect tallied with that of Volkov just after the end of World War II, mentioned previously. This information was used by the witch-hunters inside MI5 to support a clamour for an investigation of the Director-General and his Deputy. This clamour was intensified by the revelations originating from VENONA cipher traffic decryption produced for MI5 by GCHQ. This traffic indicated the presence of more Soviet moles spread around the world, though in all cases exact identity was hidden by the use of code-names. But patient work enabled the analysts to pin-point at least five of the code-names and establish their real identities. In his book *Mole-Hunt* Nigel West states that 'Wright maintained that in 1956 [when the Soviets suddenly changed all their procedures, thus eliminating the source] Mitchell had recommended that MI5 stop investigating leads from VENONA. Apparently, "GCHQ said they didn't think they were getting anything from it and Mitchell said OK." ... In retrospect, it seemed odd that Mitchell should have been so keen to terminate such a productive source.'[9]

The answer to this may well be that a counter-espionage service can quite easily be swamped by such material as VENONA produced. There is no doubt that just as all Security and Intelligence Services know that vital messages can be deciphered by the opposition until changes in ciphers are made, so there is also scope for disinformation in the traffic passed. A situation could arise when a service such as MI5 allowed itself to become bemused by such traffic and neglected vital surveillance on its own territory as a result. Much of the VENONA material was more important to the counter-espionage section of MI6 than to MI5. That is the probable answer to Mitchell's suggestion that a halt be called.

Even when he was being questioned by MI5, Blunt was still totally in control of himself, confident that there was insufficient evidence for him to be prosecuted. Knowing that it was only through the persistence of Goronwy Rees that MI5 had originally come to have doubts about him, Blunt, when questioned, hit back by alleging that Rees was a Soviet agent. This allegation was, of course, a constant theme from then on of Rees's detractors. In fact Rees, as we have seen, was the man who not only indicated Burgess in the very beginning, but later pointed to Blunt and others in what is rather less known as the 'Oxonian Connection'.

Once again denials by those questioned made it impossible to bring prosecutions. Nevertheless, Robert Zaehner (one of the names Rees submitted) was eventually proved to be a Soviet agent and there was some concern when it was discovered that he was working for MI6 under diplomatic cover as acting Counsellor in the British Embassy in Teheran. Zaehner had actually been recruited by the Cambridge Soviet network and then organised his own cell at Oxford where he had been Senior Scholar at Christ Church.

Mole-hunting within its own ranks had become a mania within MI5 and it would seem that discipline as well as morale was affected. Two leaders of this witch-hunt were Peter Wright and Arthur Martin, both of whom took the view that neither Hollis nor Mitchell was paying sufficient attention to Soviet infiltration of the service. They sought support for their views outside the service and inside MI6. Unfortunately and almost outrageously, such support they managed to get. As a result the witch-hunters were told to tackle Hollis personally and to suggest to him that his Deputy, Mitchell, was a Soviet spy.

Hollis decided to hold an informal conference on the subject away from the offices of MI5, choosing his home in Campden Hill Square. Present at that meeting were Arthur Martin and Martin Furnival

Jones, a senior member of MI5. As a result of this a discreet investigation of Mitchell was carried out under the code-name of PETERS. Peter Wright was one of the investigating team. He had joined MI5 as a technician from Marconi and his work in this field had been so impressive that he had been offered the post of scientific adviser.

Nobody has yet come up with any impressive evidence against Mitchell. There is the somewhat vague suggestion that he 'lived on the edge of Chobham Common and usually caught the same train each evening from Waterloo, but he often took elaborate precautions to prevent anyone tailing him to the railway station'.[10] Didn't someone have the sense to guess that Mitchell had rumbled what was going on by this time and that he intended to fool his shadowers if only as a matter of revenge? After all he must have had some hints that he was being investigated. A special closed-circuit camera was rigged behind a two-way mirror over his office door to monitor him while he was at work. On one occasion he was overheard to say out loud 'Why are you doing this to me?'

Mitchell was alleged to have given clearance to Pontecorvo many years earlier; another complaint against him was, as I have mentioned, that he played postal chess with the Russians, the implication being that this was used for passing on messages! Once people start on an undisciplined witch-hunt, anything goes.

It should be stressed that at this time, while some had doubts about Hollis, Graham Mitchell was the chief suspect. It was after Hollis had been told that the Director-General himself called the meeting at his own home. Without doubt he had already guessed that he was one of the suspects, and for this reason he insisted that if Mitchell was to be investigated he should also be included in any probe. He gave permission for a full inquiry to be conducted and allowed the seven-man committee, code-named FLUENCY, to investigate both himself and his deputy. The results were confusing and inconclusive: in short there was no worthwhile evidence against either man, only a mish-mash of theories. As an example of the latter it was alleged that Mitchell was drinking heavily and gave all the appearance of being under great stress. If so, this could easily and more sensibly be attributed not to fear of being unmasked, but the strain of knowing he was under suspicion while at the same time in poor health. Mitchell retired in 1963, having been awarded the CBE in 1957 and died in 1984.

Though there are still some who suspect Mitchell of being a Soviet agent (as indeed is also the case with Hollis), he has been cleared in further independent investigations and in 1987 the Prime Minister, Mrs Thatcher told MPs 'the conclusion reached at the end of that investigation was that he had not been an agent of the Russian intelligence services.'[11] Even Chapman Pincher, who first directed attention to Hollis as top mole in MI5, has described the allegations against Mitchell as 'grotesque'.[12]

This was all a sad and cruel end to Mitchell's life, even though he was told he had been completely cleared before he died. One of the claims made by Peter Wright against Mitchell was that when the waste-bin at his home was examined they found a hand-drawn map of Chobham Common nearby, marked 'RV'. Wright's suspicious mind suggested that this might suggest a rendezvous with a KGB officer, or even a DLB. When confronted with this information, Mitchell said he regularly drew maps for weekend walks with his grandchildren on Chobham Common.

The Never-ending 'Trust'

Glasnost means publicity rather than openness ... *Glasnost* is important not only as a means of re-assessing the authority and prestige of the CPSU and its leadership, but as a propaganda tool to fool the West by creating a new image of the USSR. *Glasnost* and 'democratisation' can be represented as a departure from Marxism-Leninism, whereas it is a term and a concept which was given currency by Lenin himself in 1918.

(Dr Françoise Thom, a French Sovietologist)[1]

The above quotation may seem somewhat purely philosophical and not directly concerned with the subject of this book. In fact it points to a host of practical problems, many of which are being ignored even in Intelligence circles. It is also a commentary on the USSR's clever development of the never-ending 'Trust' and its subtle exploitation of 'One Worldism'. Just as in Trust Number Two the Curiel network, named after Henri Curiel, the founder of the Egyptian Communist Party, was initially developed as a joint asset of the Nazis and the Comintern, so Trust Number Three is quietly but effectively manoeuvring behind the idea of a 'United States of Europe'. Behind the debate on the 'European Domestic Market, 1992' and plans for European integration lies an attempt gradually to impose a dominant Soviet interest not only in Eastern Europe, but Western Europe, too.

Hollis retired in 1965, and this must have been a great relief for him after the tensions of the past few years. Quite apart from the convictions resulting from MI5 operations, MI5's watch on British communists had been so rigorous that Gordon McLennan, a top CPGB official, in 1982 demanded an inquiry into what he termed as 'the infiltration of my party by MI5'.[2]

Refusing offers of various jobs in and out of Whitehall, Hollis settled in Wells for a while with his first wife, and regularly attended Sunday morning services at Wells Cathedral where he became a Governor of Wells Cathedral School. According to his housekeeper, 'they lived quite frugally there. No champagne or caviar.'

This was but a brief interlude in his retirement. In 1968 there was a divorce and Hollis married his secretary, Miss Valentine Hammond. They went to live in the village of Catcott, near Bridgewater. Here he soon became quite a popular and respected figure. Within a year he had been elected to the Bridgewater Rural District Council as an Independent, unopposed, where he was appointed to the Plans Committee. He was also a governor of some local schools. He continued to play golf and was an energetic captain of the local club, the Burnham and Berrow Golf Club. Said one club member: 'He was very good company and quite an exceptionally good golfer. He played off a handicap of four and I recall that when the club played away in county competitions, he insisted that we learned all about the characteristics and peculiarities of any opposition side we had to face.'

Sir Roger had one son by his first marriage, Adrian, a Fellow of Keble College, Oxford, a classical scholar and a national grade chess player. This latter pursuit brought him in touch with Graham Mitchell who also took a keen interest in his progress, even though Mitchell had long since given up correspondence chess. Sir Roger was delighted with his son's progress and all seemed set for a happy retirement until the 'Young Turks' (as the witch-hunters of MI5 came to be known) started making mischief again. This now came from a former MI5 man who had switched to MI6 after incurring Sir Roger's displeasure at his tactics, but it was supported by others inside MI5. A further inquiry into the theory that he was a Soviet mole was demanded and it resulted in Hollis being called from his home in Catcott to face accusers in a house in Mayfair, with Peter Wright listening secretly through earphones next door. This squalid and very nearly ridiculous affair lasted for two days in 1970.

It may well be asked at this stage whether there was something in Hollis's make-up or personality which caused him to have enemies. There is no obvious answer to this. Perhaps he was one of those with whom subordinates found it difficult to establish a rapport, but the answer to this is that he had slowly disciplined himself to change from a rather hearty and somewhat dissolute undergraduate to Chief of MI5 in the Cold War period: in short, he had cultivated reserve. Almost from the beginning of his term of office as Director-General he had had to cope with tensions in his work, the suspicions of colleagues and to some extent tensions of his first marriage. In some ways he was a man of great paradoxes. Never an intellectual, he nevertheless possessed a shrewd and quick mind. He could be stiff and formal in the office, occasionally ill at ease in a group of people and he found it hard to relate to his junior staff. Yet he got on extremely well when he travelled on official business, enjoying good relations with his transatlantic colleagues, especially the always difficult Edgar Hoover, but equally with security people in Australia, Africa and Canada. Behind all this was the fact that Sir Roger was trapped in an unhappy marriage – a man of honour who felt bound to resign as a school governor on announcing his divorce.

It would appear that it was partly as a result of the further inquiry concerning Hollis that Wright somewhat moderated his previously harsh attitude towards Hollis. By this time his view was that he found Hollis's testimony entirely satisfactory except for 'the two missing years' from 1936 to 1938, which was a period in which Hollis was ill and awaiting a new post.

The final episode in the persecution of Hollis must have taken its toll health-wise. At the beginning of 1973 he had a stroke and nine months later he died, six weeks short of his sixty-eighth birthday. Even then the 'Young Turks' insisted on continuing with their investigations against both him and Mitchell. In 1974 Sir Burke Trend, a former Cabinet Secretary, conducted an independent inquiry and could still find no evidence against Hollis. It was after this that Stephen de Mowbray, a former MI6 liaison officer in Washington, approached the Prime Minister with details of the case. In 1980 Chapman Pincher as a result of information given him by Lord Rothschild (a wartime member of MI5 and a friend of both Burgess and Liddell as will be recalled) and an introduction by the latter to Peter Wright, produced his book, *Their Trade is Treachery*, which suggested that Hollis was a Soviet mole.[3] Despite a statement by Mrs Thatcher that same year that 'Hollis was not an agent of the Russian intelligence service', the allegations continued both against Hollis and Mitchell, the latter being named as the probable top mole by Nigel West in his book, *Mole Hunt*.[4]

In the end there was some climbing down by some of the witch-hunters. Even Arthur Martin went on record as saying that 'my recollection is that, while Hollis fitted the circumstantial evidence more closely than any other candidate, the case against him was not conclusive . . .' Support for Hollis came from such informed commentators as Sir Patrick Reilly, Lord Sherfield and Lord Trend. There was also a letter to *The Times* on 21 October 1981, from Sir Martin Furnival Jones and Anthony Simkins, two senior members of MI5, which read:

Up to the time we retired there was not a shred of evidence that

Sir Roger Hollis had been disloyal at any time, or in any way, let alone evidence that he had been a spy. Moreover, throughout his career his positive contribution to security was outstandingly valuable and his wartime record makes ludicrous any suggestion that he might have been sympathetic to the USSR.

That kind of evidence can, of course, be dismissed as a typical example of the British Establishment closing ranks and defending itself. As we have seen, there were similar defences put up by Establishment figures for Guy Liddell. What I find more impressive is the response of Oleg Gordievsky, the former KGB head of station in London, who defected in September 1985, when he was asked if Hollis had been a long-term penetration agent. His reply was unequivocal: 'Of course not. But when the KGB saw the chaos caused by the allegations against Hollis, their laughter made Red Square shake.'

Furthermore Mr Daniel J. Mulvenna, a leading member of CASIS (the Canadian Association of Security & Intelligence Studies), who has made a deep study of these matters, writes: 'I agree with you totally on the Hollis allegations. Furthermore, I have proof that Hollis was not a Soviet agent: this is wrapped up in the DEW WORM – LONG KNIFE affair. It has never been published.'[5]

It is not possible to go further into these coded operations at the moment, as they do not appear to have been recorded on file in Canada, at least not officially. It can, however, be explained that DEW WORM was an electronic penetration operation mounted against the Soviet Embassy in Canada round about 1953-6. Hollis, Mitchell and Liddell knew about this operation.

This Canadian operation and others linked to it were known to the British under the code-name KEYSTONE. The RCMP had a double agent who had infiltrated KGB networks in both Canada and the USA, but had disappeared when he went back to Moscow in 1955. It has been suggested that he was betrayed to the Russians by a 'well-placed traitor' and there are even hints that this could have been from someone inside MI5, but again nobody has come forward with any proof of this.

I have mentioned earlier in this book how Colonel Mikhail Goleniewski, that most remarkable of all defectors to the Western World, regarded me as being used as a tool of the KGB. This was on account of my taking the view some years ago that he was himself a purveyor of Soviet disinformation. I was wrong then and Goleniewski was right. I am happy to make amends, especially as there is massive evidence to confirm that the information he brought with him to the West has long since been confirmed one hundred per cent. Regardless of his claim to being the son of Tsar Nicholas of Russia (for which there can be many explanations if one analyses his particular case), his testimony on events is astonishingly accurate. Even he cleared Hollis. Edward J. Epstein, a specialist American writer on intelligence matters, refers to a meeting with Goleniewski in Harry's Bar in New York in 1981. 'I ended our lunch by asking Romanoff [Goleniewski] about Hollis, who had been head of MI5 at the time of his defection. Did he think that Hollis might have been a KGB mole? "I don't think it would have been very probable," he said. He then ticked off very precisely all the Soviet agents whom MI5 had captured due to the information he had personally provided. "If the KGB had a mole at the head of MI5 then, you can be sure all these men would have escaped." He suggested that the report that Hollis was a mole was more likely to have been a piece of disinformation circulated by the KGB in order to discredit British Intelligence.'

Yet even as late as 1987 there was alleged to be damning evidence against Hollis unearthed in the USA, this time the suggestion being that Hollis helped:

> dozens of Communist spies infiltrate the British and American intelligence networks immediately after World War II . . . by providing false or misleading background dossiers on Nazis recruited from eastern European countries by the British Secret Service. These men, many of whom were passed on to America, were recruited to set up an underground force to fight communism in their homelands. But a number turned out to be Communist double agents.[6]

This allegation came from a former US Justice Department investigator, John Loftus, who gave evidence to a US Congressional Committee investigating Nazi war criminals in the USA. Loftus alleged that 'each of the British liaison officers for post-war Nazi operations has now been identified as a Communist double-agent' and he named Hollis as one of these officers.[7] No doubt some double-agents slipped through in those days when so many were trying to escape to the West at all costs: it would be surprising if this had not happened. Loftus' claim seems to be out of all proportion to realities, and in any case it would be a matter in which Hollis would only be marginally concerned, especially if such people were being vetted in West Germany for passage to the USA. Nevertheless it is only proper to record such evidence for what it is worth, while at the same time stressing that majority opinion now is that the allegations against both Hollis and Mitchell were largely based on Soviet disinformation. This is a view which was certainly accepted inside the CIA during the period in which William Colby was chief and, as far as one can gather, afterwards, too.

Grahame Greene, who served in MI6 in Africa during World War II, in response to a letter from me, wrote 'my own impression, which has no value, is that he [Hollis] has been the victim of a disinformation campaign from the East.'[8] Here, I cannot help thinking, is a rather more important and dispassionate viewpoint, as Greene is a former communist and, though a Roman Catholic, still somewhat sympathetic to the USSR and corresponded with Philby until the latter's death.

Indeed, the weight of evidence points towards a campaign of disinformation to protect the real culprits – a campaign waged almost equally by the USSR and the British Establishment.

Why should the ultra-suspicious Peter Wright have been so adamant that allegations against Liddell were absurd – unless he had been urged to accept such a premise? He had already known about Liddell's undesirable friendships when he was so ill-advisedly promoted within MI5 in 1953. When the allegations against Hollis were made, Oldfield, then head of MI6, was convinced that this was a Soviet-inspired plot and smear to detract attention from the real villain in MI5. He took the view that, alive or dead, the Fluency Committee should have examined the question of Liddell as well. This view he repeated in measured terms to reliable American Intelligence sources. He also made his views known about the MI5 witch-hunt both to members of that service and some within his own. This made Oldfield unpopular with the witch-hunters, who responded by trying to smear him.

Disinformation at this time was not coming solely from cleverly placed bogus defectors from the USSR, but also from some of the former British members of MI5 and MI6 who were trying to divert attention from their own actions or those of some of their colleagues. Thus Philby was busily trying to defend Blunt and trying to clear him of any Soviet allegiance when he had his last interview with an MI6 interrogator in Beirut. At the same time Philby is reported to have suggested that one of his oldest friends from schooldays at Westminster onwards, Ian Innes Milne, had been a fellow-conspirator in the Soviet espionage network. This was, of course, an outrageous and untrue statement and it took MI6 very little time to dismiss the allegation as totally baseless.

A few years ago, obviously as a result of reading some of my earlier books, an anonymous communication mainly in Russian was posted to me from Hamburg. No address was given and there was no clue as to the identity of the writer. However, it seemed as though my mysterious correspondent wished to impress upon me that he had access to inside information on Russia as he included a detailed transcript of all that was said at a secret meeting of the Soviet Praesidium conducted by Brezhnev. The vital part of this letter was that Liddell had been an informant to the Soviet Union since the late 1920s and that he was the man whose code-name was 'Elli':

> Usually when someone is very important such code-names are changed every few years. This was not done for Liddell because we simply used the same code-name for other people. Later on we were hugely amused to note that the letters 'ELLI' could be found in the names of both George Mitchell, Charles Ellis [another MI6 officer accused of being a Soviet agent] and Kathleen Willsher. This has caused a great deal of confusion. Liddell was very much a GRU man and therefore better protected than other agents. He was in many respects far more valuable than the agents inside British services who followed him, but his belief that in the long-term the Soviet Union would guarantee the peace of the world was pathetic.

I am fully aware that this could have been planting of disinformation by the USSR. There have been some instances where such blatant use has been made of *samizdats* that the reason behind them is obvious. If there is a dissident writer in Russia who, though claiming to be a good communist, is critical of the regime, a member of the KGB will concoct a manuscript, partly genuine, written by the man in question, but into which is interpolated in skilfully imitated handwriting violent attacks on the Soviet Government and communism as a creed. This will be smuggled out of Russia to an intermediary who poses as a friend of the writer and promptly sends it to a Western newspaper or magazine, or even passes it on to some Western writer. When it is published, the KGB use this as an excuse to arrest the writer of the original on charges of treason. In view of this I had the correspondence I received checked and analysed by a graphologist. I had a lengthy reply, the gist of which was that 'there is a strong probability that the two documents show the normal handwriting of the same person'.

Liddell could not have escaped detection without the British Establishment's habit of closing ranks and pretending to have noticed nothing unusual whenever one of their members is either caught out, or suspected. It is a disastrous trait which, alas, is still perpetuated in all walks of life, leading to unnecessary covering up of the truth. It is true that Americans tend to go to the other extreme: not only to fight out every such issue in public, but even to express their suspicions about some person in public life before he has been caught out, and sometimes, of course, when he has not even done anything wrong. Occasionally a good man may be lost in this way, but on the whole it is so useful a fault that it can be a real asset. James Jesus Angleton, former director of the CIA, certainly spotted the defects and signs of unreliability in both Philby and Liddell long before Philby was finally unmasked and even in Liddell's hey-day.

Angleton, even before he joined the CIA, was perplexed at the 'diligent interest' Liddell took in affairs which were not in his province:

> His whole handling of the Tyler Kent case puzzled me. I was also surprised when studying various documents later on at his quite intense interest in the Sidney Reilly case when he was in the Special Branch at Scotland Yard. This was hardly a matter for Liddell, unless he had some other interest in Reilly of his own account. Altogether he increasingly became a suspect, and, when I say this, I am not merely relying on the testimony of Anatoli Golitsin as so many people in Britain seem to think.[9]

Though Liddell remained throughout his life very much an Establishment figure to most of his colleagues, they should have heeded the damaging friendships which he cultivated among both the homosexual Mafia and the subversives. Had he been in the FBI or the CIA such associations would have caused him to be removed from office long before his ultimate delicately covered up dismissal. In support of the Soviet Union Liddell adopted what can best be called aristocratic machiavellianism – the traditional mode of conduct of the class of courtiers to which he belonged. He revelled in the secrecy of it all and the knowledge that this chicanery gave him a power and influence which extended far beyond these shores. Whatever help he gave to the Soviet cause was cautiously done without allowing himself to be linked directly to any USSR network, though it would seem that he had indirect links with the GRU. Probably Baroness Budberg and Baykalov were his chief intermediaries.

Sometimes the people who seem to love flirting with treachery, or even simply delight in intrigue, either switch sides or play along with both. By doing so they occasionally become heroes. One such manipulator was Mountbatten. There is no doubt that at one time, despite his then cleverly disguised left-wing views, he toyed with the idea of some kind of a deal with Germany, using all his contacts in that country and his friendly relationship with the Duke of Windsor to pursue that aim. As soon as he found the Duke no longer an asset in this aim he quite ruthlessly isolated himself from him. One of his undercover contacts was undoubtedly Guy Liddell of whom he had known from his earliest years through court circles. It was, according to Peter Murphy, Peter Churchill and others, Liddell who provided him with an information link with the Countess (sometimes called Princess) Carlos de Rohan, more generally known to her friends as 'Dill', who had her own private intelligence network which extended to Germany, France, Austria, Spain and Morocco. Not only was she an authority on Germany but on the Ukraine as well and especially on secret plans then being launched to obtain independence for that satellite of the U.S.S.R. This was the woman with close friends in high places in Germany who was surprisingly nominated by Brendan Bracken to take over the Swiss desk at the Ministry of Information in World War II. At the same time Mountbatten was putting out inquiries to contacts inside the Soviet Union, including some Russian naval officers, whom he had met informally during service in the Royal Navy and also through his close friend the Marxist, J. D. Bernal, who introduced him to a dining club called the Tots and Quots which functioned during the war. Bernal was unfortunately employed by Mountbatten as scientific adviser to Combined Operations. Bernal was considered sufficient of a security risk that he was actually excluded from the war room for sometime before D-Day and precise plans and date for the invasion of France were kept from him. Through such contacts Mountbatten acquired rather more knowledge this way than many politicians and diplomats. It should be remembered that it was Mountbatten who insisted that the USSR would hold out against Germany and eventually defeat that nation in 1941 when Churchill and most of his advisers were taking the opposite view. By then Mountbatten had abandoned his ideas of a negotiated settlement with Germany and not only cut off his contacts there, but even abandoned his friend, the Duke of Windsor.

From that moment onwards one had the picture of Mountbatten the naval hero, sometimes, one suspects, sacrificing a ship in the cause of sheer bravado and love of publicity. Certainly the late Admiral of the Fleet Andrew B Cunningham regarded him as a 'Mediterranean play-boy with extravagant ideas'. His active service record consisted of little more than having his ship HMS *Kelly* sunk in the Mediterranean – a disaster which was turned into an epic by skilful propaganda. Leslie Gardiner, author of a history of the Admiralty, recalls a sailor observing while the Kelly was off Crete: 'If Lord Louis persists in manoeuvring a new ship at maximum revolutions under full helm in that panic-stricken fashion, she won't be afloat much longer.' The late Vice-Admiral Sir Geoffrey Robson testified to his alarm at what he thought was Mountbatten's rash behaviour in flashing long and unnecessary signals with a bright light off an enemy coastline.[10]

A member of the HMS *Kelly* Survivors' Association, formed after the war, gave some indication of the arrogance of Mountbatten when he recalled his captain's comment in an address to the crew: 'Every man in this ship is important, but some are more important than others.'[11] Similarly later on when he was sent to Burma he told the troops: 'You are not the forgotten army . . . no one has ever heard of you. They've heard of *me* at home, so now *I'm* with you, they'll have heard of you.'

Admiral of the Fleet Sir Caspar John always blamed Mountbatten for the running down of the Naval Intelligence Division, at one time the most powerful of all British Intelligence services and the equal of, if not superior to, MI6. Not only did it collect vital naval intelligence, but a wealth of commercial intelligence, too, which, if properly used could have more than justified the cost of retaining a powerful NID by the financial gains it could have created for the nation.

The question was the integration of the intelligence services of all the Armed Forces. Whereas in the USA both the CIA and the FBI had their say on similar integration proposals before they were implemented, in Britain neither the SIS, nor MI5, seems to have been consulted. Worse still, during the period preceding integration, the NID was allowed to run itself down. Caspar John was very wary when taking up his appointment as Vice Chief of Naval Staff, doubting whether Mountbatten as First Sea Lord was the right man for him to serve under. 'He deplored the flamboyance, the self-promotion, above all the deviousness of the First Sea Lord,' wrote John's daughter . . . 'Mountbatten was known as "Tricky Dicky" throughout Whitehall.'[12]

There have been at least three people who have claimed to be children of the last Tsar of All the Russias, despite the reports (still queried by some historians) that the whole of the Russian Imperial family were assassinated at Ekaterinburg. Mountbatten personally disputed the claims of two, yet as far as can be ascertained he never raised any query concerning Colonel Mikhail Goleniewski, which seems somewhat inconsistent since as a youth he knew the Tsarevich intimately. As to whether his silence on Goleniewski's claim was due to fear of what the latter might reveal can only be conjecture. One can only say that this silence did not stop Goleniewski from giving information not only privately to American Intelligence sources, but in his news-letter, *Double Eagle*, about the admiral. In the December, 1979 issue of this news-letter, after Mountbatten's death, he wrote of 'Red spies being now deprived of such a powerful protector, began to run in panic, and a mixture of disinformation books and of manipulated news media is an expression of the many attempts to cover up the real terrifying status of Communist espionage in Great Britain.' He referred to Mountbatten's friendship with Blunt and what he called 'the Soviet Agents Club at Buckingham Palace.' It is not without some significance that it was only a few months after Mountbatten's death that Blunt was officially declared to have been a Soviet agent.

In this same issue of *Double Eagle* Goleniewski told how intelligence had come from 'a member of Imperial Underground of Tartarian nationality who under Chinese cover-identity infiltrated the Red Chinese Intelligence for more than twenty years. For reason of his age he was compelled to leave his underground position in Red China and to retire to another non-Communist country [in Asia].' As a result of his information about Chinese infiltration of the Soviet Army, it was learned that some high-ranking officers of the USSR had been recruited as agents for the Chinese. 'Consequently,' wrote Goleniewski, 'one of the leading members of the Imperial Underground in Western Europe, elaborated a plan to use this information in other ways and to make a test if Lord Mountbatten was involved in cooperation with the Soviets or not. .... this information was brought to the attention of Lord Mountbatten through one of his close contacts, and in a way concealing the real task of this operation.'

The object, Goleniewski asserted, was to find out whether Mountbatten would pass on this intelligence of Chinese infiltration of the Red Army to the Soviets. If he did this, it was calculated that the USSR would take immediate action. Shortly afterwards it was reported that a number of Soviet senior officers had mysteriously died or disappeared. Four of these generals had been mentioned in the information about Chinese infiltration of the Red Army which Mountbatten had received in conditions of complete confidentiality two months before. Goleniewski named one of these officers as General Nicolai A. Silayev.

Defenders of Mountbatten may dismiss Goleniewski's allegations as disinformation or imaginative nonsense. But it is foolish to dismiss what he says so lightly in view of the fact that his intelligence led to the uncovering of Philby, Blake, Heinz Felfe, the West German traitor, Colonel Israel Beer of Israel, Stig Wennerstrom, the Swedish air attaché in Washington and many other spies in Britain, the USA and other parts of Europe. What is more it is clear from various records that British Intelligence not only took heed of his information in many instances, but actually sought him out. Since much of his evidence affected British security the CIA sent an experienced counter-espionage officer to London at the end of 1959 to brief his British counterparts. This was a year before Goleniewski crossed over into West Berlin and revealed himself personally to the Americans.

Goleniewski commented in his December, 1979 news-letter that 'it was surprising that ten years later in March, 1973, when this Editor [i.e. himself] did not have any contacts with CIA, he had been called up by the chief of British Security in Washington D.C., who, making reference to an approval by competent US authorities, urgently asked this Editor for renewed consultantions in "old matters" because some progress had been reached in investigations of "important cases". After a verification of the US Governmental approval through FBI in New York City, a series of confidential meetings took place in New York with an assistant to the Director of British Security Service, Christopher H, who arrived from London, a few times between April 2, 1973 and May 6, 1975. Among the consultations the key affair was the matter of the Soviet agent penetrating the British MI5.

'Later one of the well informed special agents of the FBI in New York City told this Editor ". . . your information and expertise were excellent. . . . The British have verified this in process of their investigations and they found a candidate to be this KGB agent. I just have doubt if they would ever arrest an aristocrat with some touch to Buckingham Palace."

It looks as though the British were still keeping in touch with Goleniewski at this actual time as the photograph of a letter to him reproduced in this book reveals. The letter was addressed not to Goleniewski, incidentally, but to 'Alexei Nicholaevich Romanoff' and it begins 'Dear Mr Romanoff, I have just heard that you have kindly agreed to meet me on my forthcoming visit to the USA. I am delighted that you are able to spare the time and I look forward to meeting you at 11 a.m. on Tuesday, 6 May, at the UK Consulate General in New York. On arrival would you please let the reception desk know so that I can be informed.' It is signed 'C. Ho.'

Greville Wynne, the self-confessed British spy who was caught by the Russians cooperating with Oleg Penkovsky in the passing of top Soviet secrets to Britain, has told of a meeting between Penkovsky and Mountbatten at an MI6 'safe house' in Coleherne Court, Chelsea, in 1961. Penkovsky, who was at that time in charge of a Russian trade delegation visiting London, had spent nightly sessions telling his secrets to MI6 officers. Then, apparently fearing a trap, according to Wynne, he demanded to meet the Queen and the Chiefs of Staff. The Queen, of course, did not meet Penkovsky, but Mountbatten as Chief of Defence Staff at the time went along to reassure the Russian. When told of this James Angleton made the somewhat abstruse comment that 'we could have done without that news'! Penkovsky, eventually caught by the Russians, was sentenced to death by a Moscow court in 1964. Wynne was sentenced to eight years' imprisonment, but was eventually exchanged for the Soviet spy, Konon Molody.[13]

This was yet another example of Mountbatten's penchant for managing to be on the inside of all manner of affairs from politics to intelligence. Sometimes this would even lead to his fantasising about actual events with a view to building up his own self-importance. A typical example of this, as well as of his own hypocrisy, was when he refused to attend the Buckingham Palace banquet for the late Japanese Emperor Hirohito in 1971. Mountbatten had always ostentatiously shown a hatred of the Japanese, yet having 'won some easy acclaim by failing to support the Queen at the banquet, he slipped into Buckingham Palace to see the Emperor the next morning – holding out a begging bowl for his pet venture, World United Colleges.'[14]

One of the most puzzling of Mountbatten's 'fantasy' stories is that concerning the disappearance of Commander Lionel Crabb in 1956 on a mission involving three Russian warships in Portsmouth harbour during the official visit of Khrushchev and Bulganin. The generally accepted story is that Crabb, an accomplished and highly experienced naval diver, was given by MI6 the mission of conducting a secret underwater examination of the Soviet cruiser *Ordzhonikidze*. During this he was detected by the Russians and killed. To substantiate this story some 14 months later the decomposed body of a man in a black diving suit, headless and handless, was conveniently found on a sandbank in Chichester harbour. At the subsequent inquest the body was identified as that of Crabb, yet one witness insisted privately that this could not possibly be true, as Crabb had hammer toes while the corpse did not.

Long afterwards a photocopy of a remarkable letter said to have been written by Mountbatten was discreetly circulated in certain circles. He was First Sea Lord at the time of Crabb's disappearance. The letter gave permission for the truth about Crabb to be told many years later. Mrs Patricia Rose, Crabb's fiancée, was convinced that the body washed up off Chichester was not that of her fiancé. She had a lengthy correspondence with me during her lifetime and she gave me a good deal of information on the whole mysterious episode with per-mission to quote.[15]

On one point, however, she was adamant: that I would not quote her on the Mountbatten story in her lifetime. As she is no longer alive I feel free now to set the record straight. Certainly the story has all the ele-ments of fantasy. Briefly, it is that Crabb was not spying on the Russians, but taking part in a security operation to protect Khrushchev and Bulganin against possible sabotage by the Americans! When he made his search under the Soviet ships he discovered American-produced limpet mines attached to them. Crabb is supposed to have killed himself while trying to remove the mines, death being due to the failure of his equipment.

Did Mountbatten encourage such a story to be discreetly circulated for some devious reason of his own, or has it an element of truth? A similar but slightly different account of the Crabb disappearance was given to Derek Jameson in 1986. He wrote about being shown 'a letter from Earl Mountbatten, marked Most Secret, which gives permission' for the story to be told one day. This story was identical with that given to me by Mrs Rose except for this statement: 'And those mines? It was all part of a plot by hardline elements in the KGB to get rid of the all-powerful Khrushchev . . . The whole thing was covered up by Mount-batten, acting on Eden's orders. [Sir Anthony Eden, as he then was, Prime Minister at the time, was said to have been furious about the leakage of the Crabb story during the Soviet mission to the UK.][16]

One could never be sure with Mountbatten whether his occasional indiscretions such as the above were deliberate or otherwise. The ex-Attorney-General, Lord Rawlinson, has told how the Admiral poured out State secrets on a train as fellow passengers listened in astonish-ment. He was on a trip to Cambridge with Lord Rawlinson when two women barged into their reserved compartment. 'Their unexpected intrusion disturbed the flow of the Admiral of the Fleet not a whit,' stated Lord Rawlinson in his memoirs, *A Price Too High*. 'The secrets, the weaponry, the statistics, the reflections on strategy, the criticisms of allies and the shortcomings of Ministers all poured out uninterrupted.' The Attorney-General left the train praying that the females were not spies.

It was a combination of vanity, egoism and a compulsive urge always to get his own way, regardless of others, which caused Mountbatten to become an agent of influence often in favour of the Soviet Union. The more he got his own way the more demanding he became. No doubt he also felt that whatever he did was also in the best interests of his country. Two examples of some of these characteristics of his will suffice. His correspondence with Driberg shows that not only did he ask Driberg of all people to show Prince Phillip round the Houses of Parliament, but actually begged Driberg to put it around among Labour MPs that the Prince was 'really on their side'! Mr Trevor Artingstoll, of Haverfordwest, has recorded that when Mountbatten was head of SEAC the gates of a level-crossing were closed in readiness for the Kandy Express. At this moment Mountbatten's chauffeur-driven car arrived at the crossing: 'Mountbatten sent his driver to order the gates to be opened. Since this was strictly contrary to regulations for perfectly obvious reasons, the signalman refused. Mountbatten bounced from his car, ran up the steps and assaulted the signalman by winding his arms about him and ordered his driver to open the gates of the crossing. After driving the car through, the driver returned and closed the gates, but not quickly enough to prevent the Kandy express ripping chunks off the partly closed gates as it tore past. Releasing the shaken signalman, the Commander SEAC, entered his car again and was driven off.'

Regarding his general attitude to the Soviet Union, initially in the late 1940s Mountbatten appeared to be in favour of the nuclear deterrent, but in retirement he gradually changed his views on this and disarmament (especially nuclear disarmament) became his policy. In this he seems to some extent to have been influenced by Lord Zuckermann and after the Cuban missiles crisis and a visit to President Kennedy he began to take a more openly pro-Soviet line. He clamoured for a naval goodwill mission to be sent to Russia and when Kosygin invited him to the thirtieth anniversary of the defeat of the Germans, Mountbatten accepted promptly with enthusiasm. In the last year of his life in a speech to the Stockholm International Peace Research Institute he referred to his sadness at the lack of achievement in disarmament, saying of the old adage that 'if you desire peace, prepare for war' was 'absolute nuclear nonsense'.

In fact, towards the end of his life Mountbatten was urging a joint

American-European-Soviet foundation for planning a nuclear-free world. This was an idea developed by Armand Hammer who helped to finance to the tune of a million dollars the International Foundation for the Survival and Development of Humanity, which was proposed by Soviet and American scientists at an international forum for a nuclear-free world and human survival held in Moscow in February 1987. Mountbatten shared Hammer's and others' views on 'One Worldism', convinced that the Soviet Union must play a major part in this.

So much did this become an obsession with him in the late 1970s that he even considered openly declaring his support for the USSR, even to the extent of revealing to the world that he had been quietly working on their side for some years. My evidence for his having considered making such a confession comes from the testimony of the homosexual mafia including some young naval officers with whom he consorted in his later years in Kinnerton Street, Belgravia. News of such indiscreet talk eventually reached the KGB who, far from welcoming such news, felt that it could rebound against them, especially as Mountbatten had made a strong point of wishing to condemn the USA for causing the 'Cold War'. From the advent of President Carter onwards the Soviet view was that such talk should be curbed and that America must be wooed rather than attacked. It was not forgotten that Mountbatten had told the Russians many years earlier that he regarded Ernest Bevin, the Labour Foreign Secretary at the beginning of the 'Cold War' as 'not a socialist, but a Reactionary Tory of the worst kind.' Peter Murphy, who testified this, added that it was a view shared by Lady Mountbatten as well.

Certainly Mountbatten behaved as though he had no fear of being blackmailed on account of his indiscreet behaviour. His modest residence at No. 2 Kinnerton Street, which he described in a letter to Driberg when inviting him there as being formerly 'the old garage of our house at 2 Wilton Crescent', was the scene of what can only be described as nocturnal orgies. Mr Ernest Frobisher, a former resident in Kinnerton Street which is slightly to the north of Belgrave Square, told the author: 'I was astonished at what went on there at nights and the type of person going in and out. Not only did some quite important people join in the parties, but there were young Servicemen as well, both naval ratings and soldiers from Chelsea Barracks. One could sometimes see the frolics through open windows as well as hear some of the shrieks of laughter. From what one could see and hear it was obvious that these were all-male sexual parties. It was hard to believe that anyone in Lord Mountbatten's position would take such risks.'[17]

There was a scandal implicating the admiral in 1975. This involved 'allegations of a homosexual vice ring involving up to a hundred members of the Household Cavalry'.[18] This concerned Chelsea Barracks, though it principally concerned the procurement and distribution of photographs of naked young soldiers in obscene poses. The Special Investigation Branch of the Military Police was asked to inquire into the matter and eventually reported that three men of national prominence were involved, Mountbatten being one of them. Their report was passed to the Security Service for further action. As a result eighteen soldiers were discharged from the Army and seventeen more, all from one regiment, were called before their CO and warned about their future conduct. The Director of Public Prosecutions became involved, which clearly indicates that certain civilians not subject to military law had been identified. *The Times* of London recorded on 29 January, 1976, that 'homosexuals who include influential and wealthy men are believed to be named in a report made by the Army's Special Investigation Bureau after irregular sexual practices involving Household Cavalry men came to light'. But no further action was taken.

There is documentary evidence that at one time Mountbatten took a keen interest in the subject of unidentified flying objects, though his biographer, Philip Ziegler comments that by 1957 the admiral had become disillusioned with the amount of rubbish published about UFOs. Previously he had even become excited about the alleged appearance of a UFO in the grounds of his own home at Broadlands. What is interesting in that it sheds another light on his sometimes curious political views is that in 1950 in a comment on UFOs he said 'The fact that they can hover and accelerate away from the earth's gravity again and even revolve round a V2 in America (as reported by their head scientist) shows they are far ahead of us. If they really come over in a big way that may settle the capitalist-communist war. If the human race wishes to survive they may have to band together.'[19]

Contrast this comment to that made by General George C. Marshall, US Secretary of State 1947-49, only six years later. Asked by Dr Rolf Alexander why such emphasis had been put on denying the existence of UFOs, Marshall replied that 'the US wanted her people to concentrate on the real menace – communism – and not to be distracted by the visitors from outer space.'[20]

When Mountbatten was murdered by a bomb placed in the boat in which he was cruising with family and friends off the Irish coast in 1979, it was generally thought that the IRA alone was responsible, though this was never proved, despite claims to this effect and a sentence of life imprisonment passed on Thomas McMahon, described as a Provisional IRA bomb-maker. Indeed, Enoch Powell took the view that the admiral had been the victim of an American assassination plot, presumably instigated by the CIA. Mr Powell's actual words written in a private letter (which he gave permission for the *Guardian* to publish) were 'the Mountbatten murder was a very high-level "job" not unconnected with the nuclear strategy of the United States . . .'[21]

The background to this is that Mr Powell had long maintained that there was an underlying and unstated objective both of Britain and the USA that the Irish should abandon its military neutrality and presumably join NATO. Only three months before his murder Mountbatten had made a controversial speech in Strasbourg about nuclear arms, expressing the view that there was a case for nuclear disarmament by the Western powers.

Another and much more probable suggestion has been mooted among some members of the Conservative Party, including one of the present Ministers: this is to the effect that Mountbatten was murdered by the IRA with support from the KGB, because they feared he was about to reveal to the world at large that he had been working for them and against the Americans. Even at that stage the long-term planners of the USSR were working on 'Trust No. 3' and 'One-Worldism' and it would not have suited their policy if Mountbatten had appeared to be backing them *against* the USA. They were well aware that this indiscretion on his part, if committed, would be more to boost his ego as the liberal elder statesman rather than to help the USSR. Thirty years earlier such a move might have been welcomed, but in the late 1970s Russia was much more sophisticated and carefully attuned to international opinion. It would not be the first time that the KGB has used a foreign terorist organization to carry out such a killing. More than once caches of Soviet-made weapons have been found in IRA hide-outs.

The mystery of the Mountbatten killing has never been satisfactorily cleared up. As recently as August, 1989, Chris Ryder, the Irish correspondent of the *Daily Telegraph*, reported that the file on the incident had not been closed and that 'an Irish businessman remains one of the prime suspects in the plot to assassinate Lord Mountbatten'. He added that despite the fact that the Mountbatten family had visited the Sligo area of Ireland every August for many years, 'there were serious doubts about one acquaintance of Lord Mountbatten's in the Irish Republic. He was a businessman who came to the notice of the security forces in Britain and Ireland after arms finds on the border.'

Mr Frank Doherty, formerly editor of the *Sunday News* of Belfast, has stated that 'The IRA spent nearly two months setting up the assassination, relying on information from Lord Mountbatten's homosexual contacts to track his movements. Lord Mountbatten was interested in what homosexuals call 'the rough trade' and liked to have contacts with working-class youths. He was particularly attracted to boys in their early teens. It was this characteristic which made him especially vulnerable to the IRA, because he needed to slip away from his personal bodyguards to keep dates with such boys, some of whom came in contact with IRA men.'[22]

'The right deed for the wrong reason'? It is in this sense that there is a distinct difference between treachery and treason. Today, far more than in the past, skilled analysis by intelligence services is needed to ascertain when what may appear to be 'the right deed' is indeed developed for the wrong reason. Only recently Mr Michael Heseltine in a speech to the Royal Institute for International Affairs in London asserted that the Soviet Union was planning to exploit Western concerns about the environment to gain access to sophisticated military technology. Kremlin strategists, he said, had identified such worries in Europe and America as an opportunity for 'mischief-making' similar to the peace movements of the early 1960s. Behind the Soviet strategy is an attempt to use the green movement to undermine Western efforts to modernise short-range nuclear weapons in Europe.

If evidence is needed to support this contention it is surely contained to some extent in *Mezhdunarodnaya Zhizn*, a Soviet Foreign Ministry publication, in 1988. This quoted Vladimir Kryuchkov, shortly to become head of the KGB, as saying that a priority of the Kremlin's foreign policy had been and would increasingly be to cultivate 'green' movements in West Germany and other nations of the West.

The infiltration of the EEC bureaucracy by agents of the Soviet Union is much more difficult to pin-point, but it should be regarded as a vital issue by both intelligence and counter-intelligence services. One wonders how de Gaulle would regard current moves in the EEC towards that deceptive policy of integration. De Gaulle certainly believed in French sovereignty however much he may have favoured the original conception of a small Common Market in which France and Germany were the major partners. When the UK entered the EEC the British Prime Minister represented it as a move that would not mean loss of sovereignty. But it did: under Articles 189 and 191 of the Treaty of Rome the EEC Commissioners were empowered to formulate directives and decisions which took precedence over national laws. The 'European Market 1992' will in effect mean extending to Western Europe something which gradually will become dangerously like the conditions under which the satellite states of the Soviet bloc exist. In an interview in *Corriere della Sera* last year Dino Grandi, Mussolini's former ally, calmly suggested that 'a unification of Europe by Russia would be both possible and desirable. Charles V, Louis XIV, Kaiser Wilhelm and Adolf Hitler had tried to achieve this but in vain. Russia today has the power and influence to do just this.[23]

It is an often-forgotten fact that fascism and communism have much in common. Sometimes this is presented under the guise of liberalism, of integrating European Union into the organisation of the United Nations, but behind it all is a scheme for *Ostpolitik*, for a closer relationship between the states which compose the EEC and the eastern bloc of the USSR. It all sounds like the initiation of a golden era of peace, but any Western intelligence service which neglects to find out the real purpose of the operatives behind all this and their motives will be failing in its duty to the people it serves.

It should be remembered that even after his declarations on *glasnost* and *perestroika* Gorbachev stated on 2 November, 1987: 'In October, 1917, we departed the old world and irreverently rejected it. We are travelling to a new world, the world of communism. We shall never deviate from this path.'[24] It is true that much has changed in Eastern Europe since then, but Gorbachev's views have not altered as his attitude towards Lithuania has shown. What he is doing is to continue what Leonid Brezhnev said in 1972: 'Military peace in no way signifies the end of our struggle. On the contrary the struggle must be intensified and we must use every means we can devise to subvert ordered governments, *especially those making a success of parliamentary democracy.*'

Summary

While this book reveals a disturbing story of treachery, incompetence and appallingly lax security in high places in Britain over a very long period, the intention is not to attack our Security and Intelligence Services, but to get at the truth as a warning for the future.

The purpose of this narrative is just as much to defend and exonerate those unfairly and, indeed, sometimes falsely condemned, as to reveal some of the treacherous characters who have been so ardently protected by the Establishment. Those who have indulged in unjustified smears have undoubtedly done some damage to the reputation of these services. On the other hand it should be borne in mind that unless two authors had set out to expose the late Anthony Blunt, thus paving the way for a question in Parliament, the probability is that he would have retained his knighthood and his privileged position to the end of his life, and maybe forever.

Others, equally important and just as treacherous, have been protected for years. Indeed, what has been both wicked and disgusting is that *innocent people have been named as traitors to detract attention from the real conspirators*. Such has been the case with Sir Roger Hollis, who is being attacked again even this year. Sir Roger was a bluff, golf-loving, lounge-bar rather than clubman type who instinctively knew what was right and what was wrong and acted accordingly all his life: a quiet, unflamboyant patriot.

His enemies came from a wide group of people, some in the Intelligence and Security Services, others occupying important positions in the Foreign and Civil Services and Armed Forces, some closely related to the Royal Family, who used their privileged positions for their own nefarious schemes, both personal and political.

They included such people as Anthony Blunt, Guy Liddell, Lord Victor Alexander ('Peter') Churchill and Admiral of the Fleet Lord Mountbatten of Burma. These vain and promiscuous 'courtiers' were dabbling in politics as much as they were in aesthetics. Investigating their activities sometimes I felt as if I was discovering a new version of

Alice in Wonderland in which all the violence and sexual perversion which some psychoanalysts have discovered in the old version had become horribly explicit.

As individuals these people all had different aims, they shared a love of intrigue, and believed that, because of their privileged position, they had a duty to their exalted conceptions of themselves which superseded the restrictions of the constitution of their country and even enabled them to favour another nation above their own, as and when they saw fit.

This naturally leads to treachery, or at the very least the risk of treachery. Therein lies an acute problem of which we should all be more aware: treachery is not necessarily treason, but it can in the long run be even more damaging. This type of individual can do far more harm over a long period than any traitor who is merely caught handing over some secret papers to a foreign agent. He, or she, is frequently immune from prosecution simply because there is insufficient evidence to bring a case, while relying on the protection of allies in the Establishment. It is a vicious circle of intrigue: such people both undermine the Establishment and eagerly seduce its members with flattery and bogus pretensions.

What should be remembered is that in today's world the highly skilled agent of influence, practised in disinformation techniques and moulding opinion behind the scenes, is increasingly more dangerous than the conventional spy. The restrictive libel laws of this country make it extremely difficult to unmask such undesirable activities by those living, but there is no excuse for not revealing the damage already done by the dead. It has frequently been the obsessive secrecy of the British Establishment from top to bottom which has enabled treachery to flourish and for constructive counter-moves to be stifled.

Notes

Chapter 1

1 *The Wilson Plot*, David Leigh, Heinemann, London, 1988, relates this story of an alleged plot.

2 Hearing before the Sub-Committee to investigate the administration of the Internal Security Act and other Internal Security Laws of the Committee on the Judiciary US Senate, Part 2, 12 April 1976, US Government Printing Office, Washington, 1976.

3 *Ibid*, but referring to Part I of this report, 18 November 1975.

4 *Ibid*, Part I.

5 *The Times*, 15 April 1988.

6 'The Phantom Mole', book review by Richard Deacon, *The Spectator*, 21 March 1987.

7 *The British Connection; Russia's Manipulation of British Individuals & Institutions*, Richard Deacon, Hamish Hamilton, London, 1979.

Chapter 2

1 *The Joy of the Snow: an autobiography*, Elizabeth Goudge, Hodder, London, 1974.

2 *The Cliftonian*, 1923.

3 *The Cliftonian*, June 1924.

4 *DNB : 1970-80*.

5 *Ibid*.

6 *The Diaries of Evelyn Waugh*, edited by Michael Davies, Weidenfeld & Nicholson, London, 1976.

7 *Ibid*.

8 Letter from Roger Fulford to the author, 25 February 1982.

9 *Views*, an article by Maurice Richardson in *The Listener*, 26 October 1967.

10 Letter from Roger Fulford to the author, 25 February 1982.

Chapter 3

1 Letter from Roger Hollis to his mother, 8 January 1935.

2 This is an undated photocopy of an article in *The Times*, some time between 1935 and 1936, entitled 'Japan on the Mainland' and attributed to 'a Correspondent'.

3 This refers to a photocopy of a printed story entitled 'A Matter of Form', by Roger Hollis, but with no indication as to which journal published it.

4 Letter from Chapman Pincher to *The Times*, 13 April 1982.

5 Letter from Roger Hollis to his mother, 8 January 1935.

6 Letter from Roger Hollis to his mother, 10 September 1935.

7 *Ibid.*
8 *Molehunt*, Nigel West, Weidenfeld & Nicolson, 1987.
9 *Sonja's Rapport*, Ruth Werner, Verlag Neues Leben, Berlin (GDR), 1977.
10 Letter from Roger Hollis to his mother, 11 October 1934.
11 *Ibid.*

Chapter 4
1 *The Conflict in China*, by Roger H. Hollis, reprinted from the *Journal of the Royal Asian Society*, vol. XXV, January 1938.
2 *DNB, 1970-80.*
3 Letter to the author from Sir Roger Fulford, February 1982.
4 *Ibid.*
5 *Ibid.*
6 *Ibid.*
7 *My Silent War*, Kim Philby, Grove Press, New York, 1968.
8 *DNB, 1970-80.*
9 *My Silent War*, Philby.
10 Public Record Office: Foreign Office 371c 4790 / 2069.
11 *Ibid.*
12 Letter from Sir Con O'Neill to the author, 25 May 1982.
13 *Ibid.*

Chapter 5
1 From a letter to *The Times*, 26 January 1980, from Mr Edward Croft-Murray.
2 *The Scene Changes*, Sir Basil Thomson, Victor Gollancz, London, 1939. Also *Queer People*, Hodder & Stoughton, London, 1922.
3 *The Last Temptation*, David Mure, Buchan & Enright, London, 1984.
4 Letter from David Mure to the author, 12 December 1984.
5 Croft-Murray letter to *The Times*, 26 January 1980.
6 *Personalia*, Rom Landau.
7 *All My Sins Remembered*, Viscount Churchill.
8 Cyril Connolly in a conversation with the author, January 1971.
9 *My Silent War*, Philby.
10 *The Last Temptation*, Mure.
11 Ministry of Defence, 8 February 1989, D/MS16/58/a/MC.
12 Letter from Mrs Sebastian to the author, 25 January 1989.
13 Sir John Ackroyd, Bart., son of Lady Ackroyd, in a statement to the author, 3 February 1989.
14 Cited by Nesta Webster, *World Revolution : The Plot Against Civilisation*, edited and brought up-to-date by Anthony Gittens, Britons Publishing Co., Chulmleigh, 1971.
15 Prologue by Sir Compton Mackenzie to *Walls Have Mouths*, Wilfred Macartney, Gollancz, London, 1936.
16 *Ibid.*
17 *Ace of Spies*, Robin Bruce Lockhart, Hodder, London, 1969.

Chapter 6
1 Churchill to Lloyd George, 6 December 1921, House of Lords Record Office,

Lloyd George MSS F/10/1/53. See also *Great Contemporaries*, Churchill, London, 1947 edition.

2 *Czechoslovak Legion Papers*, Geneva, and Savinkov archives, International, Institut voor Soziale Geschidenis, IIV SG /Sol, Amsterdam.

3 This particular telegram was sent in cipher by Lansing to the American Consul-General in Irkutsk on 23 September 1918, and is on microfilm in State Department records.

4 Internal CIA Study on 'The Trust', March 1969, entitled 'Historical Intelligence Collection'.

5 *Ibid.*

6 *Daily Express*, 23 July 1930.

7 The statement about 'Sidney Berns' was made by Krivitsky to his American friend and adviser, Isaac Don Levine.

8 *Reilly : The First Man*, Robin Bruce Lockhart, Penguin Books, London, 1987.

9 *Ibid.* Much the same view is expressed in Hill's *Reminiscences*.

10 *Reminiscences*, Hill.

11 *Reilly : The First Man*, Bruce Lockhart.

12 *Ibid.*

13 *Secret Servant*, Ilya Dzhirkvelov, Collins, London, 1987.

Chapter 7

1 *Walls Have Mouths*, Mackenzie.

2 *Ibid.*

3 Information from Krivitsky to Isaac Don Levine. The late Mr Levine has been somewhat unfairly dismissed as a sensationalist by some writers on the subject of Intelligence, but it should be stressed that it was Levine who first alerted the British Embassy in Washington to Krivitsky's identification of Capt. King as a Soviet agent. The verdict of Mr Robert T. Crowley, co-author of *The New KGB*, makes an apt point: 'If Levine resorted to sensationalism, it was largely because most of the American officials, whom he first warned, had shown little interest in the problem of Soviet penetration of the US Government.'

4 *Episodes & Reflections*, Sir Wyndham Childs, Cassell, London, 1930.

5 US Embassy, London, papers, 800 B, 29 March 1926. From this admittedly slight evidence it would seem that there had been discussions between Scotland Yard and the American Embassy for months before the ARCOS raid was made.

6 *Walls Have Mouths*, Mackenzie.

7 Supt Askew to the author.

8 *Ibid.*

Chapter 8

1 *The Times*, 30 September 1933.

2 *Ibid.*

3 Personal statement by the widow of the late H. Challinor James, now the author's wife. Statement dated 1977.

4 Ilya Dzhirkvelov, author of *Secret Servant: MyLife with the KGB and the Soviet Elite*, Collins, London, 1987, states that 'we learned from an NKVD agent inside the Rumanian counter-intelligence service that all Agabekov's visitors were searched by his bodyguards and any potential weapons removed.'

5 *Murder & Kidnapping as an Instrument of Soviet Policy* : Hearing before the Sub-committee to investigate the administration of the Internal Security Act and other security laws, 89th Congress, 1st Session, 26 March 1965.

6 Annexes of the SR (*Service de Renseignement*), 23 June 1934. The French view seems to have been that Oldham might have been murdered by the British, though admittedly this could be construed as being based on theory rather than fact.

Chapter 9

1 Chancery Division reports : C.A. 1936, 25 February.

2 Chancery Division reports : C.A. 1936 : Liddell's Settlement Trusts.

3 *The Times* obituary of Moura Budberg of 2 November 1974, stated : 'For nearly four decades she was in the centre of London's intellectual, artistic and social life. She shared homes with H.G. Wells, Maxim Gorky and Sir Robert Bruce Lockhart.'

4 *Reilly : The First Man*, Bruce Lockhart.

5 Papers of Lord Davidson, House of Lords Library.

Chapter 10

1 Driberg Papers, Christ Church College, Oxford.

2 *One Girl's War*, Miller.

3 *The Spectator*, 23 July 1988.

4 Documents & Materials Relating to the Eve of World War II, Dirksen Papers (1928-39) vol. ii, Foreign Languages Publishing House, Moscow. Dirksen was German Ambassador to the UK.

5 Statement made in the William Hickey Column of the *Daily Express*.

6 *Albany at Large* column in the *Sunday Telegraph*, 27 November 1988.

7 Public Record office : HO 45 10 144 and HO 283 series.

8 *Ibid.*

9 Vansittart Papers, March-April 1938, in Churchill College, Cambridge.

10 *Ibid.*

11 US State Department Archives for 1940.

12 *'C' : A biography of Sir Maurice Oldfield*, Richard Deacon, Macdonald, London, 1985.

13 'Francis Herbert King : A Soviet Source in the Foreign Office', by D. Cameron Watt, *Intelligence & National Security*, vol. 3, no. 4.

14 *Ibid.*

15 *Daily Telegraph*, 17 February 1989.

16 *Ibid.* Kennedy was pessimistic about British chances of victory, but he was not a lone figure in this respect. Kennedy's son, Robert Kennedy, when he was Attorney-General in the 1960s, kept back files dealing with help given by his father to German industrialists in registering their patents with Mexican-based American companies.

17 *A Man Called Intrepid*, William Stevenson, Macmillan, London, 1976.

Chapter 11

1 Maxwell Knight's anti-communist section became an immediate target for critical and derisory remarks by Liddell and his new allies in 1940, and Liddell was foremost in getting Knight's report *The Comintern is not Dead*, rejected.

2 Letter to the author from Dr Montgomery Hyde, 19 October 1988.

3 Interview with Christopher Harmer by Simon Freeman, 1985, cited in *Conspiracy*

of Silence, Simon Freeman and Barrie Penrose, Grafton Books, London, 1986.

4 *My Silent War*, Philby.

5 Personal statement to the author, 12 September 1977.

6 *The Double-Cross System*, Masterman.

7 Personal statement to the author, 14 September 1977.

8 *The Double-Cross System*, Masterman.

9 Personal statement to the author by the late Professor Pearson.

10 From 'Tomás Harris (1908-64)', Anthony Blunt, article in the Courtauld Institute Galleries Catalogue, 27 February – 31 March, 1975.

11 Personal statement to the author, 3 October 1977.

12 Personal statement to the author.

13 Personal statement to the author, 21 June 1978.

14 Cited in *Conspiracy of Silence*, Penrose and Freeman.

15 *The Second World War Diaries of Hugh Dalton*, edited by Ben Pimlott, Jonathan Cape, London, 1984.

16 *Spy / Counterspy*, Dusko Popov, Weidenfeld & Nicolson, London, 1974.

17 Statement to the author by David Mure, 1980.

18 *Spy / Counterspy*, Popov.

19 *Memoirs of Marshal Zhukov*, Marshal of the Soviet Union G.K.Zhukov, Jonathan Cape, London, 1971.

20 *Kurskaya Bitva*, Marshal of the Soviet Union I.S. Konev, Institute of Military History, USSR Ministry of Defence, Nauka, 1970.

21 *The Soviets and Ultra*, article by Geoff. Jukes in *Intelligence & National Security*, 1988.

Chapter 12

1 See *Socialism versus Capitalism*, A.C. Pigou, Macmillan, London, 1937.

2 The Pigou diary of 1905 was based on a 9-cell key in which the letters of the alphabet are disposed in groups of 3. The entries cited are for 21 and 24 August. Pigou seems to have had a secret, almost schoolboyish, hankering for the life of a conspirator: maybe it was an escape from academic life.

3 *Pilgrim to the Left: Memoirs of a Modern Revolutionist*, S.G.Hobson, Edward Arnold, London, 1938.

4 Personal statement to the author.

5 *Ibid.*

6 *Sonja's Rapport*, Werner.

7 *Ibid.*

8 *Ibid.*

9 *Ibid.*

10 Statement to the author from Professor Ger Harmsen, 16 December 1977.

11 *The Double-Cross System*, Masterman.

12 Personal statement to the author, 2 October 1977. See also Dr de Jong's World War II history series: vol. v, *The Kingdom of the Netherlands during the Second World War*.

13 *The Game of the Foxes*, Farago.

14 See *After the Battle*, no. 11, Battle of Britain Prints International, London.

15 Personal statement to the author.

16 Personal statement to the author.

17 See *After the Battle*, no. 11.
18 Letter to the author, 3 February 1978.

Chapter 13

1 Report of the Canadian Royal Commission on Gouzenko findings, pp. 616-20.
2 The *Toronto Telegram*, 29 January 1966, in an editorial.
3 *Their Trade is Treachery*, Chapman Pincher, Sidgwick & Jackson, London, 1981.
4 Letter of 2 February 1982.
5 Memorandum by Igor Gouzenko, 6 May 1952, to RCMP Intelligence.
6 Report entitled 'Canadian evidence of 1945 "mole" in London,' by John Best and Peter Hennessy, *The Times*, 16 October 1981.
7 *Secret Servant*, Dzhirkvelov.
8 This further confirmation of the story of an Enigma machine being given to the Russians appeared in the *Daily Telegraph*, 7 January 1988, in the Peterborough Column. In a letter connected with this report, also published in the *Daily Telegraph*, the historian, Peter Calvocoressi, raised the question as to whether if, given their spectacular successes in 1943, it might be time to ask the Russians for an explanation.

Chapter 14

1 PRO : FO 371/47897.
2 Baykaloff Archives, Amsterdam.
3 Churchill College Archives : VNST II 1/41, Vansittart Papers.
4 A personal statement to the author by the late Lady Rhondda. Koestler himself wrote to the author saying that he learned some of these details 'from the late Ellen Wilkinson who had been an intimate friend of Willi and Otto [Katz].'
5 *Cloak Without Dagger*, Sir Percy Sillitoe, Cassell, London, 1955.
6 Personal statement to the author by Mr Anthony Sillitoe.
7 *Ibid.*
8 *Cloak Without Dagger*, Sillitoe.
9 *Handbook for Spies*, Alexander Foote, Museum Press, London, 1949.
10 This statement by Alexander Foote was made to a British MP long since dead and a British newspaper editor sometime in the middle fifties (it is undated). It was given to the author by Foote's sister, Mrs Anne Stiassny.
11 *Ibid.*
12 *The Friends*, Nigel West, Weidenfeld & Nicolson, London, 1988.
13 Obituary notice of Sir Percy Sillitoe, *The Times*, 6 April 1962.
14 *Cloak Without Dagger*, Sillitoe.

Chapter 15

1 *Cloak Without Dagger*, Sillitoe.
2 PRO : FO 371 34416 C 13941.
3 Cable to the author by Sir William Stephenson, 13 February 1982.
4 *Cloak Without Dagger*, Sillitoe.
5 *A Chapter of Accidents*, Goronwy Rees, Chatto & Windus, London, 1972.
6 British United Press report, 16 June 1961.
7 Personal statement to the author, 5 July 1978.
8 Personal statement to the author, 28 January 1978.
9 *Ibid.*

10 Article entitled 'The Brotherhood of Bentinck Street', telling how Goronwy Rees revealed to Andrew Boyle how Burgess and Blunt involved Guy Liddell in their treachery, *Observer*, 20 January 1980.

11 *Ibid.*

12 *Special Office Brief*, Kilbrittain Newspapers, Ltd., Dublin, Issue No. 226, 24 March 1983.

13 See also: 'Tribute to Goronwy Rees' by Donald McCormick, *Encounter*, January 1981.

14 Personal statement to the author.

15 Information from Dr Kitty Little, of Oxford, who was a close friend of Blanche Clayton for many years.

16 *Ibid.*

17 Cadogan Papers : 1 / 22 Diary, 1951.

Chapter 16

1 *I Spied Spies*, Major A.W. Sansom, Harrap & Co., London, 1965.

2 Interview with Sir Charles Spry by Anthony McAdam, entitled 'How Petrov case shows Wright is wrong', *Sunday Telegraph*, 14 December 1986. 'To my certain knowledge,' added Sir Charles, 'Hollis had nothing to do with appointments to ASIO. In no way, shape or form did he introduce or recommend anyone to join ASIO.'

3 Driberg Papers.

4 *Ibid.*

5 *Ibid.*

6 Cited by John Costello in his book, *Mask of Treachery : The First Documented Dossier on Blunt, MI5 and Soviet Subversion*, Collins, London, 1988. This was a comment by Mr Peter Liddell, Liddell's son.

7 *Daily Telegraph*, 5 June 1987.

8 *Spycatcher*, Wright.

9 *Mole-Hunt*, Nigel West, Weidenfeld & Nicolson, London, 1988.

10 *Ibid.*

11 *Daily Express*, 14 March 1987. This statement was made at the same time as an Australian judge threw out the British government's attempt to ban publication of Peter Wright's memoirs.

12 *Sunday Times*, 'Spectrum' Column, edited by Barry Penrose, March 1987.

Chapter 17

1 *Gorbachev, Glasnost & Lenin, Behind the New Thinking*, by Françoise Thom & David Regan, Policy Research Publications, London.

2 *Daily Telegraph*, 25 January 1982.

3 *Their Trade is Treachery*, Pincher.

4 *Mole-Hunt*, West.

5 Letter to the author from Mr Daniel J. Mulvenna, 4 April 1988.

6 'Spy Chief Hollis in new scandal', by Chris Logan, *Sunday Express*, 23 August 1987.

7 *Ibid.*

8 Letter from Mr Graham Greene to the author, 9 March 1982.

9 A communication from Mr James Angleton to the author, 12 January 1984.

10 See letter to *Private Eye* from Leslie Gardiner, 12 October 1979, and also obitu-

ary of Vice-Admiral Sir G. Robson, *Daily Telegraph*, 29 December 1989.

11 BBC TV *Nationwide* programme, 8 September 1979.

12 *Caspar John*, Rebecca John, Collins, London, 1987.

13 *Daily Telegraph*, 2 October 1981.

14 'Albany at Large' column, by Kenneth Rose, *Sunday Telegraph*, 15 January 1989.

15 Mrs Patricia Rose made statements to me on various occasions both verbally and in letters during the latter part of 1985. She also allowed me to hear and check out various tape-recordings of people she had spoken to. Some of this material, but not of course that contained in this chapter, was published in my book, *The Truth Twisters*, Macdonald, 1987, while Mrs Rose was still alive.

16 *Today*, 29 March 1986.

17 Statement to the author, 29 March 1990.

18 *The Times*, 21 October 1975.

19 *Mountbatten: the official biography*, Ziegler.

20 *Above Top Secret*, Timothy Good, Sidgwick & Jackson, London, 1987.

21 *The Guardian*, 9 January 1984.

22 *Now Magazine*, September 1989.

23 *Corriere della Sera*, Rome, July 1988.

24 Cited in *Why Has the Country not been told?* Cdr. M.J.L. Blake & Col. B.S. Turner, Bloomfield Books, 1989.

Bibliography

BURTSEV, Vladimir: *Ispoved Savinkova* (The Confessions of Savinkov), *Segodnya*, Riga, 18 October, 1927.

COSTELLO, John: *Mask of Treachery*, Wm. Morrow & Co., New York, 1988.

DARLING, Donald: The Escaping Game, William Kimber, London, 1977.

DZHIRKVELOV, Ilya: *Secret Servant: My Life with the KGB & the Soviet* Elite, Collins, London, 1987.

DAVIDSON, J.C.C.: *Memoirs of a Conservative: J.C.C. Davidson's Memoirs*, ed. Robert Rhodes James, Weidenfeld & Nicolson, London, 1969.

FARAGO, Ladislas: *The Game of the Foxes*, Hodder & Stoughton, London, 1972.

FLOWER, Ken: *Serving Secretly*, John Murray, London, 1987.

FOOTE, Alexander: *Handbook for Spies*, Museum Press, London, 1949.

FREEMAN, Simon, & PENROSE, Barry: Conspiracy of Silence, Grafton, London, 1987.

HMSO Publications: *Parliamentary Papers*: Cmd. 2682, 22 June, 1926: Documents selected from those obtained on the arrest of the communist leaders on 14 and 21 October, 1925. CMD. 2874, 1927: Documents illustrating the hostile activities of the Soviet Government and the Third International against Britain, documents found by the police in their search of Soviet House.

HOUGH, Richard: *Mountbatten: A Hero of Our Time*, Weidenfeld & Nicolson, London, 1980.

HOWARTH, T.E.B.: *Cambridge Between the Wars*, Collins, London, 1978.

JOHN, Rebecca: *Caspar John*, Collins, London, 1987.

KENDALL, Professor Walter: *The Revolutionary Movement in Britain: 1900-21*, Weidenfeld & Nicolson, London, 1969.

KLUGMANN, James: *History of the Communist Party of Great Britain*, vols. i and ii, Lawrence & Wishart, London, 1968-69.

KRIVITSKY, Walter G.: *I Was Stalin's Agent*, Hamish Hamilton, London, 1954.

LOCKHART, Robin Bruce: *Ace of Spies*, Stein & Day, New York, 1968. *Reilly the First Man*, Penguin Books, London, 1987.

McCARTNEY, Wilfred: *Walls Have Mouths*, Gollancz, London, 1936.

MASTERMAN, Sir John: *The Double-Cross System in the War of 1939-45.*

MILLER, Joan: One Girl's War, Brandon Books, Dublin, 1986.

MUGGERIDGE, Malcolm: *Chronicles of Wasted Time*, vols. i & ii, Collins, London, 1973.

MURE, David: *The Last Temptation*, Buchan & Enright, London, 1984.

PHILBY, Kim (H.A.R.): *My Silent War*, Grove Press, New York, 1968.

PINCHER, Chapman: *Their Trade is Treachery*, Sidgwick & Jackson, London, 1981.

POPOV, Dusko: *Spy/Counterspy*, Weidenfeld & Nicolson, London, 1974.

RADO, Sandor: *Codename Dora*, Abelard, 1975.

REES, Morgan Goronwy: *A Chapter of Accidents*, Chatto & Windus, London, 1972.

SILLITOE, Sir Percy: *Cloak Without Dagger*, Cassell & Co., London, 1955.

THOMSON, Sir Basil: *The Scene Changes*, Victor Gollancz, London, 1939; *Queer People*, Hodder & Stoughton, London, 1922.

VOLKOV, Fyodor: *Secrets From Whitehall & Downing Street*, Progress Publishing, Moscow, 1980.

WAUGH, Evelyn: *The Diaries of Evelyn Waugh*, Weidenfeld & Nicolson, London, 1976.

WERNER, Ruth: *Sonja's Rapport*, Verlag Neues, Leben, Berlin, 1978.

WEST, Nigel: *MI5: British Security Service Operations 1909-45*, The Bodley Head, London, 1981. *Mole-Hunt*, Weidenfeld & Nicolson, London, 1987.

WEST, Dame Rebecca: *The New Meaning of Treason*, Penguin Books, London, 1965.

WHITE, John Baker: *The Big Lie*, Evans Bros., London, 1955.

WILLIAMS, David: *Not In the Public Interest: the Problem of Security in Democracy*, Hutchinson, London, 1965.

ZHUKOV, Marshal: *Memoirs of Marshal Zhukov*, Jonathan Cape, London, 1971.

ZIEGLER, Philip: *Mountbatten: the Official Biography*, Collins, London, 1985.

Also Consulted:

Martin Dies Special Committee on Un-American Activities of the House of Representatives, Sept.-Oct., 1939.

US Government Printing Office: Communist Bloc Activities in the USA; Hearings before the Sub-Committee to investigate the administration of the Internal Security Act and other Internal Security Laws of the Committee on the Judiciary US Senate 94th Congress, First Session, 18 Nov., 1975, 12 April, 1976.

The Report of the Royal Commission appointed by the Canadian Government in February, 1946, to investigate the facts relating to and surrounding the communication by public officials and other persons in positions of trust, of secret and confidential information, to agents of a foreign power.

Various FBI and CIA Papers obtainable under the Freedom of Information Act, USA; British Parliamentary Papers, documents of the British Foreign Office, War Office, Ministry of Defence and Cabinet Papers released to the Public Record Office; Papers in the Imperial War Museum.

Lord Davidson's Papers in the Record Office of the House of Lords; Czechoslovak Legion Papers in Geneva; the Wiseman Papers, E.M. House Collection, Yale University; Archives and Papers of the Hoover Institution, USA; the Driberg Papers, Christ Church, Oxford; the Vansittart and Cadogan Papers, with acknowledgement to the Master and Fellows of Churchill College, Cambridge.

Index